HUSO 2019

The Fifth International Conference on Human and Social Analytics

June 30 – July 4, 2019

Rome, Italy

HUSO 2019 Editors

Dennis Folds, Lowell Scientific Enterprises, USA

Els Lefever, LT3, Ghent University, Belgium

Ralucca Gera, Naval Postgraduate School, California, USA

Véronique Hoste, LT3, Ghent University, Belgium

Printed from e-media with permission by:

Curran Associates, Inc.
57 Morehouse Lane
Red Hook, NY 12571

Some format issues inherent in the e-media version may also appear in this print version.

Printed by Curran Associates, Inc. (2019)

International Academy, Research, and Industry Association (IARIA)
412 Derby Way
Wilmington, DE 19810

Phone: (408) 893-6407
Fax: (408) 527-6351

petre@iaria.org

Additional copies of this publication are available from:

Curran Associates, Inc.
57 Morehouse Lane
Red Hook, NY 12571 USA
Phone: 845-758-0400
Fax: 845-758-2633
Email: curran@proceedings.com
Web: www.proceedings.com

Table of Contents

Towards a Psychologically Grounded Emotion Dictionary for Russian 1
Polina Panicheva and Olga Bogolyubova

Sentiment Analysis of French Political Tweets: #MacronPresident 5
Antoine Vanrysselberghe and Els Lefever

Towards an Empirically-Grounded Framework for Emotion Analysis 11
Luna De Bruyne, Orphee De Clercq, and Veronique Hoste

Measuring the Impact of Sentiment for Hate Speech Detection on Twitter 17
Nina Bauwelinck and Els Lefever

Digital Disqualification, Digital Suffering, Digital Reliance - The Case of French Retired People over Sixty Years Old 23
Eloria Vigouroux-Zugasti and Christian Bourret

Response Patterns during Child-Robot Interaction of Children with Cognitive Impairments 33
Luthffi Idzhar Ismail, Tony Belpaeme, Fazah Akhtar Hanapiah, and Francis Wyffels

Theory and Development of Tool Frameworks for Interactive Knowledge and Data Visualization in Computational Social Science 37
Thomas McDermott and Molly Nadolski

Data for Healthy Decisions: Computation for Passive Monitoring of Medium-Risk Individuals at Home 43
Dennis Folds

Understanding Societal Well-Being Through the Eyes of the News World Media 48
Vasiliki Voukelatou, Luca Pappalardo, and Fosca Giannotti

A Survey on Studying the Social Networks of Students 50
Akrati Saxena, Pratishtha Saxena, Harita Reddy, and Ralucca Gera

A Recommender Model for the Personalized Adaptive CHUNK Learning System 58
Daniel Diaz, Ralucca Gera, Paul Keeley, Matthew Miller, and Nickos Leondaridis-Mena

An Adaptive Education Approach Using the Learners' Social Network 66
Ralucca Gera, Alex Gutzler, Ryan Hard, Bryan McDonough, and Christian Sorenson

CHUNK - Curated Heuristic Using a Network of Knowledge 73
Ralucca Gera, Michelle Isenhour, D'Marie Bartolf, and Simona Tick

Adaptive Personalized Network Relationships in the CHUNK Learning Environment 79
Shane Smith, Maria Smith, Mario Andriulli, Ralucca Gera, and Michelle Isenhour

HUSO 2019

Foreword

The Fifth International Conference on Human and Social Analytics (HUSO 2019), held between June 30 – July 4, 2019 - Rome, Italy continued the inaugural event bridging the concepts and the communities dealing with emotion-driven systems, sentiment analysis, personalized analytics, social human analytics, and social computing.

The recent development of social networks, numerous ad hoc interest-based formed virtual communities, and citizen-driven institutional initiatives raise a series of new challenges in considering human behavior, both on personal and collective contexts.

There is a great possibility to capture particular and general public opinions, allowing individual or collective behavioral predictions. This also raises many challenges, on capturing, interpreting and representing such behavioral aspects. While scientific communities face now new paradigms, such as designing emotion-driven systems, dynamicity of social networks, and integrating personalized data with public knowledge bases, the business world looks for marketing and financial prediction.

We take here the opportunity to warmly thank all the members of the HUSO 2019 Technical Program Committee, as well as the numerous reviewers. The creation of such a high quality conference program would not have been possible without their involvement. We also kindly thank all the authors who dedicated much of their time and efforts to contribute to HUSO 2019. We truly believe that, thanks to all these efforts, the final conference program consisted of top quality contributions.

Also, this event could not have been a reality without the support of many individuals, organizations, and sponsors. We are grateful to the members of the HUSO 2019 organizing committee for their help in handling the logistics and for their work to make this professional meeting a success.

We hope that HUSO 2019 was a successful international forum for the exchange of ideas and results between academia and industry and for the promotion of progress in the area of human and social analytics.

We are convinced that the participants found the event useful and communications very open. We also hope that Rome provided a pleasant environment during the conference and everyone saved some time for exploring this beautiful city.

HUSO 2019 Chairs

HUSO Steering Committee

Els Lefever, Ghent University, Belgium
Dennis J. Folds, Georgia Tech Research Institute, USA
Nitin Agarwal, University of Arkansas at Little Rock, USA
Chen Ding, Ryerson University, Canada

Liz Bacon, University of Greenwich, UK
Jan Ole Berndt, University of Trier, Germany
Christian Bourret, University of Paris East - Marne la Vallée (UPEM), France
Meena Jha, CQUniversity Sydney, Australia
Xiaolong Jin, 靳小龙, Chinese Academy of Sciences, China

HUSO Industry/Research Advisory Committee

Baden Hughes, Glentworth Consulting, Australia
Yi Shan, SDE II, Electronic Arts, Seattle, USA
Fan Yang, eBay Inc., USA
Massimiliano Zanin, The Innaxis Foundation & Research Institute, Madrid, Spain
Zhiwen Fang, Microsoft, USA

HUSO 2019

Committee

HUSO Steering Committee

Els Lefever, Ghent University, Belgium
Dennis J. Folds, Georgia Tech Research Institute, USA
Nitin Agarwal, University of Arkansas at Little Rock, USA
Chen Ding, Ryerson University, Canada
Liz Bacon, University of Greenwich, UK
Jan Ole Berndt, University of Trier, Germany
Christian Bourret, University of Paris East - Marne la Vallée (UPEM), France
Meena Jha, CQUniversity Sydney, Australia
Xiaolong Jin, 靳小龙, Chinese Academy of Sciences, China

HUSO Industry/Research Advisory Committee

Baden Hughes, GWI, Australia
Yi Shan, SDE II, Electronic Arts, Seattle, USA
Fan Yang, eBay Inc., USA
Massimiliano Zanin, The Innaxis Foundation & Research Institute, Madrid, Spain
Zhiwen Fang, Microsoft, USA

HUSO 2019 Technical Program Committee

Paul Abbiati, Founding Fellow of ELI - The European Law Institute, Austria
Nitin Agarwal, University of Arkansas at Little Rock, USA
Rodrigo Agerri, University of the Basque Country (UPV/*EHU*), Spain
Harry Agius, Brunel University London, UK
Samer Al-khateeb, Creighton University, USA
Ahmad T. Al-Taani, Yarmouk University, Irbid, Jordan
Hafizi Muhamad Ali, Yanbu University College, Saudi Arabia
Alessandro Ansani, Sapienza University of Rome, Italy
Alessio Antonini, Università degli Studi di Torino, Italy
Saïd Assar, Telecom Ecole de Management, France
Arnulfo P. Azcarraga, De La Salle University, Philippines
Liz Bacon, University of Greenwich, UK
Lakshika Balasuriya, Kno.e.sis Center | Wright State University, USA
Panagiotis D. Bamidis, Aristotle University of Thessaloniki, Greece
Balbir Barn, Middlesex University, London, UK
Stefano Berretti, University of Florence, Italy
Shreyansh Bhatt, Kno.e.sis | Wright State University, USA
Christian Bourret, University of Paris East - Marne la Vallée (UPEM), France

Copyright Information

Towards a Psychologically Grounded Emotion Dictionary for Russian

Polina Panicheva

National Research University Higher School of Economics
16 Soyuza Pechatnikov st.,
St. Petersburg, 190121, Russian Federation
Voronezh State Pedagogical University
86 Lenina st., Voronezh, 394043, Russian Federation
Email: ppanicheva@hse.ru

Olga Bogolyubova

Department of Psychology, Faculty for Social Wellbeing
University of Malta
Tal-Qroqq, Msida, MSD 2080, Malta
Email: olga.bogolyubova@um.edu.mt

Abstract—**In Natural Language Processing, there is currently a trend towards analyzing subjective language, one of the important topics being emotion detection from text. There have been a number of successful attempts of developing emotion dictionaries in the English language based on emotion theories well established in psychology. However, such resources in Russian are lacking. In the current work, we propose a roadmap for developing a psychologically grounded emotion dictionary in Russian. Based on the related work overview, we propose an emotion classification theory by Carroll Izard including ten basic emotions as a framework for building emotion dictionary. We outline a number of lexical resources for compiling word candidates for the dictionary. Finally, we describe the annotation procedure by volunteers and experts, and psychometric evaluation to measure internal consistency and external validity of the dictionary. The dictionary will be used in emotion detection tasks, compared to other available lexical resources, and supplemented with context-dependent statistical algorithms.**

Keywords–Emotion dictionary; Russian language; affective language; subjectivity analysis; basic emotions.

I. Introduction

In recent Natural Language Processing (NLP) applications subjectivity analysis, e.g., identification and interpretation of information related to personal private states, has become extremely popular. Resources and algorithms of subjectivity, sentiment and emotion detection in text are numerous. They are applied to analyze the ever-growing body of texts in the World Wide Web, including social networks, news, political debates and product reviews.

The first line of research in this field stems from psychology, with the seminal work by authors of Linguistic inquiry and Word Count [1]. This body of research adheres to the framework of psychological science, with lexicons compiled and annotated manually in a top-down manner, and dictionary categories originating from well-established research on psychology of emotions and appraisal [2]. Moreover, the resulting dictionaries are thoroughly tested in terms of their psychometric properties. The other research line is linguistically oriented: a word is supposed to fall into a sentiment or emotion category if there holds a certain formal relation between the word meaning and the category. Sometimes, the word should include a certain emotion or sentiment in its connotation [3][4], or imply an affective response as a result of common-sense logical operations [5]. Such linguistically motivated dictionaries are often developed (semi-)automatically by analyzing word usage in context [4], or rely on existing world knowledge thesauri [6][7].

Although there exist a number of sentiment and emotion dictionaries in Russian, they are mostly linguistically grounded. Some attempts have been made to translate English psychologically grounded emotion dictionaries to Russian, however, with no psychometric evaluation. In the current work, we set out to fill this gap by creating a psychologically grounded emotion dictionary of Russian. The psychological orientation of the dictionary implies the following:

- The dictionary categories are based on emotion categorization well established in the literature;
- The words belonging to emotion categories explicitly and objectively mean the expression of emotion in question, e.g., *неожиданность - surprise, шокированный - shocked, удивлять - to amaze, чудесно - wonderful,* ruling out the connotation-based, context-dependent and common-sense-derived lexica, e.g., *война - war, ужасно - awfully, ложь - lie*;
- The dictionary must be evaluated for internal consistency and external validity.

The paper is organized as follows. In Section 2, existing emotion dictionaries in Russian are described, and their limitations are discussed. In Section 3, a framework for building a psychologically grounded emotion dictionary in Russian is presented. Section 4 contains our conclusions and future work on annotation and experimental validation of the suggested dictionary.

II. Related Approaches to Emotion Dictionaries in Russian

A. Linguistic Inquiry and Word Count

The first widely known linguistic approach to representing emotions is Linguistic Inquiry and Word Count (LIWC) [1]. Work on this tool has been going on since 1993, with the latest version released in 2015. The original idea behind LIWC was to compile a dictionary of words denoting basic emotional and cognitive dimensions, which are often studied in sociology and psychology.

Originally, the LIWC dictionary is compiled for English. The latest version includes around 90 variables, covering almost 6,400 words. The LIWC dictionary is organized hierarchically and contains, among other dimensions, 21 linguistic categories (mostly parts of speech) and 41 categories tapping psychological constructs. The former include, for example, *function words, pronouns, typed personal pronouns, articles, prepositions, auxiliary, common verbs*, etc. The latter include *affective, social, cognitive, perceptual, biological processes, time orientations, relativity, personal concerns* and *informal language*. The *affective processes* contain *positive* and *negative emotions*, the latter being divided into *anxiety, anger* and *sadness*. Unfortunately, other emotions are not included in LIWC, and the choice of these emotions is not grounded by the authors. Probably, the reason for this is that LIWC is not specifically aimed at covering emotion vocabulary. The dictionary has been composed following an elaborate procedure involving 2-8 judges and recourse to common emotion rating scales and English dictionaries. Thereafter, internal consistency and external validity have been assessed for every category.

Internal consistency of a word category is a measure of all the words belonging to a category actually meaning the same thing psychologically. It is calculated with the Cronbach's alpha [8], showing to what degree words of the same category tend to co-occur in the same texts.*External validity* of a word category shows how much the words in question are actually related to the undelying psychological phenomena. It is measured by correlating word usage with manual ratings by judges on the underlying dimensions [1].

The 2007-version dictionary was translated in Russian [9]. The Russian dictionary includes 61 categories and around 5,900 words organized in a flat category structure. The categories include *positive* and *negative affects*, as well as *anxiety, anger* and *sadness*. The Russian LIWC dictionary has never been validated for internal consistency or external validity. However, Russian LIWC has been used in a few recent studies [10][11], where some dictionary categories were additionally populated.

B. Emotive Lexicon

In Russian language studies, an attempt to categorize emotional lexica was made as early as 1989 [3]. The key feature of the resulting dictionary is a purely linguistic approach to its development: the author draws a distinction between emotion words, emotional words and emotive lexica, with the dictionary capturing the latter. Emotive meaning refers to a meaning containing an emotive seme, whether in it's lexical, connotative or logical meaning.

The main idea behind the Emotive Lexicon is to identify words which contain a reference to emotion in their description in a standard Russian dictionary, e.g., *рай - paradise, баловать - to indulge.* Thus, around 8,500 words were included in the lexicon, divided into 37 categories corresponding to basic emotive meanings identified in the dictionary, e.g., *беспокойство - anxiety, вдохновение - inspiration, вера - faith, надежда - hope, недовольство - discontent, неприязнь - dislike, одиночество - loneliness, одобрение - approval, протест - protest, радость - joy,страх - fear, удивление - surprise.* Every category was further divided into 6 functional classes: emotional state, state development, influence, attitude, expression, characterization; for example, category *стыд - shame* includes the following words: *конфуз - embarrassment, смутиться - to be embarrassed, клевета - slander, закраснеться - to blush, застенчивый - shy, совестливость - conscientiousness,* respectively.

C. WordNet Affect

WordNet Affect was developed as an extension of WordNet Domains in [6]. It is based entirely on the WordNet original structure, with one or more affective labels assigned to some synsets. The core of Word-Net Affect was developed manually with the help of dictionaries. Then it was further expanded using WordNet relations. The original WordNet Affect contains 2,874 synsets and 4,787 words, annotated with a complex hierarchy of mental states and other affect-related phenomena. The affective label hierarchy provides a reference to one or more of the three main kinds of theories on emotion representation: discrete theories (based on the concept of cognitive evaluation), basic emotion theories and dimensional theories; see [12] for discussion.

A successful attempt at translating WordNet Affect into Russian and Romanian is described in [7]. It is based on the part of WordNet Affect annotation capturing 6 basic emotions: joy, fear, anger, sadness, disgust, surprise [13]. First, all the words in the English synsets denoting one of the six emotions were automatically translated in Romanian and Russian with an electronic English-Romanian and English-Russian dictionary. Second, irrelevant and duplicate translations were removed manually. Finally, the Russian and Romanian synsets were formed manually by three independent translators using Russian and Romanian thesauri and bilingual dictionaries. In the absence of Russian WordNet, the synsets in Russian were handcrafted so as to closely resemble the meaning of the original English synsets, based on the glosses of the latter. Some words were added to or deleted from the Russian synsets at this stage. The final dictionary contains 2,199 Russian affective words. The average pairwise inter-translator agreement for the Russian synsets ranged between 0.57 and 0.61, with the three-translator agreement reaching 0.29.

The Russian WordNet Affect was used in dataset filtering for sentiment analysis in [14]. However, no evaluation or validation of the resource has been performed to date.

D. RuSentiLex

RuSentiLex is a recently created sentiment lexicon in Russian [4]. It was created in three stages. First, sentiment words were extracted and manually filtered from a list of domain-specific sentiment words. Second, 55 lexico-syntactic patterns were applied to a text collection of 2 million news articles, to extract words with sentiment connotations. Finally, a supervised model of sentiment word extraction was applied to 1 million Tweets to infer Twitter-specific sentiment words.

The resulting database contains information on the sentiment orientation (positive, negative, neutral, or positive/negative, the latter meaning highly context-dependent) and the source of the sentiment. The source of the sentiment can be explicit *opinion*, negative or positive connotation (*fact*) or *feeling* (private state). The current version contains sentiment ratings for over 12,000 words and expressions. It has been successfully used in a number of NLP applications [15][16].

E. Limitations of the Existing Emotion Dictionaries in Russian

There has been a number of emotion lexicons developed for Russian, or sentiment lexicons containing additional useful information. There have also been reports on translating English-based emotion lexicons [15][17]. However, the translated parts only contain sentiment ratings for Russian words.

These are the main reasons why we have rejected the existing available Russian lexicons in our work:

- Most of the lexicons are based on purely linguistic, rather than psychological, grounds:

  - Sentiment scores instead of emotion ratings.
  - The emotive lexicon is based on emotive lexica concept, appealing to the semantic structure of words.
- WordNet Affect and some other resources are a direct translation of an English dictionary, preserving the English-based structure.
- None of the emotion lexicons in Russian have been validated for internal consistency or external validity.

Some examples of the listed issues are the following:

- Russian LIWC linguistic categories only contain parts of speech and a few pronoun types. However, the rich morphology in Russian allows to identify other grammatical categories, such as tense, voice, gender, number, etc. These are commonly identified with morphological parsers [18][19].
- In LIWC, lemmatization is accounted for by only listing word stems in the dictionary. Morphological parsing allows to lemmatize words more accurately.
- The Emotive Lexicon contains 37 linguistically grounded emotive categories. Some of them are hard to differentiate from the psychological point of view. For example, there are two distinct categories for *грусть - sadness* and *горе - grief*, which are hardly distinguishable psychologically.
- The concepts of emotive, affective and sentiment lexicons clearly include words which do not express emotion explicitly, e.g.:
  - *жар - heat, жить - to live, чувство - feeling* (Emotive Lexicon, *love* category);
  - *застенчивый - shy, скромный - modest, бесчувственный - heartless* (Russian WordNet Affect, *fear* category);
  - *уверовать - to believe, увлекаться - to be fond of* (RuSentiLex, *positive, feeling* category).

As a result, application of the existing emotion resources for Russian appears ineffective from the linguistic point of view and difficult to interpret psychologically.

III. Emotion Dictionary in Russian

A. Framework

The goal of the current work is to create a psychologically motivated dictionary of emotion words in Russian.

In psychology, numerous theories have been proposed to explain and describe emotions. Discrete emotions theories are a subgroup of these theories postulating that there are several *basic* emotions, which are distinct from one another, and that these core emotions reflect biologically determined affective responses, observable across cultures. The number of these basic emotions varies from 6 to 10, depending on the particular theory of discrete emotions. The most well-known discrete emotions theories were proposed by Ekman [20], Plutchik [21], and Izard [22]. While discrete emotions approach has been criticized, it remains the most popular and intuitively clear approach to classifying emotions. In Human-Computer Interaction research (HCI) and NLP it has been widely used for constructing emotion lexicons [6][7][2].

The first step in creating an emotion lexicon that fits within the framework of psychological science is the selection of a theoretical model of emotion classification. Within the general framework of discrete emotions theories and their existing applications to NLP and HCI, we will follow the classification of emotions proposed by Carroll Izard, which includes *anger, contempt, disgust, fear, guilt, interest, joy, sadness, shame*, and *surprise* [22]. We have chosen this classification, because it includes *shame* and *guilt*, which we find essential for further research.

We will be focusing on overt expression of emotions only. Ascribing emotional meaning to words and phrases outside of explicit expression of emotion is wrought with difficulties, as it is highly subjective and context-dependent. At the current stage, we aim at building the core of emotional expression words in Russian, which is fully motivated psychologically. However, the following steps will include identifying various linguistic ways of emotional expression, including connotation and neutral facts in view of common-sense knowledge.

For this reason, we are only concerned with lexical information, containing words and multi-word expressions. Interaction with context, including negation, is an essential step in subjective language analysis, which will be addressed in our future work.

B. Development

1) Dictionary Sources: The next step would be to identify the sources of words and phrases to annotate. Sources of words and expressions for annotation include existing Russian thesauri.

1) Words in the Russian LIWC dictionary [9] tapping the following psychological constructs:
   - Affective processes;
   - Informal language.
2) Russian WordNet Affect words [7] in the *emotion* category.
3) RuSentiLex words with the *feeling* source [4].
4) Emotional expressions in the Russian phraseology dictionary [23].

The resulting list of words will be filtered by frequency [24]: very infrequent words will be excluded from the annotation process. Thus, a set of around 5,000 words and expressions is expected to be compiled from the above thesauri.

An important question is whether to take slang words into consideration. On the one hand, slang is often related to expressing emotions. On the other hand, there are no dictionaries of emotional slang available. Also, existing Russian slang dictionaries contain over 30,000 words and expressions [25], which is a too large number to annotate manually.

2) Annotation: We will employ a two-step manual annotation by lay volunteers and experts.

1) A large group of volunteers will manually annotate the set of words and expressions pulled from the existing resources. The annotation procedure will be carried out using the Yandex.Toloka service [26] (a Russian counterpart of Mechanical Turk). Yandex.Toloka has been effectively used for crowdsourcing annotation of various semantic tasks in Russian [27][28]. The annotators will first be provided with the definitions of ten basic emotions by Izard [29]. Then, they will answer questions on whether a particular word denotes expression of every basic emotion, similar to [30]. Every word-emotion pair should be annotated by at least three annotators.

2) A small group of experts will review the annotation results, decide on the points of contradictions and make corrections, where necessary.

3) Psychometric Evaluation: As pointed out by Pennebaker et al. [1], reliability and validity testing of natural language instruments poses a number of challenges. In line with the procedures described by these authors, we will test reliability of the dictionary categories by representing each word within the category as a percentage score (words per text in selected corpora, such as blog posts, online forum entries, etc.) and conducting Cronbach's alpha calculations with Spearman-Brown prediction formula correction [1]. Validity testing will be achieved by correlating data from self-report questionnaire, targeted emotional writing tasks, and dictionary-based automated analysis in a series of studies.

IV. Conclusions and Future Work

We have outlined a framework for developing a psychologically grounded Russian emotion dictionary. First, existing approaches to emotion and sentiment dictionaries in Russian have been reviewed, and their limitations discussed. Second, we have identified the basic emotion classification by Izard, which will be used to define the dictionary categories. We have chosen a number of existing lexical resources to compile word candidates for emotion annotation. Finally, we have outlined the annotation procedure for volunteers and experts to classify words into emotion categories.

Our immediate future work includes carrying out the annotation experiment and evaluating the consistency and validity of the resulting word categories.

More distant future work will focus on real-world emotion expression in texts: narratives and social network posts will be analyzed in terms of the dictionary words attested against the ground truth provided by human judgments. The developed emotion dictionary will be compared to other emotion lexicons in Russian. Context-dependent features, such as negation and implicit emotion, will be added in order to develop a statistical emotion identification algorithm.

References

[1] J. W. Pennebaker, R. L. Boyd, K. Jordan, and K. Blackburn, "The development and psychometric properties of liwc2015," Austin, TX: University of Texas at Austin, 2015.

[2] M. D. Sykora, T. Jackson, A. O'Brien, and S. Elayan, "Emotive ontology: Extracting fine-grained emotions from terse, informal messages," International Journal on Computer Science & Information Systems, vol. 8, no. 2, 2013, pp. 106–118.

[3] L. G. Babenko, Lexical means of designation of emotions in the Russian language: monograph [In Russian: Leksicheskie sredstva oboznacheniia emotsii v russkom iazyke: monogr.]. Izd-vo Ural. un-ta, 1989.

[4] N. V. Loukachevitch and A. Levchik, "Creating a general Russian sentiment lexicon," in Proceedings of the Tenth International Conference on Language Resources and Evaluation LREC. European Language Resources Association (ELRA), 2016, pp. 1171–1176.

[5] A. Balahur, J. M. Hermida, A. Montoyo, and R. Muñoz, "Detecting implicit expressions of affect in text using emotinet and its extensions," Data Knowl. Eng., vol. 88, 2013, pp. 113–125.

[6] C. Strapparava and A. Valitutti, "WordNet Affect: an affective extension of WordNet," in Proceedings of the Fourth International Conference on Language Resources and Evaluation, LREC. European Language Resources Association (ELRA), 2004, pp. 1083–1086.

[7] V. Bobicev, V. Maxim, T. Prodan, N. Burciu, and V. Anghelus, "Emotions in words: Developing a multilingual wordnet-affect," in Computational Linguistics and Intelligent Text Processing, 11th International Conference, CICLing, 2010, pp. 375–384.

[8] L. J. Cronbach, "Coefficient alpha and the internal structure of tests," Psychometrika, vol. 16, no. 3, 1951, pp. 297–334.

[9] A. Kailer and C. K. Chung, "The Russian LIWC2007 dictionary," LIWC.net, Tech. Rep., 2011.

[10] T. Litvinova, O. Litvinova, and P. Seredin, "Dynamics of an idiostyle of a Russian suicidal blogger," in Proceedings of the Fifth Workshop on Computational Linguistics and Clinical Psychology: From Keyboard to Clinic. Association for Computational Linguistics, 2018, pp. 158–167.

[11] T. Litvinova, P. Seredin, O. Litvinova, T. Dankova, and O. Zagorovskaya, "On the stability of some idiolectal features," in Speech and Computer. Springer, 2018, pp. 331–336.

[12] G. L. Clore, A. Ortony, and M. A. Foss, "The psychological foundations of the affective lexicon," Journal of Personality and Social Psychology, vol. 53, no. 4, 1987, pp. 751–766.

[13] C. Strapparava, A. Valitutti, and O. Stock, "The affective weight of lexicon," in Proceedings of the Fifth International Conference on Language Resources and Evaluation, LREC. European Language Resources Association (ELRA), 2006, pp. 423–426.

[14] O. Kanishcheva and V. Bobicev, "Good news vs. bad news: What are they talking about?" in Proceedings of the International Conference Recent Advances in Natural Language Processing, RANLP, 2017, pp. 325–333.

[15] E. Kotelnikov, T. Peskisheva, A. Kotelnikova, and E. Razova, "A comparative study of publicly available Russian sentiment lexicons," in Conference on Artificial Intelligence and Natural Language, AINL, 2018, pp. 139–151.

[16] D. Pisarevskaya, T. Litvinova, and O. Litvinova, "Deception detection for the Russian language: Lexical and syntactic parameters," in Proceedings of the Workshop Natural Language Processing and Information Retrieval, 2017, pp. 1–10.

[17] S. Shaikh et al., "ANEW+: automatic expansion and validation of affective norms of words lexicons in multiple languages," in Proceedings of the Tenth International Conference on Language Resources and Evaluation LREC. European Language Resources Association (ELRA), 2016, pp. 1127–1132.

[18] M. Korobov, "Morphological analyzer and generator for Russian and Ukrainian languages," in Analysis of Images, Social Networks and Texts. Springer, 2015, pp. 320–332.

[19] I. Segalovich, "A fast morphological algorithm with unknown word guessing induced by a dictionary for a web search engine," in Proceedings of the International Conference on Machine Learning; Models, Technologies and Applications. CSREA Press, 2003, pp. 273–280.

[20] P. Ekman, "Basic emotions," in Handbook of Cognition and Emotion. John Wiley & Sons, Ltd, 2005, pp. 45–60.

[21] R. Plutchik, "A general psychoevolutionary theory of emotion," in Theories of Emotion. Elsevier, 1980, pp. 3–33.

[22] C. E. Izard, Human Emotions. Springer US, 1977.

[23] R. I. Yaranzev, Russian phraseology: dictionary: around 1,500 phraseologisms [In Russian: Russkaya fraseologiya: slovar'-spravochnik: okolo 1,500 fraseologismov]. Russian language, 1997.

[24] O. N. Lyashevskaya and S. A. Sharoff, Modern Russian frequency dictionary [In Russian: Chastotnyi slovar'sovremennogo russkogo yazyka]. Azbukovnik, 2009.

[25] V. M. Mokienko and T. G. Nikitina, Big Dictionary of the Russian Slang: 25,000 words, 7,000 expressions [In Russian: Bolshoy slovar'russkogo zhargona: 25,000 slov, 7,000 ustoychevyh sochetanij]. Norint Publ, 2000.

[26] "Yandex Toloka," 2019, URL: http://www.somewebpage.org/ [accessed: 2019-03-06].

[27] D. Ustalov, "Expanding hierarchical contexts for constructing a semantic word network," in Dialogue, vol. 16, 2017, pp. 369–381.

[28] A. Panchenko et al., "RUSSE'2018: A shared task on word sense induction for the Russian language," in Proceedings of the 24rd International Conference on Computational Linguistics and Intellectual Technologies (Dialogue'2018), vol. 17, 2018, pp. 547–564.

[29] C. E. Izard, The Psychology of Emotions. Springer US, 1991.

[30] S. Mohammad and P. D. Turney, "Crowdsourcing a word-emotion association lexicon," Computational Intelligence, vol. 29, no. 3, 2013, pp. 436–465.

Sentiment Analysis of French Political Tweets: #MacronPrésident

Antoine Vanrysselberghe and Els Lefever
LT[3], Language and Translation Technology Team
Ghent University, Belgium
Groot-Brittanniëlaan 45, 9000 Ghent
Email: {antoine.vanrysselberghe,els.lefever}@ugent.be

Abstract—**The perpetual democratization of the Internet has made web user opinions on a wide range of topics continuously grow in value. As a result, many approaches to automatically analyse this user generated data have emerged over the last two decades. Sentiment analysis, in particular, aims to detect the presence of positive or negative sentiment within text. In this pilot study, we implement sentiment analysis on 615 political French tweets that all relate to the current French president, Emmanuel Macron. The experimental results show a satisfying performance of the supervised machine learning approach given the moderate size of the corpus. At the same time, the results reveal that the unequal distribution of the sentiments within the corpus (66% negative sentiment labels) considerably impacts the performance of the system for the positive and neutral sentiment labels. This pilot study shows, however, that supervised machine learning is a viable way to detect the global opinion of the French citizens on their president.**

Keywords–sentiment analysis; French political tweets; social media analysis.

I. Introduction

For a long time, mankind has eagerly tried to understand how people feel and how to decipher hidden meanings behind any type of utterance. The advent of the web 2.0 has without any doubt helped us to get closer to these goals. In that respect, sentiment analysis refers to an automatic Natural Language Processing (NLP) method that aims to detect the presence of a sentiment or an emotion in text and to classify this text according to a certain polarity (positive, negative or neutral). In addition, this field of research incorporates a great deal of additional dimensions. Researchers have, for example, created systems that are able to detect subjectivity, the type of expressed emotion or even the intensity of the emotion in question [1].

According to Pang and Lee [2], automatic sentiment analysis starts to draw the attention in 2001. The many opportunities that this method brings to the table and the many doors that it could end up opening start to catch the interest of various domains such as the political, sociological, financial, governmental, publicity and marketing domains. As Boullier and Lohard [3] point out, sentiment analysis now forms "an evident resource for any marketing or communication team of a brand". That being said, this steadily growing interest is not only linked to the development of sentiment analysis. The progress in the field of machine learning, the expansion of the web together with the rise of 'Big Data', as well as the ever increasing ability to vent your personal opinion on the internet have all played a considerable role towards that development [4].

Social media platforms like Facebook and Twitter have become increasingly popular in the NLP research community. In fact, this scientific interest can be regrouped under multiple primary reasons. First of all, the content on these networks is almost entirely user-generated, which also potentially means that any message that has been posted contains an opinion or some trace of subjectivity. Additionally, the user is free to post whatever he wants, what leads to a wide array of themes and subjects that, for the most part, are generally linked to current events. This can, for example, be seen via the 'trending hashtag' section on the Twitter homepage. Boullier and Lohard [3] observe that this cluster of opinions at a certain point in time can also be used to analyse the evolution of opinions on a certain subject, given that such analysis occurs on a regular basis. Secondly, the application programming interface of the vast majority of these social media platforms is openly accessible, which makes data collection very easy, as stated by Fang and Zhan [5]. Finally, the amount of people that generate content online is massive. As an example, Twitter and Facebook together boast more than 1500 million active users a day (100 million and 1400 million, respectively) [6]. Such social media platforms can therefore be seen as gigantic data mines that allow researchers, businesses as well as other individuals to collect data on a wide spectrum of different subjects. These parties have the opportunity to analyse the behaviour of shareholders within the stock market, the political tendencies of specific countries or even the development of new internet phenomena such as GIFs (Graphics Interchange Format) and memes [7]. In addition, specialised websites have even been created to gather the opinion of web users on a multitude of specific domains. Some examples are IMBD, Rotten Tomatoes, the video-gaming platform Steam or even Myanimelist for everything related to manga and Japanese animation. Multiple companies have created a core business out of annotating data for sentiment analysis. On the one hand, businesses have specialised themselves in data collection for their clients. On the other hand, companies, such as Indico, AYLIEN and Nexosis offer software that allow other companies to easily collect and analyse data themselves. Moreover, phone apps allow for an even easier data collection because of their Application Programming Interface (API). Furthermore, as Chevalier and Mayzlin [8] point out, customer reviews that are present on commercial websites influence the choice of future customers. A great deal of positive reviews on a certain product is therefore considered a major asset that encourages a purchase. Some online price comparison tools even present their users with an overview of positive and negative reviews for the requested product.

In the political field, which is also the main field this study focuses on, sentiment analysis can be employed to detect the public opinion, to recognize the sentiments expressed about a certain candidate, to predict the outcome of an election or even

to predict the coalitions that will be formed during or after the elections.
The remainder of the paper is organized as follows. Section II gives a brief overview of existing research and methodologies of sentiment analysis, while Section III describes the corpus that was compiled and manually annotated. Section IV describes our experimental setup and the different feature groups we used. In Section V, we report on the results of our sentiment analysis classifier and perform a detailed error analysis. Section VI concludes this paper.

II. Related research

Two main paradigms have been applied to conduct sentiment analysis [7]. The first method is the lexical-based approach, where sentiment analysis is performed by looking up word combinations and the sentiment that these combinations evoke within a sentiment lexicon. The major flaw of this approach, which is still widely applied within commercial sentiment analysis systems, lies in the fact that the list of words that are used do not include any kind of context. As a result, ambiguous words are especially difficult to map. An example of a well-performing lexicon-based approach is VADER (Valence Aware Dictionary and sEntiment Reasoner) [9], a rule-based model using lexicons, which are more sensitive to sentiment expressions in social media contexts. The second approach, which is also the one that has been put into practice during this research, is the corpus-based approach. The latter approach is for the most part integrated in machine learning, and aims to develop systems trained on (labeled) data that are able to independently attribute sentiment labels to new data, and this without any kind of human intervention. Various types of supervised approaches have been applied for sentiment analysis (a.o. Support Vector Machines, Nave Bayes, decision trees), incorporating a variety of lexical, syntactic and topical features [10]. More recently, deep learning approaches, which are inspired by the structure of the biological brain, have emerged as powerful machine learning techniques that have successfully been applied to sentiment analysis [11]. At the same time, researchers have started to investigate sentiment analysis at a more fine-grained level. Aspect-based Sentiment Analysis (ABSA) [12] [13], aims to extract (and summarize) the opinion people have on specific entities and on the aspects of said entities. It might, for instance, be the case that a user rating a new smartphone likes the battery, but thinks negatively of the screen. Although the general sentiment on the product can be positive or negative, the user might have different opinions on the different aspects of the product. This fine-grained ABSA is a challenging task, requiring automatic aspect extraction, aspect categorisation and sentiment analysis. Other important initiatives driving the sentiment analysis research are the multiple joined sentiment analysis projects that have emerged, such as SemEval (Semantic Evaluation) and DEFT (le Défi fouille de textes). These projects, that often take the form of conferences and workshops, focus among other things on hot topics within the field of sentiment analysis, such as for instance ABSA. Because of the nature of these joint projects, multiple research teams try to develop systems that aim to find the best solution for one of the many research questions, which results in some kind of friendly internal competition. All of this ultimately leads to an important amount of new research data and a comparative overview of all the systems which allows the community to unravel the methods that work best for a given task. Despite the fact that these projects have, for the most part, focused on English data, the spotlight has recently been turned on multiple foreign languages, such as Arabic, French, Dutch and even Chinese [12].
Conducting sentiment analysis on data collected from social media is bound to a couple of global difficulties that are generally not present in other data or document types. This is, for the most part, due to the fact that the core message of a tweet is often strengthened by elements that are not made up of words, such as images, GIFs and links to videos on other online platforms, for example. Furthermore, web users write, for the most part, in a rather informal way. Because of that, abbreviations that are typical of the web 2.0 surface, such as 'wdym' (what do you mean), 'ic' (I see), 'imma' (I will / I am about to), etc. While frequently used abbreviations can easily be transformed back to their original or more formal form, the web is also a dynamic place where codes, ways of writing and habits keep evolving. For the past few years, more and more abbreviations with a foreign origin keep finding their way into the French internet language. Words such as 'afk' (away from keyboard), 'omg' (oh my god) and 'wtf' (what the fuck) are starting to appear way more frequently on social media. Moreover, compared to official or professional documents, user generated data may contain spelling mistakes and wrong grammatical constructions. Frequently recurring mistakes are for example made against the indefinite articles 'tout' and 'tous' as well as mistakes against the conjugation of verbs that follow each other consecutively. When the present perfect is used, for example, the past participle is often conjugated as a simple infinitive (*j'ai manger ma pomme*). The typical social media symbols, namely hashtags, at signs, smileys and emojis, on the other hand, do not pose a real problem. As a matter of fact, hashtags and at signs can be used to determine the frequency with which they appear in the corpus. This can, among other things, be used to detect which ones often appear together. Moreover, Barbosa and Feng [14] have proven that, by exploiting the typical social media functionalities to create new features, which they call microblogging features, their sentiment analysis system performs better.
Sentiment analysis has also been applied under different angles within the political domain. Williams and Gulati [15], for example, have analyzed the impact of Facebook during the presidential elections in the United States in 2008. This study shows that the electoral support that a runner up for the White House receives on Facebook accurately reflects the success of his electoral campaign. A correlation even exists between the online electoral support of a candidate in a certain country and the final voting results. Tumasjan et al. [16] have analyzed political tweets during the federal elections in Germany in 2009. This research showed that Twitter is indeed used as a platform for political debate and that this particular social media even reflects the political mainstream that is present in the physical world. They also note that the political tweets are not only used to vent personal opinions but are also a way to share and engage with the political opinions of the other users. Additionally, a correlation between the total number of tweets (100.000) and the final results of the elections was also found. The political parties that often emerged together in the tweets reflected the coalitions that were present at that moment in time. Nonetheless, it is important to note that a small number of users (4% in that particular analysis) were responsible for 40% of the tweets within the compiled corpus.

That being said, the task of sentiment analysis is more complex than it looks like. Compared to a human being, a machine struggles to detect figures of speech, ironic or sarcastic data. As Cambria and White [17] point out, sentiment analysis now embodies a unique domain that focuses on semantics and existing sentiments, which is situated somewhere between natural language processing and the understanding of that natural language.

In this paper, we conduct a pilot study to discover the efficiency of supervised machine learning to implement sentiment analysis on French political tweets. Emmanuel Macron, the current French president is the main topic of this research. His election and his proactive policy have led to a huge amount of tweets that can be analysed to detect the global opinion of the French citizens on their president.

III. Corpus

To test the viability of sentiment analysis on French political tweets, a corpus of 615 French political tweets relating to the French president Emmanuel Macron has been manually compiled and annotated. Furthermore, two versions of the corpus were created: the first corpus contains the tweets stripped from smileys and hashtags, unless the hashtags is an integral part of a sentence. The second corpus contains the same tweets including smileys and hashtags. These two versions will allow us to analyze the impact of smileys and hashtags on automatic sentiment analysis.

As we intend to sample a global overview of the French opinion on Emmanuel Macron, tweets that were not linked to the president in any way were purposely excluded. To discover what the French think about him on different aspects, tweets were collected for four different categories: (1) the global opinion on Macron (hashtag #Macron was used together with the keyword 'Macron', 135 tweets), (2) the opinion on one of his newest laws, the housing-tax reform (hashtag #taxed-habitation and keywords 'taxe', 'habitation' and 'Macron', 124 tweets), (3) the opinion on his appearance during an exclusive interview on France 2 (#Macronjt20HWE, 210 tweets) and (4) the opinion about Macron during the elections (hashtag #macronprésident, 146 tweets).

All tweets were labeled with a sentiment label (positive, negative, neutral) and with an indication of whether a trace of irony was present in the tweet or not. Figure 1 shows the distribution of the sentiment labels. The large amount of negative labels might be surprising given the fact that Macron has been elected president with 66.1% of the votes. It is good to keep in mind, though, that the French presidential election procedure consists of different rounds. In the first round, Macron's new political party *En Marche!* and Marine Le Pen's *Front National* pulled 24,01% and 21,3% of the votes, respectively. In the second round, a lot of French citizens voted for Macron to simply block Le Pen from ascending [18].

Some general observations could be made during the corpus compilation and annotation process. Similarly to [16], a specific part of the users was responsible for many different tweets on the given subject. As the opinion of a tweeter generally does not change in a few hours between the posts, it was decided to restrict the data inside the corpus to one tweet per user. As this present study attempts to extract the global opinion of the French citizens on their new president, including multiple positive, negative or neutral tweets of a single user would inevitably skew the representation of a global opinion. Similarly, various members of different political parties, both for and against Macron, have vented their opinion on Twitter. Logically, Macron's opponents reacted negatively towards him while his adherents were supporting him in a positive way. In spite of this, retaining only one tweet per user quickly balanced out this phenomenon.

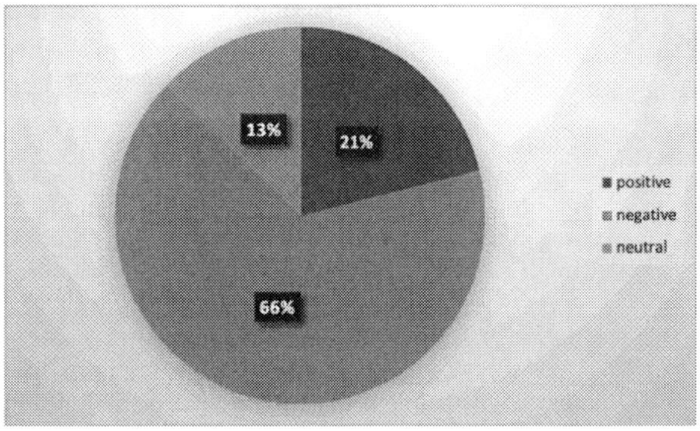

Figure 1. The distribution of the different sentiment labels in the corpus.

Moreover, around 5% of the tweets within the corpus are ironic. The vast majority of these ironic tweets also contain graphic elements, especially satires, to convey spot more efficiently. The system trained for this study, however, did not take into consideration these visual elements, which might have had a negative impact on its learning phase. Because the social media platform decided to double the character limit of a tweet from 140 to 280 characters two years ago, a very specific tweet pattern often recurred concerning the presidents interview on France 2. As the maximum amount of character increased and that the topic in question is an interview, users often inserted a specific quote of the president followed by their own opinion. Finally, when a refined search was used to further develop the corpus using the popular hashtags #macronprésident and #MacronJT20HWE, multiple spambots were encountered. These spambots abused the popularity of the hashtags to efficiently broadcast their off-topic messages. As the corpus was compiled manually, this type of data was successfully avoided.

IV. Experimental Setup

We evaluated the feasibility of sentiment analysis of French political tweets by means of a supervised classification-based approach. We opted for the LIBSVM [19] with a linear kernel as our classification algorithm. In order to train and test the system, 10-fold cross-validation was implemented, where the data is divided into 10 equal folds, allowing 90% of the data to run as training and 10% of the data to run as test within each fold. The k Cross-validation method turns out to be especially efficient within the context of this study for two main reasons. First of all, the compiled corpus remains rather small and selecting one fixed test set could lead to less reliable results. Secondly, there is a notable imbalance of sentiments within the corpus (80 neutral tweets, 130 positive tweets, 405 negative tweets). To determine the efficiency of the system, the accuracy, precision, recall and F-scores (weighted average of precision and recall) were used as performance measures.

As a preprocessing step, all posts were tokenised using the

LeTs Preprocess Toolkit [20], and the following linguistic features were constructed:

1) **Token and character n-grams**. As a great deal of comparative studies have already demonstrated, basic linguistic features are simple yet very efficient [21]. Token-n grams (varying from 1 to 3 words) as well as character n-grams (ranging between 3-4 characters) were included for the experiments.
2) **Flooding**. Textual flooding happens when a user writes the same characters or words over and over again or when he abuses punctuation marks. This can also be used as a feature to detect a certain sentiment in a text. An unsatisfied user can, for example, repeat negatively connoted words to vent his opinion as in *"Les hommes politiques ne tiennent jamais leurs promesses, j'en ai marre marre marre marre marre marre !!!!!!!!" (English: Politicians never keep their promises, I've had enough!)*. Two features based on textual flooding were extracted: token flooding and punctuation flooding.
3) **Capitalisation**. Writing complete words or even sentences in capitals can refer to a specific sentiment. In the following example, the capitals are used to further convey the dissatisfaction of the user: *"LES MENSONGES DE MACRON S'ACCUMULENT ..." (English: "MACRON'S LIES ARE ACCUMULATING...)*.
4) **The NRC lexicon**. To capture sentiment words, the French part of the NRC lexicon [21] was included in the pipeline. This lexicon, developed as a shared project, proposes a list of more than 25.000 manually annotated English terms. Each term is also linked to a certain emotion as well as to a sentiment (positive or negative). This list has been automatically translated via Google Translate into more than 100 languages, including French. The lexicon is used for the look-up of all tokens in the tweet and stores the number of retrieved positive, negative and neutral words, as well as the polarity sum as features in the pipeline.

V. Results and Analysis

Given the moderate size of the corpus (615 instances) and the unbalanced representation of each sentiment (with the negative sentiment being the most prominent), the system achieves satisfying classification results. Table I shows the experimental results per fold for the corpus where smileys and hashtags have been removed, and the difference in performance (between brackets) with the corpus including smileys and hashtags. The value between brackets was calculated by subtracting the results of the second corpus from the first one (results corpus 1 - results corpus 2). Consequently, positive values indicate that the results of the first corpus were higher whereas negative values indicate that the results of the second corpus were higher.

Overall, the system achieves convincing accuracy results, with an average accuracy of around 70%. The accuracy of the corpus without smileys and hashtags averages 68.71% compared to an average of 69.19% for the corpus including these elements. While the smiley-hashtag corpus only achieves better results twice (in the first and tenth fold), the differences amount to 5% and 4.48%, which ultimately favors it.

A first striking observation concerns the zero values, which appear for two sentiments, viz. the positive and neutral sentiments. Because the positive and neutral sentiments only represent a third of the total corpus, two possible reasons can explain these zero values. Firstly, as the system had access to less positive and neutral training data, it seems to have had a harder time identifying these two sentiments. Secondly, the zero values for the positive sentiments only appear in the first and third folds, which contained very few positive tweets (five positive tweets and one single positive tweet in the first and third fold, respectively). This offers the system an extremely small error margin. The zero values for the neutral sentiment can be explained the same way. From the 300 tweets that these five folds contain, only 24 tweets contain a neutral sentiment. Moreover, the neutral sentiment remains the least represented sentiment in the corpus. Two actions could be taken to circumvent this problem. The first option would be to equally allocate the amount of positive, negative and neutral tweets in each fold. The second option would obviously be to expand the corpus to collect more positive and neutral tweets. This would allow the system to be better prepared for the detection of these two (underrepresented) sentiments.

It is clear that the system that was trained for this pilot study achieves much better results when it comes to the detection of negative sentiments. The third fold even contains results exceeding 90%. Furthermore, this fold only contains two non-negative tweets, which explains this almost flawless results. Similarly, folds 4 and 7 propose above average results. Yet, the precision of folds 1, 8 and 10 are rather mediocre (66.67%; 58.70% and 59.30%, respectively). The system often makes the same type of mistake inside these folds: it has a hard time attributing the correct label to tweets that are formulated as questions as well as to positive tweets that contain negatively connoted words. In the latter case, the system falsely labels the tweet as containing a negative sentiment, as is the case for the following example: *L'ingratitude est le signe des leaders implacables. Aurait-on enfin un bon président? (English: Ingratitude is the sign of relentless leaders. Would we finally have a good president?)*.

In fold 8, the system often failed to predict a positive label. As a result, we can observe a mediocre precision of the negative sentiment (58.70%), which correlates with the mediocre recall of the positive sentiment (40.63%). Once again, these errors appear most of the time when a positive tweet contains negatively tainted words: *Non, pas d'accord. Il a été pertinent. Comme d'habitude (English: No, I disagree. It was relevant. As usual.)*.

Finally, the system also struggled to analyze tweets containing abbreviations and figurative language, as in the following two examples: *L'itw de #MacronJT20HWE un grand coup de com sur un fond de politique d'austrit (English: The #MacronJT20HWE itw(interview), a publicity stunt hidden behind a political background focusing on austerity)* and *" Un âne aurait l'étiquette En Marche, il aurait été élu." (English: Should a donkey wear an 'En Marche' sticker, it might very well be elected)*.

Despite the system achieving very high results for the prediction of the negative sentiment throughout the analysis, this is not the case for the positive and neutral sentiment. Apart from the zero values that have already been discussed, the majority of the results for the positive sentiment vary between 25% and 50% with some performance peaks in the last three

TABLE I. ACCURACY, PRECISION, RECALL AND F-SCORES FOR THE POSITIVE (POS), NEGATIVE (NEG) AND NEUTRAL (NEU) SENTIMENT LABELS (IN PERCENTAGE) FOR THE SYSTEM WITHOUT SMILEYS AND HASHTAGS. THE VALUES BETWEEN BRACKETS REFLECT THE DIFFERENCE IN PERFORMANCE WITH THE SYSTEM INCLUDING SMILEYS AND HASHTAGS.

Fold	Accuracy	P_POS	R_POS	F1_POS	P_NEG	R_NEG	F1_NEG	P_NEU	R_NEU	F1_NEU
1	61.67 (-5.0)	0.00	0.00	0.00	64.71 (-2.0)	86.84 (-7.9)	74.15 (-4.1)	44.45 (-22.2)	21.05	28.57 (-3.4)
2	63.93 (1.6)	25.00 (5.0)	50.00	33.33 (4.8)	70.83 (0.6)	85.00 (4.5)	77.27 (2,3)	44.44	21.05 (-1.2)	28.57 (-1.1)
3	88.52	0.00	0.00	0.00	96.43 (-0.1)	91.53 (-3.0)	93.91	0.00	0.00	0.00
4	73.77 (1.6)	28.57 (3.6)	25.00	26.67 (1.7)	79.63 (0.4)	97.73 (2.3)	87.76 (1.2)	0.00	0.00	0.00
5	63.93	25.00 (1.9)	30.00	27.27 (1.2)	75.00 (-1.6)	81.82	78.26 (0.9)	0.00	0.00	0.00
6	70.49 (1.6)	52.94 (2.9)	64.29 (14.3)	58.06 (8.1)	82.5 (1.6)	76.74 (-2.3)	79.52 (-0.5)	25.00 (5.00)	25.00	25.00 (2.8)
7	70.49	53.85 (-4.5)	43.75	48.28 (-1.7)	76.60 (3.1)	92.31	83.72 (1.9)	0.00	0.00	0.00
8	65.57	92.86	40.63	56.52 (-1.3)	57.45	96.43 (-1.0)	72.00	0.00	0.00	0.00
9	70.49	73.33 (6.7)	57.89 (-5.3)	64.71 (-0.2)	69.77 (-2.7)	85.71 (2.9)	76.92 (-0.4)	66.67	28.58	40.01
10	58.21 (-4.5)	71.43 (-14.3)	20.00 (-4.0)	31.25 (-6.3)	55.93 (-3.4)	94.29 (-5.7)	70.21 (-4.3)	100.00	14.29	25.01

folds, especially fold 8 with an accuracy of 92.86%. As was already mentioned, these low results can be attributed to two deciding factors: the small corpus size and the unbalanced representation of the sentiments within the folds. The five first folds, which also contain the lowest results, only contain 25 positive tweets in total. The last folds, however, provide much higher results as many more positive tweets are present within the data. These results show that when the system determines that a tweet is positive, the given tweet is in fact positive. Yet, all the folds contain low recall scores.

A next point of analysis concerns the impact of smileys and hashtags on the sentiment analysis. Globally, the differences in performance between the first corpus (without smileys or hashtags) and the second corpus (with smileys and hashtags) are minimal. When looking at it in more detail, two major differences can be noted. First of all, the system trained on the first corpus is better at predicting positive sentiments. Secondly, the second system performs better when it comes to detecting negative sentiments.

The performance gaps are especially noticeable for the positive sentiment, and more specifically for fold 6 (a difference of 14.29% for the recall and 8.06% for the F1-score), fold 9 (a difference of 6.66% for the precision and 5.27% for the recall) as well as for fold 10 (a difference of 14.28% for the precision and 6.25% for the F-score). The performance gaps for the negative sentiment, on the other hand, are more discreet and hover around 2% to 3%. The recall results, however, fluctuate noticeably on three occasions. In fact, a 7.90% difference can be observed in the first fold, a 4.51% disparity in the second fold as well as a divergence of 5.71% in the last fold. The results for the negative sentiment, in comparison, barely differ. Despite 1%-3% differences appear here and there, the major gap resides in the precision of the first fold. In this case, a 22.22% disparity is present in favor of the second corpus.

This enhanced performance for the detection of the negative sentiment can be attributed to two determining factors. Firstly, the corpus contains many negative tweets, which entails that more negatively tainted hashtags and smileys have been added in comparison to the other sentiments within the second corpus. Furthermore, a more detailed comparative analysis has shown that users are more inclined to use emojis to express a so-called negative sentiment. The most common smileys are: the angry emojis, the crying emojis as well as the crying of laughter emojis (to express some kind of disbelief). The latter is often accompanied by a touch of irony.

As was already mentioned, figures of speech such as irony can pose a problem for machine learning systems that have not specifically been configured for it. In total, the corpus for this pilot study contains 30 ironic tweets (e.g., *Vive le roi ! (English: Long live the king!)*). In total, the system attributed a wrong label to an ironic tweet six times out of 30. In other words, the system attains an accuracy of 80% on ironic tweets. Three of the six mistakes were made when labeling a neutral tweet. In the following example, the system has attributed a neutral label to a negative tweet: *#Macron souhaiterait remplacer la taxe d'habitation par un nouvel impot qui serait plus juste mais comparable à la taxe dhabitation. Ce mec est un génie. (English: #Macron would like to replace the housing tax with a new tax that would be fairer yet comparable to the housing tax. This guy is a genius.)*. The first sentence indeed conveys a neutral sentiment at first glance. The second sentence, on the other hand, arguably conveys a negative sentiment that mocks the French president (*Ce mec est un génie*). Another example concerns a positive label that has been wrongly attributed to a negative tweet: *Ne dérangez pas Macron cette semaine , il finit de libérer la Syrie avec ses petits bras et il règle la faim dans le monde courant 2018 (English: Leave Macron alone this week, once he has finished freeing Syria with his little arms, he will have solved world hunger in the course of 2018)*. In this example, the irony clearly misleads the system. After having identified positive words such as 'libérer', the system labeled this tweet as being positive. Yet, 'ses petits bras' and mentioning the impossible task in such a short time-lapse clearly point towards mockery and discontent.

Another interesting example is the following one: *Quelle ébouriffante nouveauté. On avait pas vu a depuis...Guy Mollet en juin 1956 (English: What a mind-blowing innovation. We hadn't seen that since... Guy Mollet in June 1956)*. This example is quite interesting as it demonstrates how difficult cultural references are for automated systems. This specific reference, pointing towards Guy Mollets interview in June 1956, was one of the first interviews where a journalist was invited inside the president's office. This was something exceptional at the time. Similarly, Macrons interview in December 2017 was also held in the president's office. Yet, this time, this was seen as something old fashioned. As a result, this tweet hides a negative sentiment that the system was unable to infer.

VI. CONCLUSION

This paper presents a classification-based approach to sentiment analysis on French political tweets. To this end, a corpus of tweets concerning the current French president Emmanuel Macron has been collected and manually annotated. The experimental results and analysis show that the system developed for this pilot study achieves fairly good results given the limited corpus size, the amount of features used as well as the imbalance of the three main sentiments present in the data. Globally, the system achieves an average accuracy of 70% for both corpora. While the system does achieve high results for the detection of the negative sentiment, various improvements can be made to enhance the performance for the positive and neutral sentiment. First of all, much more data could potentially be added to the corpus as the 'Emmanuel Macron' topic generates a constant flux of new data. A larger corpus would also translate into much more training data concerning the positive and neutral sentiment. Secondly, ensuring an equal representation of each sentiment in each fold could potentially eliminate zero values and provide more streamlined results across all sentiments. Thirdly, incorporating more advanced linguistic features, such as common-sense knowledge [22], could help to improve the sentiment analysis accuracy.

A manual error analysis has revealed multiple causes for the wrong prediction of positive and neutral tweets. The presence of negatively connotated words inside a sentence, tweets formulated as a question, abbreviations, cultural references as well as figurative language all seemed to complicate the correct prediction of sentiments. Although irony usually poses a major problem in sentiment analysis, the system achieved convincing results with an accuracy of 80%.

Despite the unbalanced distribution of the sentiment labels in the corpus and the resulting classification problems, the lack of positive and neutral data on the current French president reflects a reality that cannot be ignored. Macron's election was a rather surprising event that occurred without a real majority vote. According to multiple sources, his election can partially be attributed to a wish to block the Front National (FN). In creating a small corpus on a specific subject, the distribution of the sentiments present in the collected data closely reflect the general opinion on the subject. In present case, a negative opinion of 70% correlates to the most recent opinion polls on Macron at the time of the study. The small corpus size can therefore be considered as a representative sample of the online public opinion. This, together with the high results for the negative tweets in comparison to the positive and neutral ones, reflect in present case the discontent and distrust of the French population towards Macron.

In conclusion, using a larger corpus for this study with a better balance of the sentiments would most certainly lead to better results, especially for the positive and negative sentiments. Overall, we can conclude that a support vector machine with a linear kernel is a viable way to perform sentiment analysis on French political tweets.

REFERENCES

[1] F. Benamara, M. Taboada, and Y. Mathieu, "Evaluative language beyond bags of words: Linguistic insights and computational applications," Computational Linguistics, vol. 43, 2017, pp. 201–264.

[2] B. Pang and L. Lee, "Opinion mining and sentiment analysis. Foundations and Trends," Information Retrieval, vol. 2(1-2), 2008, pp. 1–135.

[3] D. Boullier and A. Lohard, Opinion mining and Sentiment analysis. OpenEdition Press, 2012.

[4] C. Van Hee, Sentiment Analysis for political tweets: a corpus study (original title: L'analyse des sentiments appliquée sur des tweets politiques: une étude de corpus). Ghent University, 2013, phD.

[5] X. Fang and J. Zhan, "Sentiment analysis using product review data," Journal of Big Data, vol. 2(1), 2015, pp. 1–14.

[6] "Twitter by the Numbers: Stats, Demographics Fun Facts," 2018, URL: https://www.omnicoreagency.com/twitter-statistics/ [retrieved: Juin, 2019].

[7] P. Gonçalves, M. Araújo, F. Benevenuto, and M. Cha, "Comparing and combining sentiment analysis methods," in Proceedings of the first ACM conference on Online social networks. ACM, 2013, pp. 27–38.

[8] J. A. Chevalier and D. Mayzlin, "The effect of word of mouth on sales: Online book reviews," Journal of marketing research, vol. 43(3), 2006, pp. 345–354.

[9] C. J. Hutto and E. Gilbert, "VADER: A parsimonious rule-based model for sentiment analysis of social media text," in Proceedings of the 8th AAAI conference on weblogs and social media (ICWSM), 2014, pp. 216–225.

[10] M. Joshi, P. Prajapati, A. Shaikh, and V. Vala, "A survey on sentiment analysis," International Journal of Computer Applications, vol. 163(6), 2017, pp. 34–38.

[11] L. Zhang, S. Wang, and B. Liu, "Deep learning for sentiment analysis: A survey," Wiley Interdisciplinary Reviews: Data Mining and Knowledge Discovery, 2018. [Online]. Available: https://doi.org/10.1002/widm.1253

[12] M. Pontiki et al., "SemEval-2016 task 5: Aspect based sentiment analysis," in Proceedings of the 10th international workshop on semantic evaluation (SemEval-2016), 2016, pp. 19–30.

[13] O. De Clercq, E. Lefever, G. Jacobs, T. Carpels, and V. Hoste, "Towards an integrated pipeline for aspect-based sentiment analysis in various domains," in Proceedings of the 8th Workshop on Computational Approaches to Subjectivity, Sentiment and Social Media Analysis, 2017, pp. 136–142.

[14] L. Barbosa and J. Feng, "Robust Sentiment Detection on Twitter from Biased and Noisy Data," in Proceedings of the 23rd International Conference on Computational Linguistics (COLING 2010), 2010, pp. 36–44.

[15] C. B. Williams and G. J. Gulati, "Facebook grows up: An empirical assessment of its role in the 2008 congressional elections," in Annual Meeting of the Midwest Political Science Association, 2009, pp. 2–5.

[16] A. Tumasjan, T. Sprenger, P. Sandner, and I. Welpe, "Predicting elections with twitter: What 140 characters reveal about political sentiment," in Proceedings of the Fourth International AAAI Conference on Weblogs and Social Media, 2010, pp. 178–185.

[17] E. Cambria and B. White, "Jumping NLP curves: A review of natural language processing research," IEEE Computational Intelligence Magazine, vol. 9(2), 2014, pp. 48–57.

[18] "Presidential Election: vote white or Macron, LR excludes abstention regarding the FN (original title: Présidentielle: voter blanc ou Macron, LR exclut l'abstention face au FN)," 2017, URL: https://www.lexpress.fr [retrieved: Juin, 2019].

[19] C.-C. Chang and C.-J. Lin, "LIBSVM: A Library for Support Vector Machines," ACM Transactions on Intelligent Systems and Technology (TIST), vol. 2(3), 2011, pp. 1–27.

[20] M. Van de Kauter et al., "LeTs Preprocess: the Multilingual LT3 Linguistic Prepro- cessing Toolkit," Computational Linguistics in the Netherlands Journal, 2013, pp. 103–120.

[21] S. Mohammad, S. Kiritchenko, P. Sobhani, X. Zhu, and C. Cherry, "Semeval-2016 task 6: Detecting stance in tweets," in Proceedings of the 10th International Workshop on Semantic Evaluation (SemEval-2016), 2016, pp. 31–41.

[22] E. Cambria, D. Olsher, and D. Rajagopal, "SenticNet 3: a common and common-sense knowledge base for cognition-driven sentiment analysis," Twenty-eighth AAAI conference on artificial intelligence, 2014.

Towards an Empirically Grounded Framework for Emotion Analysis

Luna De Bruyne, Orphée De Clercq and Véronique Hoste

LT^3, Language and Translation Technology Team
Ghent University
Groot-Brittanniëlaan 45, 9000 Ghent, Belgium
Email: {luna.debruyne, orphee.declercq, veronique.hoste}@ugent.be

Abstract—**The first step in training a system for automatic emotion detection consists of manual data annotation. Because there is no consensus on a standard emotion framework, we established a label set which is justified both theoretically and practically. Frequency and cluster analysis of 229 tweet annotations resulted in a label set containing the 5 emotions *Love*, *Joy*, *Anger*, *Nervousness* and *Sadness*. Our label set shows fair resemblance to Ekman's basic emotions, but due to our data-driven approach, our label set is much more grounded in the task (emotion detection) and the domain (Dutch tweets).**

Keywords–Emotion Detection; NLP; Emotion Annotation.

I. Introduction

Emotions play a central role in how we perceive the world and how we communicate with it, making them a prominent object of study in many research fields, including psychology [1], linguistics [2], and neurobiology [3]. In Natural Language Processing (NLP), emotion analysis has attracted interest the last decades because of its myriad of applications, including market analysis and customer satisfaction for business intelligence [4], educational and pedagogical applications [5], analysing political tweets and public sentiment [6], crisis communication [7], and mental health applications [8].

Our overall objective is to create an automatic emotion detection system for Dutch. As emotion detection has mainly been studied for English data [9], [10], [11], but only to a limited extent for some other languages, our first step will consist in manually labeling Dutch textual data with emotions following a certain framework. Notwithstanding the long history of theoretical emotion research in psychology and its recent surge in NLP, there is currently no consensus on a standard emotion framework. Categorical models, mostly offering a set of basic emotions, and dimensional representations (see Section II) coexist, and even within those models, different sets of basic emotions and dimensions can be found. This wide spectrum of frameworks impedes the exchange of data and knowledge resources (e.g., annotated datasets and emotion lexicons), which are crucial to train supervised machine learning approaches for emotion detection, and makes it difficult to compare different NLP systems handling emotions. Moreover, the motives on which a particular emotion framework is selected in studies on automatic emotion detection are often unclear, and the frameworks seem to be chosen rather arbitrary.

In this paper, we wish to establish an emotion framework which is justified both theoretically and practically to perform automatic emotion detection on Dutch tweets. To this end, we start from theories about emotion in psychology (more specifically, the work of Shaver et al. [12]), but, contrary to research in the psychological tradition, we work with real-life data instead of words in isolation. This real-life data comes from the same distribution as the data on which we will perform the ultimate task of emotion detection. This ensures that our framework is empirically grounded, which would not be the case if we arbitrary adopted a framework from psychological emotion theory.

To this purpose, we collected a large dataset of Dutch tweets comprising at least one emoji, and we annotated 300 tweets by labeling all possible emotion categories as conveyed by the author of the tweet. First, we performed an Inter-Annotator Agreement (IAA) study by having a small subset of the data (50 tweets) annotated by three different annotators, and we found that for most categories a moderate to substantial agreement could be observed. Subsequently, the remaining 250 tweets were annotated and a cluster analysis was performed. This leads to a reduced, empirically grounded emotion framework consisting of the 5 emotions *Love*, *Joy*, *Anger*, *Nervousness* and *Sadness*.

The remainder of this paper is organized as follows: in Section II, we describe the related work. Section III presents the data collection, IAA study, annotations and explains the clustering technique that was used. In Section IV, we present the results and Section V concludes this paper.

II. Related Work

In emotion theory, two main approaches for emotional representation coexist, namely, (i) representation based on a categorical model and (ii) based on a dimensional model.

In the dimensional approach, emotions are seen as a vector in a multidimensional space, e.g., with the two dimensions *Valence* (from *Displeasure* to *Pleasure*) and *Arousal* (from *Calmness* to *Excitement*) [13], the three-dimensional *Valence-Arousal-Dominance* model [14] or even a four-dimensional model which also takes *Unpredictability* into account [15].

Categorical representation models, however, involve cognitive labeling of emotions, typically using a set of basic emotions, with the theories of Ekman [16] and Plutchik [17] being the most influential ones. Ekman reports that *Joy*, *Surprise*, *Anger*, *Fear*, *Disgust* and *Sadness* are the six most basic emotions and that these can be linked to universal facial expressions. Plutchik added *Trust* and *Anticipation* to Ekman's set, resulting in a set of eight emotions. Basic emotion frameworks have been provided by many other theorists, ranging from 2 to 14 emotions. Table I gives an overview of different basic emotion frameworks. This list is adapted from [18].

More extensive frameworks exist, but then the categories are not mere basic emotions. Often, they contain secondary emotions, which are more complex categories and can be seen

TABLE I. BASIC EMOTION FRAMEWORKS.

	Author	*Basic Emotions*
[19]	Arnold (1960)	Anger, aversion, courage, dejection, desire, despair, fear, hate, hope, love, sadness
[16]	Ekman (1992)	Anger, disgust, fear, joy, sadness, surprise
[20]	Frijda (1986)	Desire, happiness, interest, surprise, wonder, sorrow
[21]	Gray (1982)	Rage, anxiety, joy
[22]	Izard (1971)	Anger, contempt, disgust, distress, fear, guilt, interest, joy, shame, surprise
[23]	James (1884)	Fear, grief, love, rage
[24]	McDougall (1926)	Anger, disgust, elation, fear, subjection, tenderness, wonder
[25]	Mowrer (1960)	Pain, pleasure
[26]	Oatley & Johnson-Laird (1987)	Anger, disgust, anxiety, happiness, sadness
[27]	Panksepp (1982)	Expectancy, fear, rage, panic
[17]	Plutchik (1980)	Acceptance, anger, anticipation, disgust, joy, fear, sadness, surprise
[28]	Tomkins (1984)	Anger, interest, contempt, disgust, distress, fear, joy, shame, surprise
[29]	Watson (1930)	Fear, love, rage
[30]	Weiner & Graham (1984)	Happiness, sadness
[31]	Epstein (1984)	Fear, anger, sadness, joy, (love, affection)
[32]	Roseman (1984)	Surprise, hope, fear, joy, relief, sorrow, discomfort/disgust, frustration, liking, disliking, anger, pride, shame/guilt, regret

TABLE II. EXTENSIVE EMOTION LISTS.

	Author	*Emotion List*
[17]	Plutchik (1980)	Aggressiveness, anxiety, awe, contempt, curiosity, cynicism, delight, despair, disapproval, dominance, envy, guilt, hope, love, morbidness, optimism, outrage, pessimism, pride, remorse, sentimentality, shame, submission, unbelief
[13]	Russell (1980)	Afraid, alarmed, angry, annoyed, aroused, astonished, at ease, bored, calm, content, delighted, depressed, distressed, droopy, excited, frustrated, glad, gloomy, happy, miserable, pleased, relaxed, sad, satisfied, serene, sleepy, tense, tired
[12]	Shaver et al. (1987)	Affection, cheerfulness, contentment, disappointment, disgust, enthrallment, envy, exasperation, horror, irritability, longing, lust, neglect, nervousness, optimism, pride, rage, relief, sadness, shame, suffering, surprise, sympathy, torment, zest
[33]	Schröder et al. (2011)	Affection, amusement, anger, annoyance, anxiety, boredom, calmness, contempt, contentment, courage, delight, despair, disappointment, disgust, doubt, elation, embarrassment, empathy, envy, excitement, fear, friendliness, frustration, guilt, happiness, helplessness, hope, humility, hurt, interest, irritation, joy, love, pleasure, politeness, powerlessness, pride, relaxation, relief, sadness, satisfaction, serenity, shame, shock, stress, surprise, tension, trust, worry

TABLE III. EMOTION DATASETS.

	Dataset	*Framework*
[10]	AffectiveText	Ekman
[11]	AffectInTweets T1, ST1-4	Anger, fear, joy, sadness
[11]	AffectInTweets T1, ST5	Plutchik + optimism, pessimism, love
[34]	Blogs	Ekman + no emotion + mixed emotion
	CrowdFlower	Ekman + enthusiasm, fun, hate, neutral, love, boredom, relief, empty
[35]	DailyDialogs	Ekman
[6]	Electoral-Tweets	Plutchik
[36]	EmoInt	Anger, fear, joy, sadness
[37]	Emotion-Stimulus	Ekman + shame
[38]	Grounded-Emotions	Happy, sad
[39]	ISEAR	E + shame, guilt
[40]	SSEC	Plutchik
[9]	Tales	Ekman (anger and disgust merged)
[41]	TEC	Ekman with posite and negative surprise

as combinations of basic emotions. The extended version of Plutchik's [17] emotion model, for example, counts thirty-two emotions, of which only eight are basic and the other twenty-four are secondary emotions (e.g., the secondary emotion *Optimism* is defined as the combination of the basic emotions *Optimism* and *Joy*). Also Russel [13] provides a list of some emotion terms, but these are rather stimuli or examples to illustrate the representation model and not basic emotions. Worth mentioning is also the emotion taxonomy proposed by Shaver et al. [12]. This taxonomy was obtained by means of a similarity-sorting task of 135 terms that were experimentally shown to be prototypical emotion words: 213 emotion words were rated by 112 psychology students for prototypicality, resulting in 135 prototypical emotion words. Then, 100 students grouped those emotion words into categories (without a predefined number of categories), which resulted in 100 135x135 co-occurrence matrices that were combined and used as input for the cluster analysis. This resulted in 25 categories, which were subsequently classified under six basic categories: *Love*, *Joy*, *Surprise*, *Anger*, *Sadness* and *Fear*. Table II presents an overview of these extensive emotion lists.

Regarding frameworks used in NLP, categorical frameworks are dominant, and both Ekman's and Plutchik's set of basic emotions are popular (see Table III for an overview of the most used English emotion datasets that use a categorical label set). Sometimes, another framework is chosen specifically based on the task/domain (e.g., [8] employ a set of 15 emotions to investigate signs of suicidal behavior). However, more often the motives on which a particular emotion framework is selected are unclear. [33] expressed the need of a standardized model for emotion detection tasks, resulting in the creation of the Emotion Annotation and Representation Language (EARL). Although this framework originates from the field of Affective Computing, its construction was not data-driven nor experimentally grounded. Moreover, we are not aware of any studies in NLP that make use of this framework.

III. METHOD

In order to establish a framework for emotion detection that is justified both theoretically and practically, we collect a corpus of real-life data which we annotate with an initial extensive emotion label set. Then, we perform a cluster analysis to reveal which categories to merge into one category, resulting in a smaller, empirically grounded label set.

A. Initial Labels

The initial label set needs to be sufficiently large to capture enough nuances between emotion categories. Most basic emotion sets are rather brief (the most popular ones, [16] and [17], contain only six and eight categories, respectively) and do not capture nuances like *Frustration* and *Envy*, which usually are subsumed under the *Anger* category. However, we think that such differentiations can be useful in certain domains. Moreover, much of the frameworks have a skewed distribution regarding sentiment polarity, with significantly more negative than positive emotions: for example, [22] has only two out of ten emotions that are unambiguously positive. In Ekman's set, only *Joy* is clearly positive, *Anger*, *Disgust* and *Fear* are negative, and *Surprise* can be either negative or positive.

Some frameworks also provide secondary emotions (e.g., [17]), which of course results in a larger emotion set. However,

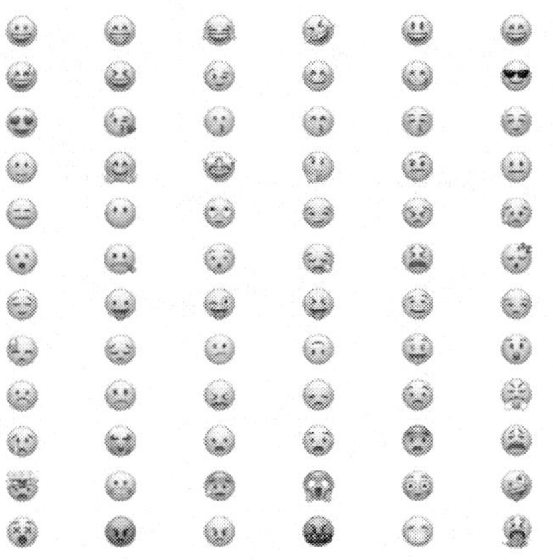

Figure 1. Emoji's used as queries for collecting tweets.

using such a set of secondary emotions as input for cluster analysis to again obtain a smaller set of categories, seems like a circular approach and is therefore not an option.

Taking this into account, we chose the emotion taxonomy of [12] as a starting point (see Table II). The main advantage of using these 25 emotion words is that the label set is not biased: although one could argue that these are secondary emotion words, they are not deducted from basic emotion categories (on the contrary, it is the other way around). This is a big difference with a framework like Plutchik's [17], where a secondary emotion word is seen as a combination of two or more basic emotion words. Moreover, this label set is independent, and not chosen to fit a certain model (unlike for example [13], where the emotion words are not prototypical, but seem to be chosen to fit the pleasure-arousal circumplex model).

Although the set of 25 emotions was already further clustered into a final set of six basic emotions in the original work of [12], our cluster analysis is no repetition of this approach. While the clustering of [12] was based on the results of a similarity-sorting task of 135 words, our analysis is performed on annotations of real-life data. As this data is similar to the data on which we eventually want to perform emotion detection, our approach ensures that our label set is more grounded in the task of emotion detection and on the domain we are interested in, instead of merely adapted from the psychology field.

B. Data

We wanted to obtain a collection of Dutch tweets that could be considered high in emotions. To increase the chance of scraping emotional tweets, we used a list of 72 emoji's (see Figure 1) as queries in the database for Dutch tweets Twiqs.nl [42]. We downloaded all tweets that the database returned from the year 2017 and took a random subset of 300 tweets. Before distributing the tweets over the annotators, we removed all duplicates and non-Dutch tweets and replaced them with another random tweet from our overall collection.

The tweets were annotated in a multi-label setup: for each of the 25 emotion words, the annotator needed to indicate whether the emotion is expressed (explicitly or implicitly) or not. Because we are interested in the emotional state of the author while writing the tweet, the annotator was asked to project oneself into the perspective of the tweet's author.

The annotation team consisted of three experienced linguists. In a first round, all three annotators labeled the same 50 tweets according to predefined guidelines. We determined inter-annotator agreement by calculating Cohen's Kappa [43] between each annotator pair and taking the mean of those two scores. IAA varied largely across emotion categories (see Table IV). For most categories, a moderate ($0.4 < \kappa < 0.6$) to substantial ($0.6 < \kappa < 0.8$) agreement can be observed. When leaving the emotions out of consideration for which at least one annotator never indicated it as present (6 categories), the mean Kappa score is 0.498 (moderate agreement). Mean Kappa score between Annotator 1 and 2 was 0.425; 0.465 between Annotator 2 and 3; and 0.533 between 1 and 3.

TABLE IV. IAA SCORES OF FIRST ANNOTATION ROUND

Emotion	κ	*Emotion*	κ
Anger	0,619	Lust	0,772
Contentment	0,525	Nervousness	-0,014
Disappointment	0,418	Optimism	0,473
Disgust	0,635	Pity	0,13
Enthrallment	0,067	Pride	0,772
Enthousiasm	0,502	Rejection	nan
Envy	nan	Relief	-0,009
Fear	0,772	Remorse	-0,007
Frustration	0,593	Sadness	0,427
Irritation	0,53	Suffering	0,219
Joy	0,492	Surprise	0,551
Longing	0,32	Torment	nan
Love	0,36		

In the second annotation round, the remaining 250 tweets were distributed among the three annotators. These annotated tweets were merged with Annotator 3's annotations of the tweets of the first round (because she had the highest agreement with both of the other annotators). Tweets for which not a single emotion was indicated as present (and thus were judged as objective), were left aside for further analysis. Our final dataset consists of 229 emotional tweets.

C. Clustering

We regarded the annotations as vectors per emotion category, resulting in 25 229-dimensional vectors. We construct a 25x25 distance matrix by measuring the Dice dissimilarity [44] between each emotion vector pair. Dice is a common metric for assessing the (dis)similarity between boolean vectors, and contrary to the similar Jaccard metric, it gives a higher weight to double positives:

$$d(A, B) = 1 - \frac{2DP}{2DP+P_A+P_B}$$

with DP the number of double positives (value of 1 in both emotion vector A and B), P_A the number of positives (1-values) in emotion vector A and P_B the number of positives in emotion vector B. Double negatives (value of 0 in both vectors) are not counted. This implies that vector pairs differing only in one value not always get the same distance score: the distance will decrease as more instances have a value of 1 in both vectors. Emotion pairs that were more frequently annotated as present will have a relatively smaller distance.

The resulting distance matrix was then used as input for a hierarchical cluster analysis. We tried seven different linkage methods: single (Nearest Point Algorithm), complete (Farthest Point Algorithm), average (UPGMA Algorithm), weighted (WPGMA), centroid (UPGMC), median (WPGMC) and Ward's linkage (Incremental Algorithm).

IV. Results

A. Frequency Analysis

Figure 2 shows that the top 3 most frequent emotions are all positive emotions (*Contentment*, *Joy* and *Enthusiasm*). The negative emotions *Irritation* and *Frustration* complete the top 5. Eight emotions (of which six are negative) appear less than 10 times in the dataset: *Suffering*, *Relief*, *Lust*, *Rejection*, *Envy*, *Fear*, *Remorse* and *Torment*. Interestingly, only three out of six Ekman emotions appear in the top 10 of most frequent emotions, namely *Joy*, *Sadness* and *Anger*. *Fear*, on the other hand, is even the third least frequent emotion in this dataset. This possibly indicates that popular basic emotion frameworks like Ekman's are not always the most suitable to apply in an NLP task like emotion detection, let alone for data coming from a specific domain or genre such as Twitter.

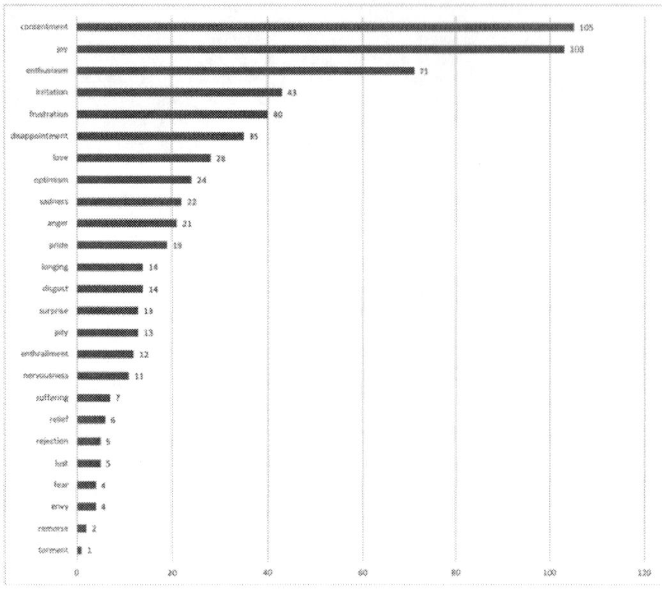

Figure 2. Frequencies of emotion categories.

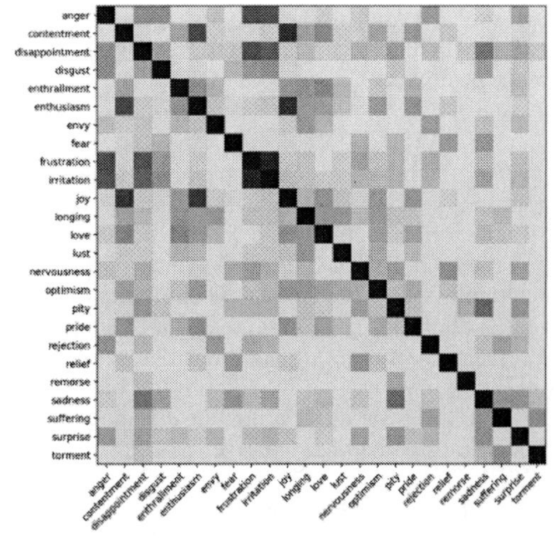

Figure 3. Distance matrix.

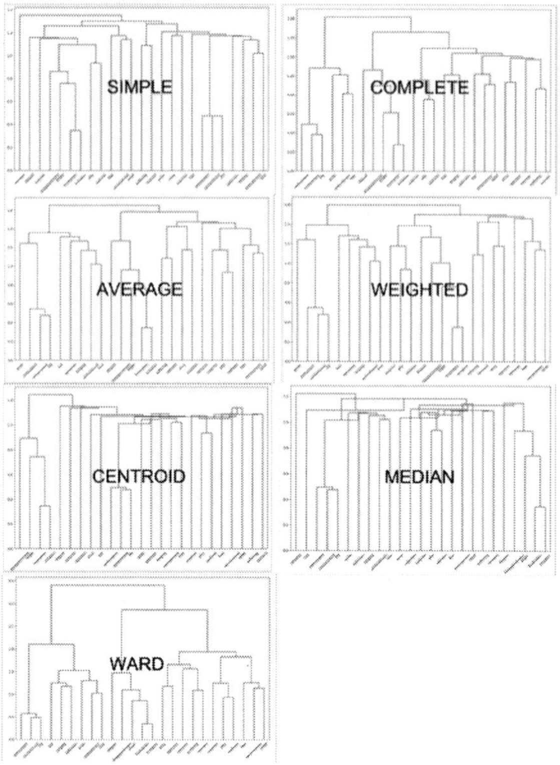

Figure 4. Dendrograms with different linking methods.

B. Cluster Analysis

Figure 3 shows the distance matrix based on the Dice dissimilarity between each emotion vector pair. This already gives some insight in which emotion categories are more related to each other. *Frustration* and *Irritation*, for example, are the most salient in terms of similarity, but also *Contentment* and *Joy* or *Enthusiasm* and *Joy* show a small distance.

We used this distance matrix as input for a hierarchical clustering algorithm. We tried seven different linkage methods, for which the dendrograms are shown in Figure 4. We asked the annotators to rank the dendrograms based on their own intuition. Their top 3 consisted of the same clusters but the order differed. After discussion, the weighted-linkage clustering was chosen as the most intuitive one. This linkage method is also known as the Weighted Pair Group Method with Arithmetic Mean (WPGMA Algorithm). At each step of the algorithm, the two clusters that have the shortest distance between each other are combined. The distance between clusters is calculated by considering the distance between each pair of elements in the clusters (with one element per cluster) and taking the arithmetic mean of those distances.

Figure 5 plots the WPGMA dendrogram with a distance of 1.3 as cut-off value. This results in eight clusters (of which one only consists of one separate emotion category: *Remorse*). Four of these clusters are related to the basic emotions of Ekman (*Joy*, *Anger*, *Sadness* and *Fear*).

However, as the frequency analysis pointed out, not all emotion categories are equally represented in this dataset. This is why we also performed a second clustering analysis excluding those emotions that were indicated less than ten

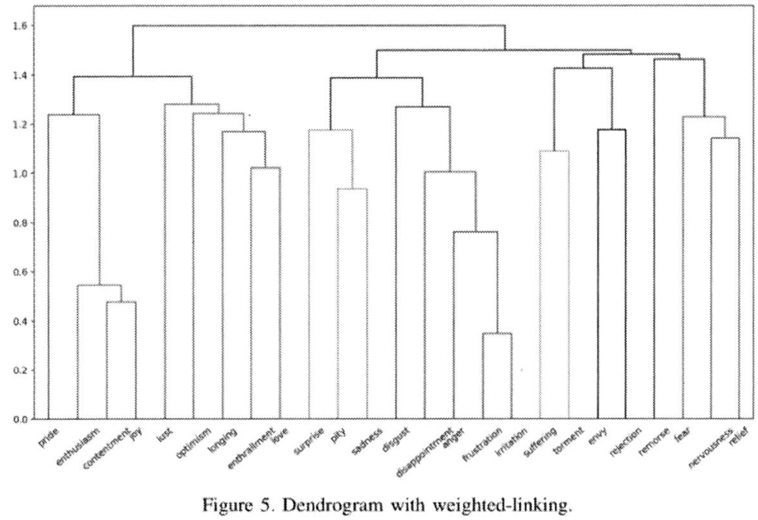

Figure 5. Dendrogram with weighted-linking.

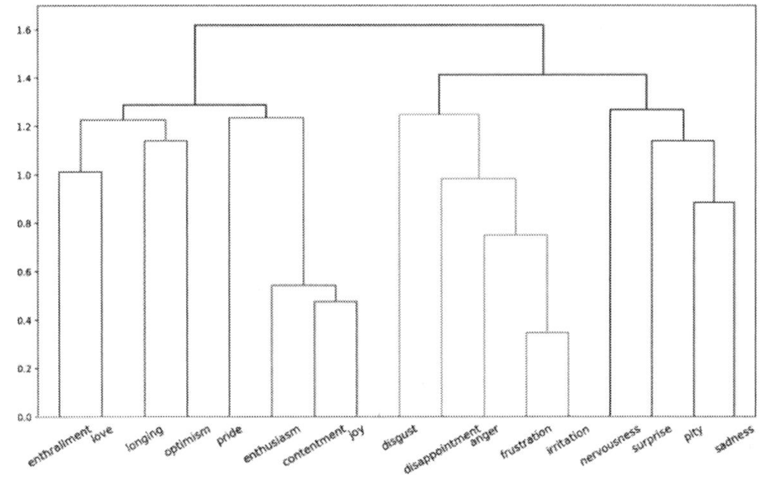

Figure 6. Dendrogram with weighted-linking without infrequent emotions.

times. This dendrogram is depicted in Figure 6. The threshold of ten might seem a bit harsh, especially since this results in the removal of the basic emotion *Fear*. However, based on Figure 5, we hypothesised that *Fear* would still be clustered together with *Nervousness* and the effect of removing it would not be problematic. We tested this and this was indeed the case. As expected, the clusters of Figure 6 are very similar to the ones in Figure 5, though only five clusters remain. Cluster 1 consists of the emotions *Enthrallment*, *Love*, *Longing* and *Optimism*, Cluster 2 comprises *Pride*, *Enthusiasm*, *Contentment* and *Joy*, the emotions *Disgust*, *Disappointment*, *Anger*, *Frustration* and *Irritation* form Cluster 3, *Nervousness* is a category on its own, and *Surprise*, *Pity* and *Sadness* are grouped together under Cluster 5.

The dendrogram nicely shows that the first two and last three categories form two distinct groups (positive versus negative emotions). Although we have a more equal distribution of negative and positive emotion clusters, our final clusters show a fair resemblance to Ekman's basic emotions.

To select an umbrella term per cluster, we take the Ekman emotion if the cluster has a term in common with the Ekman set. Otherwise, we select the emotion word with the highest frequency. This results in a final label set with *Love*, *Joy*, *Anger*, *Nervousness* and *Sadness* as emotion categories.

V. CONCLUSION AND FUTURE WORK

We established an emotion framework which is justified both theoretically and practically to perform automatic emotion detection on Dutch tweets. Frequency and cluster analyses of 229 tweet annotations resulted in a label set containing the 5 emotions *Love*, *Joy*, *Anger*, *Nervousness* and *Sadness*. Unlike many emotion frameworks directly borrowed from psychology, this label set has a more equal distribution over positive and negative emotions and due to our data-driven approach, it is much more grounded in the task (emotion detection) and the domain (Twitter). There is still a fair resemblance between Ekman's basic emotions and our labels, but we are the first that give an empirical motivation for the use of these categories.

For future work, we will use a similar approach to define

a label set for two other domains, namely subtitles of reality TV and crisis communication data and verify whether these label sets even deviate more from the popular basic emotion frameworks. In this respect, mainly the crisis communication data will be interesting due to its topic specificity (in contrast to the more general character of tweets). Moreover, we will include dimensional annotations and aggregate these into a varied corpus to be used for Dutch emotion detection.

ACKNOWLEDGMENT

This research was carried out with the support of the Research Foundation - Flanders under a Strategic Basic Research fellowship.

REFERENCES

[1] L. F. Barrett, "Are emotions natural kinds?" Perspectives on Psychological Science, vol. 1, no. 1, 2006, pp. 28–58.

[2] J. Harkins and A. E. Wierzbicka, Emotions in Crosslinguistic Perspective. De Gruyter Mouton, 2001.

[3] J. Burgdorf and J. Panksepp, "The neurobiology of positive emotions," Neuroscience & Biobehavioral Reviews, vol. 30, no. 2, 2006, pp. 173–187.

[4] R. Bougie, R. Pieters, and M. Zeelenberg, "Angry customers don't come back, they get back: The experience and behavioral implications of anger and dissatisfaction in services," Journal of the Academy of Marketing Science, vol. 31, no. 4, 2003, pp. 377–393.

[5] S. Mac Kim and R. A. Calvo, "Sentiment analysis in student experiences of learning," in Educational Data Mining, 2010, pp. 111–120.

[6] S. M. Mohammad, X. Zhu, S. Kiritchenko, and J. Martin, "Sentiment, emotion, purpose, and style in electoral tweets," Information Processing & Management, vol. 51, no. 4, 2015, pp. 480 – 499.

[7] Y. Jin, B. F. Liu, D. Anagondahalli, and L. Austin, "Scale development for measuring publics emotions in organizational crises," Public Relations Review, vol. 40, no. 3, 2014, pp. 509–518.

[8] B. Desmet and V. Hoste, "Emotion detection in suicide notes," Expert Systems with Applications, vol. 40, no. 16, 2013, pp. 6351–6358.

[9] C. O. Alm, D. Roth, and R. Sproat, "Emotions from text: Machine learning for text-based emotion prediction," in Proceedings of the Conference on Human Language Technology and Empirical Methods in Natural Language Processing. Association for Computational Linguistics, 2005, pp. 579–586.

[10] C. Strapparava and R. Mihalcea, "Semeval-2007 task 14: Affective text," in Proceedings of the Fourth International Workshop on Semantic Evaluations (SemEval-2007), 2007, pp. 70–74.

[11] S. Mohammad, F. Bravo-Marquez, M. Salameh, and S. Kiritchenko, "Semeval-2018 task 1: Affect in tweets," in Proceedings of The 12th International Workshop on Semantic Evaluation, 2018, pp. 1–17.

[12] P. Shaver, J. Schwartz, D. Kirson, and C. O'Connor, "Emotion knowledge: Further exploration of a prototype approach," Journal of personality and social psychology, vol. 52, no. 6, 1987, pp. 1061–1086.

[13] J. A. Russell, "A circumplex model of affect," Journal of Personality and Social Psychology, vol. 39, no. 6, 1980, pp. 1161–1178.

[14] A. Mehrabian and J. A. Russell, An Approach to Environmental Psychology. MIT Press, 1974.

[15] J. R. Fontaine, K. R. Scherer, E. B. Roesch, and P. C. Ellsworth, "The world of emotions is not two-dimensional," Psychological Science, vol. 18, no. 12, 2007, pp. 1050–1057.

[16] P. Ekman, "An argument for basic emotions," Cognition & Emotion, vol. 6, no. 3-4, 1992, pp. 169–200.

[17] R. Plutchik, "A general psychoevolutionary theory of emotion," in Theories of Emotion, R. Plutchik and H. Kellerman, Eds. Academic Press, 1980, pp. 3–33.

[18] A. Ortony and T. J. Turner, "What's basic about basic emotions?" Psychological Review, vol. 97, no. 3, 1990, pp. 315–331.

[19] M. B. Arnold, Emotion and Personality. Columbia University Press, 1960.

[20] N. H. Frijda, The Emotions. Cambridge University Press, 1986.

[21] J. A. Gray, "Précis of the neuropsychology of anxiety: An enquiry into the functions of the septo-hippocampal system," Behavioral and Brain Sciences, vol. 5, no. 3, 1982, pp. 469–484.

[22] C. E. Izard, The Face of Emotion. Appleton-Century-Crofts, 1971.

[23] W. James, "What is an emotion?" Mind, vol. 9, no. 34, 1884, pp. 188–205.

[24] W. McDougall, An Introduction to Social Psychology. Methuen & Co, 1926.

[25] O. Mowrer, Learning Theory and Behavior. John Wiley & Sons Inc, 1960.

[26] K. Oatley and P. N. Johnson-Laird, "Towards a cognitive theory of emotions," Cognition and emotion, vol. 1, no. 1, 1987, pp. 29–50.

[27] J. Panksepp, "Toward a general psychobiological theory of emotions," Behavioral and Brain Sciences, vol. 5, no. 3, 1982, pp. 407–422.

[28] S. S. Tomkins, "Affect theory," in Approaches to Emotion, K. R. Scherer and P. Ekman, Eds. Lawrence Erlbaum Associates, 1984, pp. 163–195.

[29] J. B. Watson, Behaviorism. University of Chicago Press, 1930.

[30] B. Weiner and S. Graham, "An attributional approach to emotional development," Emotions, Cognition, and Behavior, 1984, pp. 167–191.

[31] S. Epstein, "Controversial issues in emotion theory," Review of Personality & Social Psychology, vol. 5, 1984, pp. 64–88.

[32] I. J. Roseman, "Cognitive determinants of emotion: A structural theory," Review of Personality & Social Psychology, vol. 5, 1984, pp. 11–36.

[33] M. Schröder, H. Pirker, and M. Lamolle, "First suggestions for an emotion annotation and representation language," in Proceedings of LREC, vol. 6, 2006, pp. 88–92.

[34] S. Aman and S. Szpakowicz, "Identifying expressions of emotion in text," in International Conference on Text, Speech and Dialogue. Springer, 2007, pp. 196–205.

[35] Y. Li, H. Su, X. Shen, W. Li, Z. Cao, and S. Niu, "DailyDialog: A manually labelled multi-turn dialogue dataset," in Proceedings of the Eighth International Joint Conference on Natural Language Processing (Volume 1: Long Papers), 2017, pp. 986–995.

[36] S. M. Mohammad and F. Bravo-Marquez, "WASSA-2017 shared task on emotion intensity," in Proceedings of the Workshop on Computational Approaches to Subjectivity, Sentiment and Social Media Analysis (WASSA), 2017, pp. 34–49.

[37] D. Ghazi, D. Inkpen, and S. Szpakowicz, "Detecting emotion stimuli in emotion-bearing sentences," in Computational Linguistics and Intelligent Text Processing, A. Gelbukh, Ed. Springer International Publishing, 2015, pp. 152–165.

[38] V. Liu, C. Banea, and R. Mihalcea, "Grounded emotions," in 2017 Seventh International Conference on Affective Computing and Intelligent Interaction (ACII). IEEE, 2017, pp. 477–483.

[39] K. R. Scherer and H. G. Wallbott, "Evidence for universality and cultural variation of differential emotion response patterning," Journal of Personality and Social Psychology, vol. 66, no. 2, 1994, pp. 310–328.

[40] H. Schuff, J. Barnes, J. Mohme, S. Padó, and R. Klinger, "Annotation, modelling and analysis of fine-grained emotions on a stance and sentiment detection corpus," in Proceedings of the 8th Workshop on Computational Approaches to Subjectivity, Sentiment and Social Media Analysis, 2017, pp. 13–23.

[41] S. M. Mohammad, "#emotional tweets," in Proceedings of the First Joint Conference on Lexical and Computational Semantics-Volume 1: Proceedings of the main conference and the shared task, and Volume 2: Proceedings of the Sixth International Workshop on Semantic Evaluation. Association for Computational Linguistics, 2012, pp. 246–255.

[42] E. Tjong Kim Sang and A. van den Bosch, "Dealing with big data: The case of twitter," Computational Linguistics in the Netherlands Journal, vol. 3, no. 12, 2013, pp. 121–134.

[43] J. Cohen, "A coefficient of agreement for nominal scale," Educational and Psychological Measurement, vol. 20, 1960, pp. 37–46.

[44] L. R. Dice, "Measures of the amount of ecologic association between species," Ecology, vol. 26, no. 3, 1945, pp. 297–302.

Measuring the Impact of Sentiment for Hate Speech Detection on Twitter

Nina Bauwelinck and Els Lefever
LT[3], Language and Translation Technology Team
Ghent University, Belgium
Groot-Brittanniëlaan 45, 9000 Ghent
Email: nina.bauwelinck, els.lefever@ugent.be

Abstract—**While social media platforms, such as Twitter offer users the opportunity to express their opinions and insights freely, there is a significant risk of users silencing each other based on prejudice by means of hateful Tweets. Since Twitter's public nature makes these messages more widely disseminated, it is important to aid in the detection of such messages, which may cause harm to targeted (groups of) users. Following current state of the art, we assume the usefulness of sentiment features for the detection of hate speech messages, which tend to exhibit a higher degree of negative polarity. Therefore, we investigate the impact of these sentiment features as well as Twitter-specific and hate speech features on the performance of a supervised classification method with Support Vector Machines (SVMs). The Twitter-specific features offer the best performance increase over our strong token n-gram baseline.**

Keywords–hate speech Detection; Sentiment Analysis; Twitter.

I. Introduction

Online platforms, such as social media networks and fora offer users a wide range of opportunities to communicate their thoughts and to share insights. Most social media platforms profile themselves as instrumental agents in promoting an Internet community in its most idealized form, namely as a space for uncensored, continuous discussion of any and all topics of interest to their users. However, the unrestricted nature of the debate possibilities on these platforms entails an inherent risk due to the unpredictability of the users' discourse. Social media sites like Twitter maintain their base principle of freedom of expression and debate, but never to the expense of the well-being of their users. The underlying idea of their intolerance towards abusive and hateful behaviour is the importance of upholding a general atmosphere of safety, thereby ensuring all users feel sufficiently able to use Twitter in a productive way. To enforce their policy, Twitter, like many other social media sites, adheres to a varied strategy. They rely on user guidelines as well as the reactions of other Twitter users to disseminate the company policy. Users are able to report posts as containing hateful language, after which they are evaluated by a team of human evaluators before punitive action is undertaken towards the offending user. The human reporting and evaluation method works particularly well for instances in which the context of the Tweet largely determines its (non-)hateful nature. The Twitter policy therefore makes a distinction between "consensual" and "non-consensual" use of hateful terms, where the latter refers to actual hate speech and the former to jocular, friendly uses of offensive terms as a "means to reclaim terms that were historically used to demean individuals" [1]. It is especially these instances of consensual and covert offensive language, which pose the greatest challenges to automatic hate speech classification.

Hate speech has been defined as any form of communication which is intended to insult, intimidate or harass an individual or a group of individuals based on some characteristic (e.g., race, gender, sexual orientation, religion, nationality, etc.). Hate speech usually also expresses stereotypical assumptions about the target. Its degree of intensity can vary greatly, since its impact can range from causing offense and upsetting the target to threatening to harm or even kill the target. Davidson et al. [2] have rightly advised researchers to not restrict themselves to the more extreme form of hate speech, which incites violence, since this would significantly decrease the amount of relevant data. Many shared tasks have been organized to tackle the challenge of hate speech detection on Twitter. HatEval is one such task and has been organized by Basile et al. [3] in the context of SemEval-2019. Participating teams were asked to develop systems for the detection of hate speech against women and immigrants on Twitter, since these two groups are common targets of hateful messages online [3]. Two classification subtasks were proposed: (1) the main binary classification of the presence or absence of hate speech and (2) the fine-grained classification of hateful tweets in terms of the tweet's aggressiveness and the target of hate (individual or group).

This paper proposes a classification-based approach to hate speech detection and is an extension of previous research performed in the framework of the HatEval task [4]. The presented research is restricted to the main HatEval task, viz. the binary prediction of presence or absence of hate speech against women and immigrants. We perform a detailed analysis of the performance of a wide range of features and combinations of features, in order to get insights in the information sources that are most useful for the task of hate speech detection.

The paper is organized as follows. In Section II, we give a brief overview of the existing research and methodologies of hate speech detection on Twitter. Section III describes our experimental setup and reports on the specifics of the experiments we carried out and the different feature groups we used. In Section IV, we report on the results of our classifier incorporating different feature groups, perform a detailed error analysis and discuss possible improvements of the system. Section V concludes this paper.

II. Related Research

The related research on hate speech detection on social media shows that most researchers consider the problem a supervised classification task. More traditional machine learning algorithms (such as Support Vector Machines (SVMs)), as well as deep learning methods have been investigated and a wide range of features have been used to tackle the task [5]. Features typically utilized in the classification of hate speech include lexical surface level features like bag of words, unigrams and n-grams, which tend to perform quite well and provide a strong baseline. As is widely known, the automatic classification of User-Generated Content (UGC) poses a large amount of spelling variation problems. In order to capture as many language variants as possible of the offensive terms, character level n-grams are considered a vital feature [5]. Surface-level features specific to Twitter have also been widely used, incorporating information, such as the occurrence and frequency of hashtags, mentions, URLs, retweets and tweet length [5]. Lexicon-based features consisting of "blacklists" of hateful and offensive terms are used to capture a variety of slurs and insults typical to hate speech messages. It has been shown that the more hateful racial and homophobic terms are present in a tweet, the more likely it is to be hate speech [2]. Syntactic information features like part-of-speech (POS) information and - on a deeper level - dependency relationships are also used to add linguistic information to the classifier. Specifically for the task of hate speech detection, the use of extra-linguistic features has been investigated. These features can be useful for the detection of the hateful intent behind the tweet, e.g., by considering the Twitter user's prior posting history and use of hateful terms. These also include information about the tweeter's ethnicity or gender, but this data is often unreliable or incomplete [2].

Sentiment analysis features have demonstrated their effectiveness in hate speech detection, based on the assumption that most instances of hate speech exhibit a higher degree of negative polarity than in cases where hate speech is not present. Such features can originate from external lexicons (in which case it is preferred that the lexicon be designed for the social media domain, such as VADER [6]). However, customized hate lexicons are also constructed through the detection of language patterns in social media corpora [3]. Gitari et al. [7] have developed their own hate speech lexicon by using sentiment, subjectivity and semantic features. They then used this lexicon to develop a rule-based classifier for detecting hate speech.

Given the constraints in post length on a platform like Twitter, it is often difficult to determine whether a tweet truly contains hate speech. In order to supply the classifier with disambiguating contextual information, knowledge-based information (e.g., from ConceptNet [8]) is used to provide generic context. Nobata et al. [9] utilize distributional semantics features, which relate to the immediate context of tweets, resulting in such informative features as the preceding comments and the commenter's past behavior or comments. Djuric et al. [10] use features derived from comment embeddings with neural language models as classification input, whereas Gao and Huang [11] used neural models to develop context-aware models. It is evident that future research on hate speech detection would benefit greatly from the incorporation of more sophisticated contextual features.

As the state-of-the-art indicates, the task of hate speech detection is complicated by the characteristics of the social media data it is applied to. Nobata et al. [9] consider the intrinsic noisiness of tweets as a helpful marker of hate speech and have developed features that capture different types of noise. As mentioned before, the spelling variation issue can hamper the performance of simple lexicon lookup features.

Finally, two major issues remain as an obstacle to fully automated hate speech detection. On the one hand, there is the difficulty of detecting hateful speech whenever it is present in its more implicit form [12], for instance, when no offensive terms are present. On the other hand, the varied use of offensive language often leads to false positives, for example, as indicated by Davidson et al. [2], when lyrics containing an offensive word are quoted, but more in general whenever a user is quoting someone else, often reporting on hate speech against their own person. This also includes all cases of what the Twitter policy on hateful conduct terms "consensual" use of hateful words. While the above overview and the current paper focus on the binary classification task of detecting the presence or absence of hate speech in tweets, it remains to be said that more and more researchers emphasize the importance of related sub-tasks, which offer up more fine-grained classification possibilities, especially for cases of implicit hate speech. Such tasks include detecting whether the hate is directed or generalized [13] and detecting the use of othering language [14], which is a particularly salient feature for detecting hate speech against immigrants. It is important that such novel fine-grained classification methods continue to be investigated, since they show a lot of promise in capturing implicit hate speech when compared to traditional lexical "blacklist" methods.

This paper presents our contribution to the field of hate speech detection by developing a supervised classification method using Support Vector Machines (SVMs) with linguistic features inspired by the state of the art. We will investigate the classification performance impact of various feature groups and more specifically, the impact of sentiment features as opposed to lexical n-gram features. Following the assumption that hate speech typically exhibits a higher degree of negative polarity, we anticipate that adding sentiment information will improve performance. We believe adding sentiment features will help to capture more implicitly hateful tweets, which may help in the detection of tweets which have been 'edited' by offenders to ensure their messages can slip through the net of current automated hate speech detection methods [10].

III. Experimental Setup

The purpose of our experiments is to find out how well our framework is able to detect hate speech and to what measure sentiment features are able to improve the system performance in this task. To this end, we built various classifiers where different features and feature combinations were used. The task was approached as a supervised classification task and we applied the Library for Support Vector Machines (LIBSVM) [15] with the standard Radial Basis Function (RBF) kernel as the machine learning algorithm. In previous research [4], we performed a grid search to find the optimal hyperparameter settings for running the SVM on this type of data, resulting in a value of $c = 8.0$ and $g = 0.001953125$. In order to train and test the hate detection system, 5-fold Cross-validation was implemented, viz. the data is divided into 5 equal folds, allowing 80% of the data to run as training and 20% of the data as test within each fold.

A. Corpus

Our corpus consists of the English training data supplied in the HatEval shared task [3] of SemEval-2019. We conflated the development and training sets to make one large training set of 10,000 tweets. Half of these had the target "women", the other half "immigrants" [3]. The distribution of the labels is as follows: for the training set of 10,000 instances, 4210 are labeled as hateful (2000 of which are targeted towards immigrants, 2210 towards women) and 5790 are labeled as non-hateful (3000 targeted towards immigrants, 2790 towards women).

For preprocessing the data, the Twitter-specific module tweetokenize was used [16]. This module took care of tokenization and converted all mentions, numbers and URLs by placeholder tags. We applied an additional function to tokenize hashtags that was able to capture camelcased hashtags correctly. Since we created external lexicons for our emoji and smiley sentiment features, we also replaced all emojis in the data with a placeholder ('emoji') followed by the Unicode code of the emoji (e.g., 'emoji0001f194'), to ensure our featurizer would be able to recognize its presence in the document.

B. *Information Sources*

We aimed to develop a rich feature set that focused on lexical information, supplied with linguistic features. This featurization pipeline is based on work in cyberbullying detection and analysis [17]. Following similar research [5], we added surface-level Twitter-specific features to capture the use of hashtags, mentions and URLs. In order to investigate the performance impact of sentiment information and following the assumption that hate speech exhibits a higher degree of negative polarity, we added several general purpose sentiment lexicons as well as Linguistic Inquiry and Word Count (LIWC) [18] for capturing psychometric information. Additionally, we also used a sentiment polarity lexicon for emojis, the Emoji Sentiment Ranking lexicon [19], consisting of the 751 most commonly used emojis and their sentiment polarity score (positive, negative, neutral). Even though emojis tend to be more common in tweets than smileys consisting of only typographical characters, we also included a sentiment polarity lexicon for smileys. Finally, we developed a set of features specific to hate speech, comprising a lexicon look-up of profanity words, a feature to capture self-referential use of commonly used offensive words and a feature capturing the combination of a mention and a profanity word present in the tweet.

1) Linguistic features:

- **Token:** token unigrams, bigrams and trigrams.
- **Char:** character bigrams, trigrams and fourgrams.
- **Linguistic:** binary lexicon look-up features for the following types of linguistic information:
  - Allness: presence of allness word (e.g., "always", "everybody").
  - Diminishers: presence of diminisher word (e.g., "almost", "meh", "little").
  - Intensifiers: presence of intensifier word (e.g., "as fuck", "awful").
  - Negations: presence of negation word (e.g., "none", "nah", "nobody").
  - Imperative: presence of imperative mood.
  - Person-Alternation: if the instance contains references to both first and second person pronouns (e.g., "my" and "ur").
  - Names: presence of a proper noun.

2) Sentiment features:

- **Sentiment Lexicons (SL):** ratio of positive, negative and objective lexicon entry matches vs. all matches for the four sentiment polarity lexicons listed below; as well as the polarity sum of all matches in document:
  - AFINN-111 [20]: 2,477 English terms with sentiment score of -5 to 5.
  - Multi-perspective Question Answering (MPQA) opinion corpus [21]: 8,222 English terms with four sentiment score labels (positive, negative, both, neutral).
  - General Inquirer [22]: 3,644 English terms with sentiment score labels (positive, negative).
  - Hu and Liu Opinion Lexicon [23]: 13,202 English terms with sentiment score labels (positive, negative).
- **Linguistic Inquiry and Word Count (LIWC) Psychometric Features:** relative frequency of 64 psychometric categories in the 2001 version of the Linguistic Inquiry and Word Count dictionary [18].
- **Smiley and Emoji Sentiment Lexicons:** ratio of positive, negative and objective lexicon entry matches vs. all matches for two sentiment polarity lexicons (one containing 125 typographic smileys; the other one being the Emoji Sentiment Ranking lexicon [19], consisting of the 751 most commonly used emojis) as well as the sum of all matches in the tweet.

3) Twitter-Specific Features:

- **Hashtag, URL, Mention:** binary feature recording the presence of a hashtag, URL and @-Mention and a count feature making the sum of all hashtags present.

4) Hate Speech Features:

- **Profanity Lexicon:** counts exact matches with a lexicon containing 2,315 single and multiword expressions commonly used as slurs.
- **Self-Referential:** binary feature recording the presence of both a first person pronoun (singular and plural) and a common profanity word (e.g., "I" and "bitch").
- **Mention and Profanity:** binary feature recording the presence of both an @-mention and a common profanity word in the tweet.

IV. Results and Analysis

In this section, we present the results of our experiments with 5-fold Cross-Validation on the training data. We start by discussing the global scores and then we discuss some of the features in isolation, focusing on the outliers. We conduct a brief error analysis, observing some of the trends and instances where classification performance was particularly good and bad. We end this section by making some suggestions towards possible improvements on our current features.

We experimented with the different feature groups and individual features described in Section III in order to get a comprehensive overview of the precise impact of each feature addition on the performance of our hate speech classifier. The scores of our systems overall indicate good performance, since there are no massive outliers and none of our systems score lower than 57.91% micro-averaged F-score. The best performing system is TWIT-2, which utilizes token n-gram and twitter-specific (hashtag, URL, mention) information. The system combining all features performs well, with an average F-score of 78.11%, making it the third best out of all of the systems we trained.

Overall, our systems score better on the NOT (not hate speech) label than on the HS (hate speech) label. For the linguistic feature groups, it can be noted that the combination of token and character n-grams works well with linguistic information (LING-3: 77.94% Avg. F1). Additionally, this system also has one of the highest F1-scores for the HS label out of all the systems. The sentiment feature groups perform poorly when compared to the other groups, since most of them overgenerate on the HS label (SENT-1, SENT-3, SENT-5, SENT-7, SENT-9). We assume that the fact that information related to sentiment is often omnipresent in tweets labeled as HS and not just those labeled as NOT, leads the classifier to consider too many instances as HS. SENT-5 presents us with the most severe case of overgenerization. This is due to a similar case of smileys and (especially) emojis being present in HS tweets as much, if not more than in non-hateful tweets.

It can be noted that the addition of token n-grams seems to balance out the scores considerably, especially for the sentiment features group. Therefore, it is no surprise that the highest scoring sentiment-informed system combines token n-gram information with sentiment features (SENT-10, with avg. F1-score of 78.05%). The LIWC feature on its own (SENT-3) overgenerates more over the HS label than the Sentiment Lexicons as a separate feature (SENT-1).

Aside from the combination system (ALL), the TWIT-2 system is the highest scoring system for the HS label (73.0% F-score) and also for the NOT label (82.3% F-score, surpassing the score of our ALL system). It makes sense that this system performs quite well, since a glance at the training data confirms that the presence of a mention is usually indicative of a hateful tweet (it assumes a target is being addressed).

(1) USERNAME You're a vapid whore; one day you'll be ugly and begging for dick scraps

Additionally, lots of the hate speech tweets targeting immigrants abound in hashtags, URLs and mentions.

(2) ey #Democrats Obama agreed wth USERNAME on ILLEGAL #Immigration Now Democrats Stop Whining and Lying and Pass a BILL Your jobs depend on it #ElectionDay #RedNationRising #Trump #MAGA #GOP USERNAME URL

Overgenerization does not solely occur for the sentiment features, however. The combination of all hate speech features, without any token n-grams (namely, HATE-4) also overgenerates for HS. For the remaining hate speech features, the addition of token n-grams once more has a balancing effect on the scores.

Having discussed the global scores for all sentiment groups, we examine some of the errors made by our best performing system (TWIT-2, with an avg. F-score of 78.59%). We observe some trends in the tweets misclassified by TWIT-2 as not containing hate speech. First of all, it is clear the Mention feature is detected in both HS and NOT-labelled instances. This is illustrated in (3), where the combination of the offensive word "cunt" and the double mention does not determine the label to be HS.

(3) USERNAME USERNAME you cunt.

Secondly, the presence of a URL is also characteristic of both labels. As illustrated in (4) and (5), this feature is often present in tweets where context is important in order to arrive at the correct classification.

(4) 30 seconds after you ' re done fucking the attitude out of her URL

(5) How basic bitches wash away their weekend sins and mistakes URL

Since a lot depends on the content that the link is referring to, it would be necessary to expand this feature to exploit this information to the full.

Thirdly, the hashtag sum feature is probably the most informative of our Twitter-specific features, since a lot of the tweets in our training data labelled as HS contain a large number of them. These are predominantly hateful tweets targeting immigrants, containing both official and unofficial campaign slogans from British ("#VoteLeave", "#Brexit") and American politics ("#EndDACA", "#DrainTheSwamp", "#BuildThatWall"); as well as hashtags like "#IllegalAlien" and aggressive imperatives, such as "#SendThemBack", "#DeportThemAll", #LockThemUp" and "#StopTheInvasion" as in (6).

(6) the cubans never assimilated in miami. thats why I left. #ThirdWorldCountry #StopTheInvasion

In order to assess the performance of all the other feature groups we experimented with, we will discuss the main trends we noted in the misclassifications made by our ALL system (where the gold standard has the label HS and our system predicted NOT), containing all feature information. Concerning our hate speech features, we observe a number of errors related to specific offensive terms, which were not present in our profanity lexicon (HATE-1), for example the term "rapefugee" as in (7) and "roachingfugee" as in (8).

(7) USERNAME He's not a refugee, he's a RapeFugee!!!Past time to PURGE the West

(8) Absurdity! The Swedes overwhelmingly voted for Democracy, Freedom, Human Rights, and the Nectar of Rapefugee welfare! I'm so moved I'm willing to fund 10 of the local Roachingfugees to fuck off there never return. I hope the Swedish Gormint funds me in this grand undertaking.

Such cases can easily be captured in future by sufficiently expanding the profanity lexicon. However, determining how far such a lexicon needs to be expanded is not straightforward, since many creative insults appear with words less commonly considered to be offensive (as is the case in (9)).

(9) USERNAME USERNAME Tina, you willfully ignorant somnabulist kunt, have a beer

Our 'Self-Referential' hate speech feature was introduced in the assumption that it would increase the classification performance on instances, which contained a type of "consensual" use of offensive terms, namely when the Twitter users are referring to themselves by means of an offensive word in a self-deprecating manner. However, all of these instances were incorrectly classified by our system as hate speech, e.g., (10):

(10) I'm such a little pussy ass bitch on my period what tha fook

TABLE I. PRECISION, RECALL AND F-SCORES FOR THE HS (hate speech) AND NOT (NOT hate speech) LABEL, AND THE MICRO-AVERAGED F-SCORE (%). RESULTS OF 5-FOLD CROSS-VALIDATION EXPERIMENTS ON THE TRAINING SET.

Feature Group	Features	P_HS	R_HS	F_HS	P_NOT	R_NOT	F_NOT	AVG_F-score
	Lexical Features							
LING-1	Token	65.7	**77.9**	71.3	86.5	77.6	81.8	77.71
LING-2	Char	69.0	75.9	72.2	84.0	78.8	81.4	77.68
LING-3	Token + Char + linguistic	69.5	76.0	72.6	84.1	**79.1**	81.5	77.94
	Sentiment Features							
SENT-1	Sentiment Lexicons (SL)	28.5	62.8	39.2	87.7	62.8	73.2	62.76
SENT-2	Token + SL	67.9	77.2	72.2	85.5	78.5	81.8	78.04
SENT-3	LIWC	3.6	73.4	6.9	99.1	58.6	73.6	58.86
SENT-4	Token + LIWC	66.7	77.8	71.8	86.1	78.0	81.9	77.93
SENT-5	Smiley and Emoji	0.1	62.5	0.2	**99.9**	57.9	73.3	57.91
SENT-6	Token + Smiley and Emoji	65.4	77.7	71.1	86.4	77.5	81.7	77.55
SENT-7	SL + Smiley and Emoji	28.2	63.3	39.0	88.1	62.8	73.3	62.87
SENT-8	Token + SL + Smiley and Emoji	67.6	77.1	72.0	85.4	78.4	81.7	77.89
SENT-9	SL + Smiley and Emoji + LIWC	28.5	63.9	39.4	88.3	62.9	73.5	63.11
SENT-10	Token + SL + Smiley and Emoji + LIWC	68.1	77.1	72.3	85.3	78.6	81.8	78.05
	Twitter-Specific Features							
TWIT-1	Hashtag, URL, Mention	**73.2**	56.5	63.8	59.0	75.2	66.1	64.95
TWIT-2	Token + Hashtag, URL, Mention	68.6	**77.9**	73.0	85.8	79.0	**82.3**	**78.59**
TWIT-3	Token + Hashtag, URL, Mention + Smiley and Emoji	68.2	77.5	72.6	85.6	78.7	82.0	78.27
	Hate Speech Features							
HATE-1	Token + Profanity Lexicon	66.6	77.7	71.7	86.0	78.0	81.8	77.83
HATE-2	Token + Self-Referential	65.6	77.7	71.2	86.3	77.5	81.7	77.59
HATE-3	Token + Mention and Profanity	65.4	77.6	71.0	86.3	77.4	81.6	77.48
HATE-4	Profanity Lexicon + Self-Referential + Mention and Profanity	16.3	69.0	26.4	94.7	60.9	74.1	61.68
HATE-5	Token + Profanity Lexicon + Self-Referential + Mention and Profanity	66.7	77.4	71.7	85.8	78.0	81.7	77.78
	All Features							
ALL	All Lexical + Sentiment + Twitter-Specific + Hate Speech Features	71.1	75.5	**73.2**	83.2	79.8	81.5	78.11

There are also instances in which it contributes to the misclassification as NOT hate speech of examples, such as (11):

(11) USERNAME USERNAME USERNAME USERNAME and I thought I was a bitch, but you are, well the worst cunt ever.

This feature did perform well in the classification of tweets as NOT hate speech, in which the user is reporting having experienced hate speech against their person (12) or someone close to them (13).

(12) This is besides the catcalls, the hey babys and calling me a slut and bitch when I wasnt interested. Fuck this shit.

(13) Who the fuck is calling my girl a whore and a bitch? She hasn't even been at that school for a whole month, people are fucking stupid

The self-referential feature has helped to correctly classify tweets containing consensual use of offensive terms in very obviously non-hateful contexts, such as birthdays (14):

(14) ::smirking face emoji:: ::dancer emoji:: ::rose emoji:: ::revolving hearts emoji:: happiest of birthdays to the main hoe I hope you have a wonderful day angel USERNAME

We also believe that the Self-Referential feature might help to capture instances containing (rap) lyrics [2], since these are often sung from a first person perspective.

Finally, even though our sentiment features led to overgeneration on the HS label, our combined system (ALL) also misclassified examples like (15). This leads us to recommend the use of a feature capturing the combination of strongly negative words like "curse' and "cunt" with smileys with positive polarity as being indicative of aggression.

(15) I saw a women driving whilst speaking on the phone I cursed that cunt :)

In order to increase the effectiveness of our lexicon look-up features, it would be useful to include bigram lexicons as well. For our sentiment features, we used general purpose sentiment lexicons. However, for future experiments, it would be useful to try out lexicons, which are more sensitive to sentiment expressions in social media contexts, such as the Valence Aware Dictionary and sEntiment Reasoner (VADER) [6]. Furthermore, our system currently lacks syntactic information. We tried to mitigate this by adding lexicons containing linguistic information, like the presence of 'allness' and 'diminisher' words, but in future research we would like to incorporate more syntactic features, like POS and dependency relationships. As illustrated by example (16), which was misclassified as NOT hate speech, the performance of our combined system would benefit from begin able to capture long-range dependencies:

(16) Anyone would think that Julie Hartley-Brewer is jealous of rape victims, the way the vacuous, malicious cunt is going on about it.

This syntactic information could also improve our performance on examples of self-referential and "consensual" use of offensive terms (cfr. Supra for (10)). Finally, we can conclude that our system managed to classify the more violence-inciting instances of hate speech correctly ((17), (18)).

(17) I'd punch that cunt in the fuckin mouth. Idgaf if she's a woman URL

(18) USERNAME Its time to give hunting licenses to border homes and make it year round open season on this invading force! Free guns and ammo to

those willing to defend our borders!!! #BuildThatWall #BuildThatDamnWallNow

V. Conclusion and Future Work

We have experimented with a supervised machine learning approach incorporating different informative features for the task of hate speech detection on Twitter, building upon our previous participation to the HatEval task of SemEval-2019. Our model employed a varied feature space, ranging from linguistic information, sentiment and Twitter-specific features, to hate speech specific features. Our best model used Twitter-specific features (hashtag, URL, mention) (Avg. 78.59% F-score) and was an expansion on our token n-gram baseline (Avg. 77.71% F-score), which appeared to be a very strong baseline, as is the case for many related Natural Language Processing tasks. The sentiment features we added ended up overgenerating on the hate speech label, but when combined with our baseline, the scores evened out. The detailed error analysis we performed on our best and combined systems has made us reflect more generally on the biases related to the tasks of hate speech detection and the use of offensive language on social media like Twitter. Aside from the subjective biases impacting the annotations of different types of hate speech [2], it is useful to consider the research bias in hate speech detection identified by Zhang and Luo [24]. According to these authors, the problem of hate speech detection is often viewed starting from the same research question, namely: how can we improve the system to ensure that non-hateful instances do not get classified as hateful? This leads to evaluations, which are biased towards the detection of non-hateful messages, rather than hateful ones [24]. It is interesting to consider how this perspective is indicative of a different focus on the use(fulness) of social media. On the one hand, the principle of freedom of expression seems to lie at the root of the bias towards detecting non-hateful tweets, since the positively evaluated detection systems are those which would not result in users innocent of the use of hate speech to be banned or to receive a warning for their "consensual" use of offensive terms. On the other hand, system evaluations which are biased towards detecting hateful tweets seem driven by another guiding principle of social media platforms, i.e., the need to maintain the assurance of a safe space for its users. We agree with Zhang and Luo [24] that the second perspective is perhaps the more urgent of the two in the context of hate speech detection, but it is our opinion that other related tasks, such as detecting offensive messages would benefit more from the first perspective.

References

[1] "Hateful conduct policy," 2019, URL: https://help.twitter.com/en/rules-and-policies/hateful-conduct-policy [accessed: 2019-06-02].

[2] T. Davidson, D. Warmsley, M. Macy, and I. Weber, "Automated Hate Speech Detection and the Problem of Offensive Language," CoRR, vol. abs/1703.04009, 2017, pp. 512–515. [Online]. Available: http://arxiv.org/abs/1703.04009

[3] V. Basile et al., "Semeval-2019 task 5: Multilingual detection of hate speech against immigrants and women in twitter," in Proceedings of the 13th International Workshop on Semantic Evaluation (SemEval-2019). Association for Computational Linguistics, 2019, pp. 54–63.

[4] N. Bauwelinck, G. Jacobs, V. Hoste, and E. Lefever, "Lt3 at semeval-2019 task 5 : multilingual detection of hate speech against immigrants and women in twitter (hateval)," in Proceedings of the 13th International Workshop on Semantic Evaluation (SemEval-2019). Association for Computational Linguistics, 2019, p. 5.

[5] A. Schmidt and M. Wiegand, "A Survey on Hate Speech Detection using Natural Language Processing," in Proceedings of the Fifth International Workshop on Natural Language Processing for Social Media, 2017, pp. 1–10. [Online]. Available: https://doi.org/10.18653/v1/W17-1101

[6] C. J. Hutto and E. Gilbert, "VADER: A parsimonious rule-based model for sentiment analysis of social media text," in Proceedings of the 8th AAAI conference on weblogs and social media (ICWSM), 2014, pp. 216–225.

[7] N. Gitari, Z. Zuping, H. Damien, and J. Long, "A lexicon-based approach for hate speech detection," International Journal of Multimedia and Ubiquitous Engineering, vol. 10(4), 2015, pp. 215–230.

[8] R. Speer, J. Chin, and C. Havasi, "Conceptnet 5.5: An open multilingual graph of general knowledge," in Proceedings of the 31st international artificial intelligence research society conference (AAAI 31), 2017, pp. 4444–4451.

[9] C. Nobata, J. Tetreault, A. Thomas, Y. Mehdad, and Y. Chang, "Abusive language detection in online user content," in Proceedings of the 25th International Conference on World Wide Web, 2016, pp. 145–153.

[10] N. Djuric et al., "Hate speech detection with comment embeddings," in Proceedings of the 24th International Conference on World Wide Web. ACM, 2015, pp. 29–30.

[11] L. Gao and R. Huang, "Detecting Online Hate Speech Using Context Aware Models," CoRR, vol. abs/1710.07395, 2017. [Online]. Available: http://arxiv.org/abs/1710.07395

[12] D. Benikova, M. Wojatzki, and T. Zesch, "What Does This Imply? Examining the Impact of Implicitness on the Perception of Hate Speech," in Language Technologies for the Challenges of the Digital Age, G. Rehm and T. Declerck, Eds., 2018, pp. 171–179.

[13] M. ElSherief, S. Nilizadeh, D. Nguyen, G. Vigna, and E. Belding-Royer, "Peer to peer hate: Hate speech instigators and their targets," in Proceedings of the 12th international AAAI conference on weblogs and social media (ICWSM), 2018, pp. 52–61.

[14] W. Alorainy, P. Burnap, H. Liu, and M. Williams, "'The Enemy Among Us': Detecting Cyber Hate Speech with Threats-based Othering Language Embeddings," ACM Transactions on the Web, 9(4), pp. 1–26.

[15] C.-C. Chang and C.-J. Lin, "LIBSVM: A Library for Support Vector Machines," ACM Transactions on Intelligent Systems and Technology (TIST), vol. 2, no. 3, 2011, pp. 27:1–27:27, ISSN: 2157-6904.

[16] J. Suttles. tweetokenize. https://github.com/jaredks/tweetokenize [accessed: 2019-06-02]. (2013)

[17] C. Van Hee et al., "Automatic detection of cyberbullying in social media text," PLOS ONE, vol. 13, no. 10, 2018, pp. 1–22. [Online]. Available: http://dx.doi.org/10.1371/journal.pone.0203794

[18] P. J. Tausczik, Y.R., "The psychological meaning of words: Liwc and computerized text analysis methods," Journal of Language and Social Psychology, vol. 29, no. 1, 2010, pp. 24–54. [Online]. Available: https://doi.org/10.1177/0261927X09351676

[19] P. Novak, J. Smailović, B. Sluban, and I. Mozetič, "Sentiment of emojis," PLOS ONE, vol. 10, no. 12, 2015, pp. 1–22. [Online]. Available: https://doi.org/10.1371/journal.pone.0144296

[20] F. Nielsen, "A new anew: Evaluation of a word list for sentiment analysis in microblogs," in Proceedings of the ESWC2011 Workshop on 'Making Sense of Microposts': Big things come in small packages 718 in CEUR Workshop Proceedings, 2011.

[21] T. Wilson, J. Wiebe, and P. Hoffmann, "Recognizing contextual polarity in phrase-level sentiment analysis," in Proceedings of the conference on human language technology and empirical methods in natural language processing. ACL, 2005, pp. 347–354.

[22] P. J. Stone and E. B. Hunt, "A computer approach to content analysis: studies using the general inquirer system," in Proceedings of the AFIPS, 1963, pp. 241–256.

[23] M. Hu and B. Liu, "Mining and summarizing customer reviews," in Proceedings of the tenth ACM SIGKDD international conference on Knowledge discovery and data mining. ACM, 2004, pp. 168–177.

[24] Z. Zhang and L. Luo, "Hate speech detection: A solved problem?the challenging case of long tail on twitter," Semantic Web, vol. 1, no. 0, 2018, pp. 1–51.

Digital Disqualification, Digital Suffering, Digital Reliance

The Case of French Retired People over Sixty Years Old

Eloria Vigouroux-Zugasti
Laboratory of DICEN IDF
University of Paris-East Marne-la-Vallée
Val d'Europe / Serris, France
Email: eloria.vigouroux-zugasti@u-pem.fr

Christian Bourret
Laboratory of DICEN IDF
University of Paris-East Marne-la-Vallée
Val d'Europe / Serris, France
Email: christian.bourret@u-pem.fr

Abstract— **Occidental society tends to be increasingly dependent on digital technologies, even for basic activities (socialization, work, administrative tasks, etc.). For instance, since 2016 in France, the tax return must be submitted online. However, does this evolution consider those who lack the required capacity? How to measure the digital divide? To explore this issue, we study the case of older adults with low technological knowledge and skills. This population presents more difficulties in using digital devices than the young generation because of the effect of digital divides and the lack of digital literacy. This situation has the potential to produce some (digital) suffering, making this population feel outdated and excluded from the social entity.**

Keywords: Elderly; retired people; digital technologies; suffering; emotional behaviour; social challenges; loneliness; reliance.

I. Introduction

Older people have to suffer from a denial of recognition from the rest of society. They do not meet the standards currently required by contemporary society. The phenomenon of ageism, a kind of stereotypes attached to older people [1], reflects a negative image of the retired population and emphasizes the discourses encompassed the value of eternal youth. This population suffers from common negative representations, referring to a certain contempt and denial of recognition from the rest of society [2].

In parallel to this denial, we observe the evolution of the digital sphere and its related capacities, with the impetus of thousands of users who define social codes that use technologies. The digital sphere tends to become a community space with its own rules, obligations and social recognition systems, enabling users to join in a system of social relationships [3]. To gain recognition and full social identity, web surfers must match their use of technology with the technical use of the online community.

The effect of this standardised uses goes beyond the digital sphere itself. Since the 1990s, we have entered an area dominated by the Information and Communication Technologies (ICTs), which are understood as a necessary requirement for a renewed exercise of democracy, making possible to break free from old hierarchies [4]. This "necessary requirement" reveals the phenomenon we want to talk about. The use of digital technologies is nowadays an implicit or explicit requirement for continuous development within society. The conventional approaches are punctuated by the obligation to use these technologies, such as taxes returns, although the French State does not provide resources to help people make a successful digital transition. Even more worryingly, public services are gradually phased out, though they could help people with low, or non-existent, digital skills. The digital teaching tasks are mainly devoted to associations, family, or friends.

It seems that retired people show different digital uses, influenced by historical and social contexts that may or may not encourage the expansion of their digital skills [5]. How can you consider yourself as a citizen, in a society whose norms do not correspond to yours? Speaking of digital norms, can not we talk about a kind of suffering, feeling experienced by those who are not embedded in the actual digital mould? By learning how to absorb social requirements, particularly in digital terms, older people would be able to (re)integrate the society. Incorporating the norms would be a solution for them not to suffer from social and digital disqualification.

To answer the questions listed above, we propose a study case. We conducted an exploratory qualitative research, interviewing thirty-one elders over sixty years old, living in the south-west of France, where the digital divide is stronger than in other parts of this country. The region was selected for its social, digital and economic features (repartition between countryside and cities, the proportion of older people, territorial digital equipment, etc.), highlighting the low level of technological knowledge and skills of older adults, resulting on issues related to social and digital disqualification.

This article will be divided into four parts. In section II, we will explain the methodology used for our investigation. In section III, we will present the actual social and technological background in western societies, related to the elderly social disqualification resulting from the massive implementation of ICTs. In section IV, we will develop the concept of digital imperative and its effects on collective and individual norms. Then, in section V, we will present the consequences of these social and digital disqualifications, namely the feelings of loneliness, suffering, and digital reliance.

II. Methodological Approach

In this section, we would like to specify the methodological approach we followed, both in terms of sampling and interviews analysis.

A. *Epistemological choices*

First of all, we would like to point out the results of this investigation do not tend to be excessively generalized. Indeed, if we seek to take some theoretical distance, from the corpus and model concepts, we also aware of the limited impact of our results.

The study is based on an exploratory approach of older people digital skills. Our purpose is to grasp the consequences of those skills on well-being, social integration and self-esteem. To this end, we choose to develop a qualitative survey. It seemed to be the most relevant way to investigate digital skills and practices, as close as possible to the realities of elderlies. Indeed, this kind of methodology is in line with our research goals, as "confrontation with the corpus is a necessary condition for the perception of social practices" [26]. The objective is to understand the symbolic appropriation of digital technology by respondents, by placing them in specific contexts, applied in particular to social cohesion and wellbeing.

We did the survey according to a comprehensive epistemological point of view. We sought to understand the meaning of elderlies' digital uses. Thus, our study aims to grasp uses as they are perceived by the interviewed people, as well as to grasp the meaning they are given in an everyday life context. The comprehensive paradigm tends to place the researcher in a position to understand his interviewed sample as closely as possible to reality [27]. This paradigm implies a work of empathy about one of the authors who, intends, during an interview or analysis by putting himself in the place of the respondent and tries to understand the world from his own point of view.

B. *Construction and justification of the sample*

The choice of the interview sample was based on two criteria. First, we investigated territories that share the same public policies, involving aging, health, institutional accesses and technological mediation management. The comparative study of public policies in different counties, while potentially interesting, is not the subject of our research. It seemed more coherent to focus on users with the same social, health and political frameworks, starting from the postulate that can be influenced by these same frameworks. We chose to consider all Aquitaine counties to vary the profile of the users we interviewed. This region offers a wide variety of living places and social aspects that allow us to diversify the profiles of respondents. Although they are all affected by the same public policy, we still considered the influence of their living environment: urban, semi-urban, rural; married, living alone, in cohabitation; from a high, medium, low social background, etc.

The selection of a retirement sample was based on socio-professional categories, limiting the disparity in lifestyles, by having only people who are no longer working.

Hereafter, we propose a summarizing table about the criteria we used to make up the corpus.

TABLE I. Distribution of the Interviewed Elderlies

Criteria	Distribution	Number	%
Gender	Male	13	41,93
	Female	18	58,07
Age	60-64	11	35,48
	65-69	10	32,26
	70-74	5	16,13
	74-78	5	16,13
Living situation	Married	21	63,63
	Alone	7	21,21
	With one children	3	9,09
	Cohabitation with other elderlies	1	3,03
Living places	0 > 2 000 inhabitants	5	15,15
	2 001 > 10 000 inhab.	5	15,15
	10 001 > 30 000 inhab.	6	18,18
	30 001 > 60 000 inhab.	6	18,18
	60 001 > 100 000 inhab.	5	15,15
	> 100 001 inhab.	4	12,12
Counties	Dordogne	4	12,9
	Gironde	14	45,17
	Landes	4	12,9
	Lot-et-Garonne	3	9,68
	Pyrénées-Atlantiques	7	19,35
Socio-professional background	Wealthy class	10	32,27
	Middle class	10	32,27
	Working class	11	35,48

C. *Interview chart and analysis*

In order to provide some details about our investigation without losing the reader in too many information, we recommend explaining three of the themes we explored, which related to our article. First, we examined the impact of generational belonging on the evolution of digital uses, questioning the time when respondents started using digital technologies and the role of relatives in digital learning. Then, we explore the ability of the Internet to respond to social expectations, such as biographical break or projection and daily-life restructuring. The third theme is devoted to understanding the subject of social recognition through online uses and digital skills. The goal of these themes, questions and topics, was to investigate the ability of digital technologies to support the social inclusion of retired people and to verify converging / diverging phenomena, according to the criteria we chose for the survey. To keep it concise and consistent, we will focus, in this article, on the most relevant results.

To analyze these results, we assume that speeches are performative, that speeches build meaning. It induces actions and implies consequences in the real world. Analyzing a discourse is trying to grasp and to identify the actions it involves. The enunciation, through its elaboration, influences and transforms the world. We so analyzed the interviews, considering that everyone, during the production of a speech, develops some special meaning [28]. This perspective corresponds to a discourse design that is appropriate for this survey. The idea that speech is an act is at the heart of our study, as we will see in the analysis chapters.

III. Social Exclusion: socio-economic issues for elderly

Digital technologies are seen as a potential for innovation to transform communities' lifestyle by influencing the way people live together. It seems that technology improves people's ability to act by expanding the panel of information resources and networked communication [6]. Not being a user of digital technologies, or more broadly of ICTs, is now a factor of exclusion and disqualification. Indeed, in a continually increasing digital civilization, the individual who is not equipped, or who does not know how to use these platforms, sees his capacity for action, knowledge and integration significantly reduced.

Connectivity appears to be a hot issue for those who want to take full advantage of their social abilities, concerning, particularly, intergenerational relations or institutional changes. The requirement to file the tax return on the Internet, for example, is representative of a numerical disqualification factor. In 2016, in France, it became mandatory, for the first tranche of taxpayers, to file their returns online. However, the institutional tends, by 2019, to get each taxpayer to do the online tax return, under penalty of having to pay a lump sum fine. This revision of declaration completion is less vital than what it implies: people who are not connected to the Internet or who do not have sufficient knowledge will be, in a few years, illegal.

A. *Elders and digital dependency*

The evolution of French social context towards an increasingly digital dependency appears to be a factor of social disqualification. This is reflected in the development of e-inclusion policies, such as in Switzerland or through projects, proposed by certain several clusters specializing in digital technology, such as Cluster *Health ICTs* in Aquitaine, in France. The "e-" brings back to electronic literacy and, more broadly, to digital culture. The term "inclusion" highlights the fracture lines, due to the digital divide, both on the technical and uses aspects. This institutional evolution is linked with the recognition of the right, developed by Axel Honneth. "If some people rights [...] are denied, this implicitly means that they are not recognized to the same degree of moral respectability as other members of society" [2]. However, with the current digital transition, institutions are changing the notion of "right".

As the digitalization of administrative procedures increases, the right to take measures without digital technology tends to decrease. This evolution means the full spread of technologies within society. However, despite the massification of ICT's in society, some digital divides remain, based, for instance, on income, education level, cultural and social capital, or even age [7]. Indeed, as shown by the Research Centre for Study and Observation of Living Conditions' (from now on called CREDOC) statistical studies and the scientific literature, there are many fault lines, as much due to lack of equipment (first-degree divide), as for the lack of digital skills (second-degree divide). The standard of living has a substantial impact on household equipment, with the purchasing power of the wealthiest making it easier for them to purchase equipment than people with low incomes. Moreover, a user must have a certain level of digital literacy to be able to develop serene and relevant digital practices [5]. However, as Charmakeh notes, some segments of the population (retired, for example) do not have such knowledge [7]. They do not have sufficient expertise and are not able to consider the opportunities offered by technologies. As a result, despite the increasing rate of the equipment, reaching almost 97% among teenagers (12-25 years old) and young adults [8]–[11], there are still social groups on the margins. The older we get, to harder it is to perform changes. Any change creates a "small crisis" and requires real personal work to change individual habits. So, making a transition from habit to a new model is difficult, sometimes impossible for adults or elderlies, by joint persistence, tenacity, comprehensibility, often reinforced by common sense, experiences or values [12].

Institutional change tends, through the firmness of these reforms, to influence the diffusion of ICTs, at the societal level. As Claude Dubar explains, it is tough, perhaps impossible, for some people to follow this evolution. This can be all the more applied to the populations that had missed the digital revolution of recent decades, as well as to some of the older generations, especially those over 80 years old [5]. Thus, the change desired by institutions tends not to take root among these groups, in which digital culture and uses remain alien. They find themselves out of step with the values and practices of the other social groups.

B. *Disruption and disempowerment: consequences of social disqualification*

Some older people can have some difficulties to feel in accordance with today's society. This feeling leads them to experience ever-increasing concern in understanding the world they live in, which no longer recognizes them [13]. However, the loss of meaning and the loss of common points, of complicity, imply phenomena of disruption (physically, psychologically and healthily speaking). This concept may be defined as the abandonment of activities or habits, by someone who is no longer able to perform them, whether for physical, cognitive or cultural reasons, as it is the case with elders of our study context. To keep in touch with the world, people must find some matching points with the environment they live in. Most of the time, it is the contradictions between people's skills or needs and the world they are surrounded by that lead them to disruption [13]. The lack of correlation leads the individual to be no longer attached to his life or the world he lives in.

Existentially speaking, it therefore seems necessary to offer meaningful activities to individuals to help them (re)connect with their environment. In today's institutional context, it appears difficult very old people to find commonalities, opportunities of commitment within the digital sphere, that tends to isolate them, generating, in this way, exclusion and social disqualification. As Vincent Caradec says, anyone should expect from a culture that it supports him, from the beginning of existence until death. This support can have many variations, from living models, stimulating policies, help to improve their abilities, etc. [14]

IV. Digital imperative: collective norms and individuality

The example of the tax return mentioned above does not concern only social exclusion. It also highlights, in a more or less subtle way, what we consider as a numerical imperative, using Fabien Granjon's terminology. It concerns a feeling of obligation, linked to the use of digital technologies. The subject, through institutional, media and social pressure, tends to develop uses to preserve social integration. For the people we interviewed, the imperative is reflected by the desire to gain recognition from the social body. Stop working and enter retirement are sometimes equated with the idea of social and identity break-up. The term "retirement" is, itself, often associated with a social withdrawal [15]. Integrating digital sphere is, then, a way to regain social esteem, as we will see later in this article, through the development of knowledge and skills in this field and an acclaimed development through media and social discourse.

A. The intergenerational implication in the elders' uses of ICTs

Digital imperative is also expressed through intergenerational relationships, particularly with descendants, whether children or grandchildren. These generations are predisposed to use online communication platforms because of their appropriation of digital technologies during their youth or working life. Their digital literacy level and the incorporation of communication habits lead them to favour this type of medium. In this way, in order to keep in touch, elderlies are encouraged to develop online communicative practices, in line with the attitudes and preferences of the person they wish to contact. Younger generations enrol the old ones in the digital sphere. The more they are equipped, the more they will propose opportunities to elderlies to join the movement of digital communication by, for instance, training them to use social platforms or offering technological gifts [16]. The term "enlisting" corresponds to the idea we want to develop here. Since the desire to maintain social bonds is stronger than traditional communication formats, elders develop new uses, by copying the uses already embedded among younger generations, who are, in turn, closely involved in the development of the digital sphere. This sphere tends to impose itself as an imperative in maintaining communication with family and close social circle. The family's use of digital technologies tends to create an incentive effect that retired people, who respond to a normative desire, in connection with a desire to maintain their socialization and their belonging to the social sphere.

B. The construction and the effects of collective and normative expectations on people

Through political, media and institutional discourses, representations or behaviours, society establishes rules of conformity, moral, technical and ethical, which individuals are required to respect from an early age and throughout their lives, to become an integral part of the social body [17]. This process of socialization results in the internalization of norms. Those norms are established from the generalization of all society members' expectations [2].

As Alex Honneth says, an individual has to understand, to learn to respect and, above all, internalize the normative social rules imposed on him. By doing so, he earns the capacity to evolve in interactions and in his environment, he lives in, to be accepted by his group or society. The norms he learns allow him to identify his rights and duties concerning the other member of the group. So, he learns to understand himself from a generalized view of others [2].

The training of someone as a member of the collective social group, therefore, implies a reflexive posture, where someone queries his habits, behaviours and values, in order to integrate collective norms and rules that he must respect to be socially accepted, both by institutions and peers.

C. Collective norms and individual construction

Individual construction is partly based on the relationship with people, primarily through other's eyes. The image that interlocutors sends back influences how we perceive ourselves. This exchange, particularly in the normative framework we are talking about, allows knowing whether or not if someone is recognized as an equal by his interaction partner. Therefore, being in interaction with someone else means being in interaction with oneself and (re)building oneself, through the perception that the interaction partner sends back.

Being oneself, within a normative framework, is like being like the other, by sharing some morality, rules and common standards. By accepting or rejecting the speaker, the speaking partner or the institution defines the condition in which the told speaker is perceived. In other terms, "the normative idea that everyone has of oneself [...] depends on the possibility that he always has of being confirmed in the other [...]. The feeling of contempt can be perceived as a threatening attack and can ruin someone's identity as a whole" [2]. Being outside a normative framework or of a society tends to place people in a position of social disqualification. In this way, social groups use this framework to develop normatively expectations, social pressure to conformity [18] to which people must submit to, in order to (still) be considered as a full citizen.

We note ambivalence in surveyed elders' speeches. On the one hand, the opportunities they discover through technology lead them to perfect their knowledge of these tools. Online practices multiply the number of communication and information channels. It offers more ways to communicate and help elders to enhance their daily life and complete the connexions they have with their environment. The entire sample we interviewed says that ICT's have developed and improve their digital literacy, as well as their lifestyle. On the other hand, this very same discourse is tinged with bitterness [5], which reminds us of the notion of digital imperative. Social pressure for compliance and the need to respond to normative frameworks are particularly intense when it comes to connecting elders with the digital sphere. There is a kind of double pressure: the first is due to the prevailing social representation attached to retirement age, the second due to the digital imperative.

D. Constraint and call of duty: when elders have no other choice than "get started"

The social and digital pressure made "digital path" unavoidable. It explains that almost twenty people of our survey feel like they had to force themselves to get "digitally started" [5]. They link this to the hope of catching up with a backlog they have accumulated in this area and which, in a way, gives them a marginal position [18]. This constraint is firmly rooted in our interviews, to the point of becoming a model statement, such as: "you have to get started", "you have to live with today's trend", "in any case, today, you can no longer do anything without ICT's", "it has become essential", etc. [29]. This social pressure does not differentiate by age or social background within our sample. The notion of imperative and pressure that underlies the interviews seems to be experienced uniformly throughout our corpus.

As we said in the beginning of this article, we currently live in a strongly ageist societal context. Thus, for the people who have accumulated many years, it seems necessary for them to develop digital practices, in order to encourage collective social recognition and, so, emancipating themselves from the cult of eternal youth. They also mark their distance from their chronological age [16], as well as from collective representations related to it. Therefore, developing digital and technological skills appears to be a way for elders to counteract negative stereotypes and to encourage their social valorisation.

It seems getting closer to the aesthetic reference model makes life simpler and easier [19] and gives full meaning to digital imperative. Being accepted by others and by society is a fundamental element of well-being. That is why accepting and complying with standards is a way of being well integrated and valued, with an absolute peace of mind. However, in the context of an actively and favourably ICT's society, becoming a digital user seems to be a way to live in peace, to be accepted and recognized as a full citizen.

V. SUFFERING AND LONELINESS: CONSEQUENCES OF DISQUALIFICATION

Sociologists, such as Vincent Caradec [20] or Serge Guérin [21], have studied the loss of meaning of life and activities at retirement age, which leads people to social withdrawal and disruption. Replying to an email, playing on a virtual farm, enjoying a replayed TV show represent many emotional investment opportunities for people suffering from loneliness. New uses for new habits allow the development of automatic processes, the anchoring of changes, offering, in this way, a meaningful restructured daily life.

As we said previously, older adults tend to be even more put aside from social and digital evolutions. We now would like to develop on some of their consequences on elderlies' everyday life, based on the results of our exploratory qualitative survey [5] [29].

A. Loneliness and suffering: social or digital issues?

We first would like to talk about the feeling of loneliness. We attribute to this notion to the feeling of not being integrated into a social community and suffering from it. Thus, an "isolated" person does not feel necessarily "alone" if it does not experience it as an annoyance [5]. This is a spread sentiment, common to twenty-two people we interviewed: "My two sons live abroad, my daughter lives hundreds kilometres from me. I have other family members here, but it's not the same. I miss them and I feel a bit alone" [29]. This seventy years old woman has a computer, but do not use it for her social activities, nor to develop her intergenerational relationships. When she is asked about this opportunity, she answers: "Yes, I know I could. My children don't stop asking me the same question. But I don't feel comfortable with it. I don't understand how it works, I don't know how to call someone, what I can publish or not. I'm afraid of doing something wrong and to break the computer. I feel alone, but I don't feel capable of using something like Facebook" [29].

This feeling of loneliness is even more paradoxical, compared to the society we live in. A society is characterized by the diversity of its technological possibilities of communication [22]. In the previous case, we note that the woman has everything she needs, from a technological point of view, to keep communicating with her children. The problem seems to be related to her capacity to use it and to understand how to use it.

In the cases we studied during our survey, the feeling of loneliness seems to be even stronger since the massive diffusion of ICTs technology, related to a need for emotional stability and a lack of recognition [22]. Indeed, having a computer, without knowing how to use it, seems to spawn feelings of worry and loneliness, more significantly in everyday life activities. As they do not share the current social ways to get in touch with distant relatives, elderlies seem to feel even lonelier. They can not talk as frequently as they want to with their family They also feel socially depreciated and rejected, with some lack of recognition [5]. This is confirmed by Cécile Tréton and Christian Bourret, according to whom "the infrastructure that offers many opportunities for communication and security can not resolve the appearance of a feeling of loneliness for a growing part of the population" [22].

What our survey also highlights is the lack of digital teaching. Even when family members know the faint abilities of elderlies, very few of them try to help. "I asked my sons, but they don't have time, with the kids and their work. They tried to teach me some things, like going on Facebook, but I need a lot of time to learn, and they were quite upset of keep repeating the same things", says a seventy-two-year-old man [29]. So, increasing technology accessibility does not involve technological adoption. It is difficult, for most elderlies, to adopt new habits, especially technological ones, as we said previously. Furthermore, they also develop some distress concerning computers and digital technologies [23]. It results in everyday difficulties and negative self-judgment, regarding their abilities to learn and use digital technologies, bringing elderlies back to a kind of social failure [5].

In our survey, loneliness seems to be related to suffering. Interviewed people seem to suffer from the digital evolution of the society and of the digital communication habits of their family. Despite e-inclusion policies, suffering keeps being a fundamental issue concerning elderlies. Suffering appears to be a consequence of the lack of recognition, both from society, family members and even from institutions' digitalization. The feeling of suffering seems to be a significant setback of the current consideration accorded to social elderlies problems, which push them to doubt of their technological self-efficacy [23] and of their adequacy with the world they live in. However, as we said previously in this article, feeling useless and disconnected from the world is one of the most severe causes of disruption among retired people. In this context, we could conclude that digitalization seems to reinforce the feelings of loneliness and suffering among elders, increasing the risks of social or cognitive disruptions.

B. *Digital reliance: consequences on self-consideration and everyday life activities*

It seems older adults are unaware of many existing digital technologies and might lack necessary digital literacy (knowledge and skills) [23]. The lack of acculturation is one of the hottest issues concerning the elderly. Indeed, acculturation is influenced by the relationship to technologies during working life [5]. However, most of the current older people were already retired when ICTs were massively spread in working places. So, they have never been acculturated to them during their professional life and still ignore most of the advantages offered by them. "I fill the taxes returns for my mother. She's ninety-five years old; she doesn't want to hear about technologies. What she doesn't want to hear is that I also need to be helped by my own daughter to fill my own taxes return", says a seventy-five years old man [29].

What we observe here is the concept of digital reliance. The man we just talked about is dependent on his daughter to fill his taxes returns and those of his mother. His lack of digital literacy unable him to be autonomous. How, in this context, can some scientists still talk about empowerment?

Our observations are confirmed by Heo and Yoon, who write that asking for help is counter-intuitive with the feeling of autonomy [23]. Digital use is becoming a common standard for online administrative and everyday life tasks (buying, searching for information, etc.). However, it raises the question of the digital dependence of unconnected or unaccustomed elderly.

This digital reliance seems to be all the more problematical as it echoes to the concepts of digital vulnerability and digital suffering. Such cases of reliance seem to worsen the negative feelings and self-judgments, as they show elderlies in a position of relational vulnerability [22].

VI. Conclusion

The limits of our study is linked the number of investigated people and on the particular contexts they live in, in the south-west of France. A broader study and some comparative point of view could confirm our observations, give more detailed and find some other phenomenon.

According to French national statistics [24], people over sixty years old would currently represent more than 25% of the total French population. This number, still according to the same source, would keep on increasing in the coming years. Digital suffering or social digital disqualification, would be even more problematical, considering the growing number of elderlies and other social groups that can not follow the current digital path (living standard, incomes, social failure, digital divide, etc.). However, French society does not seem to take into account the number of people made disadvantaged by its digitalization and the consequences it has on well-being, by imposing new technical, technological and social norms, without paying attention to the crucial need of supporting digital transition, from a social, financial and technical point of view. A country can not encourage such an evolution, without giving its people the support the need to follow it.

This path could be considered as quite solutionist [25]. Digital public policies mean to resolve all the problems, health failure among others, by implementing technologies, without paying attention to the importance of social, technological (also considering digital practices levels) and human surroundings. Moreover, talking about elderlies' digital reliance, can not we consider these solutions as fundamentally paradoxical, as they propose to solve dependence issues by creating another form of dependence through digital reliance?

Acknowledgement

The authors would like to thank the MAIF foundation, which allowed them to develop their exploratory qualitative survey.

References

[1] M. Lagacé, "Ageism: understanding and changing the social view of aging", Laval University Press, 2010.
[2] A. Honneth, "The struggle for recognition", Gallimard, 2013.

[3] S. Proulx, 'Thinking about the uses of information and communication technologies today: challenges - models - trends', in "ICT issues and uses: social and cultural aspects", Bordeaux University Press, vol. 1, p. 7-20, 2005.

[4] F. Granjon, "Recognition and use of the Internet: a critical sociology of connected computing practices", Transvalor-Mine Press, 2012.

[5] E. Vigouroux-Zugasti, "The digital experience of elderly: Challenges and limitations of technological solutionism", Vol 1, Bordeaux Montaigne University, Bordeaux, 2017. [Online]. Available from: https://tel.archives-ouvertes.fr/tel-01764923/document [Accessed: 23-May-2019].

[6] C.-A. Rivière and A. Brugière, Ageing well thanks to digital technology, FYP Editions, 2010.

[7] H. Charmarkeh, "Older people and the "second degree" digital divide: the contribution of the critical perspective in communication", French Journal of Information and Communication Sciences, no. 6, Jan. 2015.

[8] CREDOC, "Aging well, retirement, dependency, fragility of seniors Representations, realities and expectations of the French population with regard to institutions", 2016. [Online] . Available from: https://www.credoc.fr/publications/la-diffusion-des-technologies-de-l-information-et-de-la-communication-dans-la-societe-francaise-2016 [Accessed : 23-May-2019)

[9] CREDOC, "The diffusion of information and communication technologies in French society (2015)", 2015. [Online] . Available from: https://www.credoc.fr/publications/la-diffusion-des-technologies-de-l-information-et-de-la-communication-dans-la-societe-francaise-2015 [Accessed : 23-May-2019)

[10] CREDOC, "The diffusion of information and communication technologies in French society (2014)", 2014. [Online] . Available from: https://www.credoc.fr/publications/la-diffusion-des-technologies-de-l-information-et-de-la-communication-dans-la-societe-francaise-2014 [Accessed : 23-May-2019)

[11] CREDOC, "The diffusion of information and communication technologies in French society (2013)", 2013. [Online] . Available from: https://www.credoc.fr/publications/la-diffusion-des-technologies-de-l-information-et-de-la-communication-dans-la-societe-francaise-2013 [Accessed : 23-May-2019)

[12] C. Dubar, The identity crisis: the interpretation of a mutation. French University Press, 2010.

[13] V. Caradec, "Sociology in the face of old age, from indifference to the exploration of aging", in "Ageing and old age, vulnerability and resources: cross-regards", Aquitaine House of Human Sciences, 2011, pp. 81–92.

[14] J. Bouisson, C. Brisset, I. Tournier, and C. Vion, "Ageing and old age, vulnerability and resources: cross-regards", Aquitaine House of Human Sciences, 2011.

[15] S. Guérin, The new senior citizens' society, Michalon, 2011.

[16] L. Le Douarin and V. Caradec, "ICTs, grandparents and their grandchildren: towards a conflict of technological generations?, in Living the ages of life, The Harmattan, 2012, pp. 253–276.

[17] M. Bahuaud, C. Destal, and A. Pecolo, "The generational approach to communication: placing audiences at the heart of the process", Communication & Organisation, no. 40, p. 5–18, Jan. 2013.

[18] D. Le Gall and C. Le Van, "Get your equipment at home. Domestic microcomputing and social cleavages", Hermès Lavoisier., 2009, pp. 89–118.

[19] P. Bourdieu, The Distinction: Social Criticism of the Judgment, Midnight Editions, 2016.

[20] V. Caradec, Ageing after retirement: a sociological approach to ageing, French University Press, 2004.

[21] S. Guérin, The invention of the seniors. Hachette Literatures, 2007.

[22] C. Tréton and C. Bourret, "Loneliness and Relational Biography", presented at the HUSO, Malta, 2015. [Online]. Available from: https://pdfs.semanticscholar.org/41a4/667ed99d3f1eb2838787a1fc8a5d87949bff.pdf [Accessed: 23-May-2019]

[23] J. Heo and J. Yoon, "Use of Smart Speakers by Elderly in Home Environment", presented at the ACHI 2019 : The Twelfth International Conference on Advances in Computer-Human Interactions, Athens, 2019. [Online]. Available from: http://thinkmind.org/index.php?view=article&articleid=achi_2019_5_20_20074 [Accessed: 23-May-2019]

[24] INSEE, "Population by sex and age group in 2019". [Online]. Available from: https://www.insee.fr/fr/statistiques/2381474. [Accessed: 23-May-2019].

[25] E. Morozov, "To solve everything click here: The aberration of technological solutionism", FYP Editions, 2014.

[26] L. Monnoyer-Smith, Laurence, For an complex epistemology of information and communication sciences, presented at the 16th SFSIC Congress, Paris. 2008 [Online]: https://www.sfsic.org/congres_2008/spip.php?article78, [Accessed: 23-May-2019]

[27] W. Feuerhahn, "Max Weber and comprehensive explanation", Philisophie, no 85, p.19-41. [Online]: http://www.cairn.info/resume.php?ID_ARTICLE=PHILO_085_0019 [Accessed: 23-May-2019]

[28] L. Bardin, "Content analysis", French University Presses, Pars. 2013

[29] E. Vigouroux-Zugasti, "The digital experience of elderly: Challenges and limitations of technological solutionism", Vol 2, Bordeaux Montaigne University, Bordeaux, 2017. [Online]. Available from: https://tel.archives-ouvertes.fr/tel-01764923/file/These_Eloria_VIGOUROUX_ZUGASTI_annexes.pdf [Accessed: 23-May-2019]

This page intentionally left blank.

This page intentionally left blank.

This page intentionally left blank.

Response Patterns during Child-Robot Interaction of Children with Cognitive Impairments

Luthffi Idzhar Ismail*†, Tony Belpaeme*‡ and Francis wyffels*

Fazah Akhtar Hanapiah

*Ghent University-imec, IDLab, Technologiepark-Zwijnaarde 126, B-9052 Ghent, Belgium
†Universiti Putra Malaysia, Faculty of Engineering, 43400 Selangor, Malaysia,
‡University of Plymouth, School of Computing, Plymouth PL4 8AA United Kingdom
Email: luthffiidzharbin.ismail@ugent.be

Universiti Teknologi MARA, Faculty of Medicine, 47000 Selangor, Malaysia

***Abstract*—Literature on Human-Robot Interaction reports that children with cognitive impairments often have engaging interactions with social robots. However, there are hardly any guidelines on how to design an interaction to achieve particular therapeutic outcomes. This paper reports on a study in which 20 children with cognitive impairments interacted with a social robot, with the aim to assess their responses and their engagement which eventually impacts on the outcomes we can achieve. The children were introduced to the robot and had three sessions during which they played therapeutic games with the robot to improve their attention skills. The overall pattern of their responses for in the sessions are reported, showing a reduction in completion time with each subsequent session. This is indicative of improved attention. This response pattern might be important in future behaviour analysis, especially as a measure for social attention skills, eye contact, and engagement analysis during child-robot interaction.**

Keywords–Robot, Cognitive Impairments, Child-Robot Interaction

Figure 1. Figure shows LUCA robot which was build based on OPSORO robot platform [4].

I. Introduction

Robots have been actively used in recent years to help children with cognitive and physical disabilities and other special needs. Research suggest that children positively engage with robots during child-robot interaction, e.g. [1], [2]. According to some carers and teachers, children with cognitive impairments (hereafter referred to as "CWCI") are known to have difficulties with remaining focused during human-human interaction, which in turn has a negative impact on interactions with peers, teachers and family members.

Conventional human-human intervention programs and therapy were proven to be effective to improve their social communication skills [3]. Teachers and therapists usually rely on additional tools, such as cards or toys, for their intervention programs or therapy sessions. Given the reliance on external props to support the sessions, and the need for focal points to practice social skills such as joint attention, deictic gaze and eye contact, it likely that social robotics can play a role here.

In this study, we use the social robot LUCA (as illustrated in Figure 1) and designed child-robot interaction modules to help CWCI to improve their social interaction skills. We hypothesize that their response towards the robot and the interaction modules shall provide us with more information and insight with which to design future child-robot interaction studies. Section 2 discusses the experimental study of our child-robot interaction, together with a description of each module. Finally, section 3 shall reports the finding of the study which elaborate the pattern of child's response in each module for each session of child-robot interaction.

II. Child-Robot Interaction Experiment

All experimental procedure has been given ethical approval on 30th July 2018 from Research Ethics Committee, Universiti Teknologi MARA (UiTM), Malaysia (REC reference number: 600-IRMI (5/1/6)). In this study, we collaborated with one of the schools in Putrajaya, Malaysia. This school has 92 children with special needs. 20 children diagnosed with cognitive impairments fulfilled our inclusion and exclusion criteria as described in Table I.

Consent to participate in our study was also obtained from their parents or legal guardian prior to start the experiment. The protocol of the experiment was clearly explained to the teachers and therapist. A teacher or therapist would come to the experimental room with one child at a time. They would knock on the door, walk into the room and sit down in front of the robot. All interactions were recorded using five video cameras for later analyses. Once the child was seated and ready, the teacher would flash a card at the robot and the interaction with the robot was initiated. Each child was exposed to the robot for 3 consecutive sessions. Each session consists of 5

TABLE I. INCLUSION AND EXCLUSION CRITERIA FOR ALL PARTICIPANTS

Inclusion criteria	Exclusion criteria
1)Age between 6 to 12 years 2)No evidence of self injury or aggressive behaviour 3)Able to speak in English or Malay 4)Diagnosed as having a Cognitive Impairment (level validated by attention skills via Children Colouring Trail Test: CCTT [5]) 5)Able to follow simple instructions in English or Malay	1)Child with mutism 2)Uncorrected hearing deficit 3)Uncorrected vision deficit 4)Unwillingness to participate

interaction modules. The 5 modules are as below:

- **Module 1: Introduction to the robot**
  The first module aimed to introduce the robot to the participant. The child was welcomed by LUCA using simple English language and some low valence non-verbal behaviour. The text to speech voice was generated using an online synthesize [6].
- **Module 2: Facial expression game**
  This module was designed as a facial expression game and has been designed to help CWCI improve their attention skills [7], [8]. The dependent variable in this module is the time taken by the child to complete the task. In this module, the researcher controlled the robot and selected a range of different facial expressions such as happy, sad, angry. The children were invited by the robot to guess the expression, and they were allowed a second try if their initial answer was wrong. If their answer was still incorrect, the correct answer was given by the robot. The children were also expected to mimic the expression of the robot while maintaining eye contact with the robot.
- **Module 3: Song with facial expression game**
  In this module, a song was added to the facial expression game in order to encourage the children to play the facial expression game and make the interaction more engaging. Some children have some difficulties in distinguishing certain facial expressions. The music was chosen to match the emotions expressed by the robot and helped the children guess the facial expression, next to enhancing their attention span.
- **Module 4: Attention task**
  This module was developed to measure the attention skills of the child. These are very important skills, central to social interaction, learning and collaboration, and robots are believed to be able to improve these skills during Child-Robot Interaction [9], [10]. This session expected the child to look at a certain shape pasted on a board placed on the right (for example, an image of rectangle) and left (for example, an image of circle) of the robot. The child would need to perform a "matching task" in which the robot gave an instruction to look at at a shape (mounted to the left or right of the robot) and fixate their gaze for 3 seconds. For example, he/she would be required to look at the rectangle for 3 seconds.
- **Module 5: Free style interaction**
  Finally, module 5 was a free style interaction between the child and the robot. The child was given the chance to ask questions to the robot. The robot answered, with answers being typed in on a keyboard by a member of the research team and spoken by the robot. If children requested the robot to move, then these actions were performed when the robot had the capability to do so.

III. RESULTS

This section reports on the overall response to the child-robot interaction for children diagnosed with cognitive impairments. Five modules were designed for this study. In module 1, children were only introduced to the robot. This is necessary in order to break the ice between the child and the robot [11], [12] and to assure the following interactions are not influenced by the child being unfamiliar with the robot or the study setting. Neither behaviour nor tasks in module 1 have been evaluated. Nevertheless, the average response time from all children was recorded to be around 60 seconds as shown in Fig. 2. In module 2, the overall response pattern showed that children took less time to complete the tasks in session 2 and 3 as compared to their average completion time in session 1. This pattern suggests that their level of concentration and attention skills has improved, considering they take less time to complete the modules over the 3 consecutive sessions. This however needs to be further investigated, as a reduction in completion time might also be caused by a practice effect.

In module 3, the overall response pattern of the children were similar to those in module 2. There was a slight improvement between session 2 and 3, as the addition of music in session 3 had a positive impact on task completion time. Earlier pilots and studies also found that music was an effective manner to draw children into the interaction [12], [13]. In module 4, there was only a slight improvement in the time needed to complete the tasks. Most of the children needed less time to complete the task in session 2 and 3 as compared to session 1, which we expected since the task were uncomplicated. Finally, the results for module 5 were difficult to generalize since it was an open and free style of interaction. The pattern for the children's response in 3 different sessions were quite scattered. This module can be very useful to gauge their interest in and attention towards the robot, which serves as a measure for their focus in social interactions [14], [15]. Their overall response varies in each session. Nevertheless, we show how unstructured interactions are still able to capture the attention of the children, with most children engaging with the robot. Most of the children showed their interest towards the robot and spent an average approximately 2 minutes in all session.

IV. CONCLUSION

We showed that children diagnosed with cognitive impairments respond well to child-robot interaction. Based on our observations, they spent an enjoyable time interacting with the LUCA robot. The tasks set by the robot were designed to uncomplicated and motivated the children to keep interacting

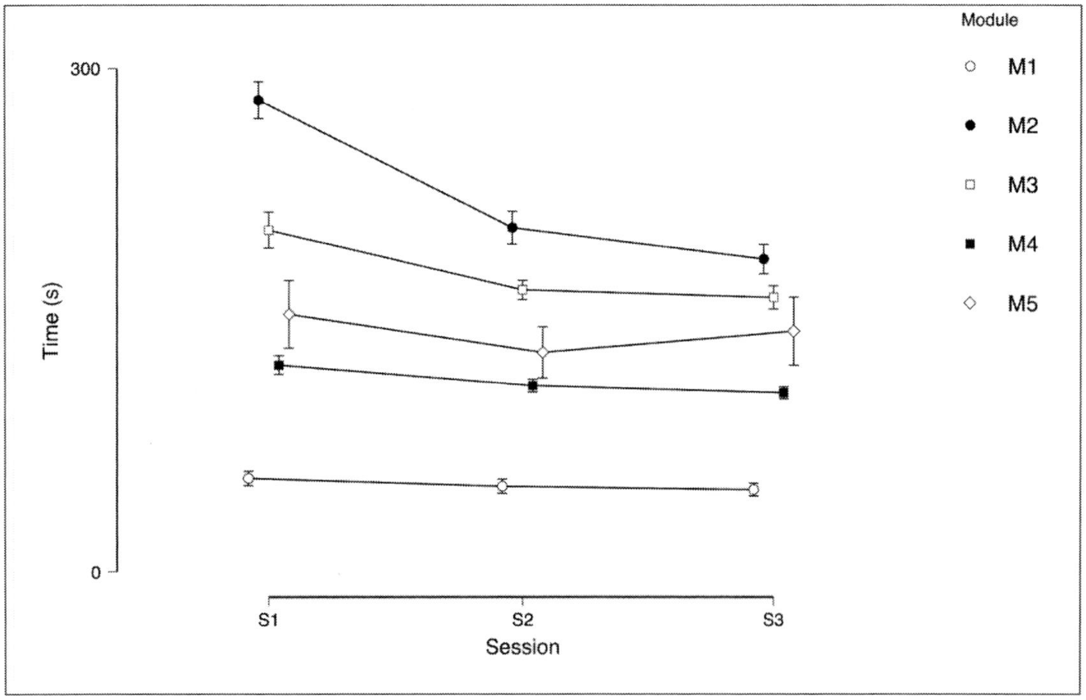

Figure 2. Figure shows the overall results of child-robot interaction time for each module in Session 1, 2 and 3.

with the robot, with no children expressing or showing disappointment with the robot. The child-robot interaction modules hold promise to help children with cognitive impairments to improve their social interaction skills. While our initial results are encouraging, further analysis is needed, especially with regards to improving the children's attention skills and transfer to human-human interaction. Time completion task analysis could be used as a proxy to indicate their improvements in attention skills in modules 2, 3 and 4 for each session. Moreover, interaction duration time could also be used as a proxy to measure their interest in the robot in module 5. This can be useful, especially for future behavior monitoring by a therapist or carer. Completion times could provide important information about the behaviour of children diagnosed with cognitive impairments (such as eye contact patterns and level of attention skills) in child-robot interaction.

ACKNOWLEDGMENT

The authors would like to thank all the funds for this project; Luthffi Idzhar Ismail received a Postgraduate Education Fund from Majlis Amanah Rakyat, MARA (MARA REF: 330407445608). This work was also partially funded by the EU FP7 DREAM project (grant 611391) and Niche Research Grant Scheme (NRGS):600-RMI/NRGS 5/3 (11/2013). Special thanks to all members of Research Ethic Committee (REC) for the ethical approval which was granted from the REC of Universiti Teknologi MARA, Malaysia (REC reference number: 600-IRMI (5/1/6)) prior to research commencement. Moreover, participant's official consent to participate in this study were granted from all parents or guardians prior to start the experiment. Thank you to all of them. The authors also want to declare that they have no conflict of interest in this project.

REFERENCES

[1] L. I. Ismail, S. Shamsudin, H. Yussof, F. A. Hanapiah, and N. I. Zahari, "Robot-based intervention program for autistic children with humanoid robot nao: initial response in stereotyped behavior," Procedia Engineering, vol. 41, 2012, pp. 1441–1447.

[2] T. Belpaeme, P. Baxter, R. Read, R. Wood, H. Cuayáhuitl, B. Kiefer, S. Racioppa, I. Kruijff-Korbayová, G. Athanasopoulos, V. Enescu et al., "Multimodal child-robot interaction: Building social bonds," Journal of Human-Robot Interaction, vol. 1, no. 2, 2013, pp. 33–53.

[3] J. A. Corbett, M. R. Trimble, and T. C. Nichol, "Behavioral and cognitive impairments in children with epilepsy: the long-term effects of anticonvulsant therapy," Journal of the American Academy of Child Psychiatry, vol. 24, no. 1, 1985, pp. 17–23.

[4] T. Vervisch, N. Doms, S. Descamps, C. Vandevelde, S. Verstockt, J. Saldien et al., "Oto–a diy platform for mobile social robots in education," in International Conference on Robotics and Education RiE 2017. Springer, 2017, pp. 257–262.

[5] A. M. Llorente, R. G. Voigt, J. Williams, J. K. Frailey, P. Satz, and L. F. DElia, "Children's color trails test 1 & 2: test–retest reliability and factorial validity," The Clinical Neuropsychologist, vol. 23, no. 4, 2009, pp. 645–660.

[6] I. Cloud. Text to speech. Accessed on July to August 2018. [Online]. Available: https://text-to-speech-demo.ng.bluemix.net/

[7] A. G. Pour, A. Taheri, M. Alemi, and A. Meghdari, "Human–robot facial expression reciprocal interaction platform: case studies on children with autism," International Journal of Social Robotics, vol. 10, no. 2, 2018, pp. 179–198.

[8] A. Adams and P. Robinson, "An android head for social-emotional intervention for children with autism spectrum conditions," in Affective Computing and Intelligent Interaction. Springer, 2011, pp. 183–190.

[9] C.-M. Huang and A. L. Thomaz, "Joint attention in human-robot interaction." in AAAI Fall Symposium: Dialog with Robots, 2010.

[10] Z. E. Warren, Z. Zheng, A. R. Swanson, E. Bekele, L. Zhang, J. A. Crittendon, A. F. Weitlauf, and N. Sarkar, "Can robotic interaction improve joint attention skills?" Journal of autism and developmental disorders, vol. 45, no. 11, 2015, pp. 3726–3734.

[11] N. Bee, E. André, and S. Tober, "Breaking the ice in human-agent communication: Eye-gaze based initiation of contact with an embodied conversational agent," in International Workshop on Intelligent Virtual Agents. Springer, 2009, pp. 229–242.

[12] L. I. Ismail, S. Shamsudin, H. Yussof, F. A. Hanapiah, and N. I. Zahari, "Estimation of concentration by eye contact measurement in robot–based intervention program with autistic children," Procedia Engineering, vol. 41, 2012, pp. 1548–1552.

[13] Y.-H. Peng, C.-W. Lin, N. M. Mayer, and M.-L. Wang, "Using a humanoid robot for music therapy with autistic children," in Automatic Control Conference (CACS), 2014 CACS International. IEEE, 2014, pp. 156–160.

[14] K. Dautenhahn, "Robots as social actors: Aurora and the case of autism," in Proc. CT99, The Third International Cognitive Technology Conference, August, San Francisco, vol. 359, 1999, p. 374.

[15] ——, "Methodology & themes of human-robot interaction: A growing research field," International Journal of Advanced Robotic Systems, vol. 4, no. 1, 2007, p. 15.

Theory and Development of Tool Frameworks for Interactive Knowledge and Data Visualization in Computational Social Science

Tom McDermott
Systems Engineering Research Center
Stevens Institute of Technology
Atlanta, Georgia
Email: tmcdermo@stevens.edu

Molly Nadolski
Georgia Tech Research Institute
Georgia Institute of Technology
Atlanta, Georgia
Email: molly.nadolski@gtri.gatech.edu

Abstract— **We present a framework and sample case study linking knowledge visualization forms with visualization of human and social data analytics. This involves integration of qualitative methods to identify and connect conceptual models with computational social science approaches for data analytics. The framework addresses two challenges: explicitly linking conceptual knowledge visualization to data analytic tools and using that linkage to explore complexity in social situations. In social or organizational change management strategies, combining new data and knowledge is critical for decision making. When the situation is complex, data must be placed in a knowledge framework to build team learning and to create new mental models for strategic change. As situational complexity increases, the role of knowledge transfer in team social networks becomes more critical, and the ability to visualize knowledge (as opposed to information) becomes paramount to insight and effective decision making. We demonstrate a framework that is derived from theories in the systems thinking and complexity thinking domains, which is then linked to how leaders and managers visualize and communicate data, information, and knowledge. A case study based on Russia's multi-domain influence in the country of Moldova is used to demonstrate explicit linkage between knowledge visualization forms and social data analytics.**

Keywords-knowledge management; complex adaptive systems; data visualization; conceptual modeling; leadership.

I. INTRODUCTION

This research explores ways to explicitly link knowledge-driven conceptual models with data-driven techniques that create insight for decision making in complex systems and situations. Visualization of knowledge in a conceptual form is primarily a qualitative process completed in group facilitation activities. It often uses data and information visualization but the linking of conceptual relationships to the data analytic tools seldom leaves the "whiteboard." With the advent of semantic data analysis and learning tools, there is more opportunity to formally link conceptual learning with data search strategies. This paper presents theory linking data, information, and knowledge visualization forms, then presents a case study exploring tools for combining visualization to demonstrate the possibilities.

The central thesis of this work is that as complexity increases, the role of knowledge transfer in social networks becomes more critical, and the ability to visualize knowledge (as opposed to information) becomes paramount to decision making and strategy. Complex situations are characterized by periods of human social learning followed by periods of stable execution. Visualization tools allow the mapping of large amounts of data to visual patterns that aid human information processing. Exploring data and designing visualization approaches requires a modeling framework as shown in Figure 1. We follow a systems thinking framework that semantically links a qualitative description of the system architecture and measurable constructs to a specification of quantitative methods for computational modeling of those measures.

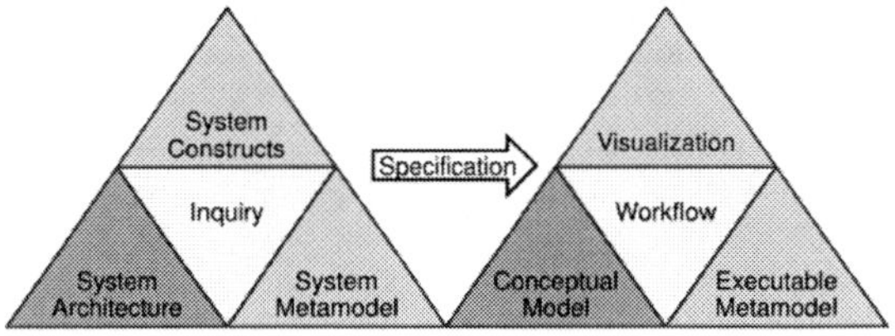

Figure 1. The bridge between qualitative analysis and social analytic model specification.

We define the qualitative aspects in Figure 1 as "System Metamodeling" using three fundamental abstraction approaches: system metamodels, system constructs, and system architecture models. These are determined in a participative and inquiry-based process. We describe quantitative aspects as "Executable Metamodeling" determined by a specification and design workflow using conceptual models, computation, and data visualization. It is useful to think about this as a tool framework. The tools support structuring the systems metamodel, creating the conceptual models, creating the executable metamodels, analyzing and visualizing the decision space, and managing the contained knowledge over time [2].

The system metamodel is described as the set of constructs and rules used to define semantic relationships across information sets, associated data sets, and methodologies or processes. The metamodel definition on the semantic side is an architectural description of the system using modeling views and stakeholder viewpoints. The executable metamodel is the dataset design and any associated computational models. This is further discussed in section III.

A research effort was conducted using the framework to explicitly deconstruct qualitative methods into a "system meta-model" in order to identify and specify "executable meta-models" using computational social science approaches.

The research domain was the study of Russian foreign and security policies. Here, the conventional focus on single-factor explanations has been challenged by the emerging cross-domain character of Russia's statecraft and pursuit of so-called "new generation warfare" in gray zone conflicts. The domain is currently dominated by the application of a narrow set of research methods, such as comparative case studies, regression analysis, expert surveys, and interviews that confront systematic problems related to limited, out of sample, and disconnected data. The case study uses the metamodeling framework to engage more holistic methods that encourage flow of knowledge across multiple domain experts and methods [3] [4].

There are a growing number of actor and event coding schemes and software tools that offer opportunity to automatically extract stakeholders, sentiments, and events related to foreign and security policy analyses. They parse a growing body of English and Russian language (and other languages) databases and media publications on daily and even real-time bases. They target actors and types of events, but struggle with visualization of complex and multi-domain relationships.

We used a combination of scenario analysis and systems thinking methods, such as narratives, taxonomies, and accompanying visual diagrams, to create the systems meta-model. The strategies and tactics within Russia gray zone operational and definitional domain and the key pressure points are identified by scenario development, which captures fundamental change in the present state. The result was a set of conceptual models, and we identified methods to bridge them to computational models via data mining to realize the executable meta-model. This is presented in section IV.

The use of the framework is recommended in periods of program complexity. Challenges of program complexity may have any or all of the following three dimensions: (1) the scale of the project and supporting enterprise, with the variety of organizational disciplines, processes, and tools that might be used to execute the program; (2) the uncertainties created by newness, originality, and innovation; and (3) the external context the program is surrounded by, including social and political factors and market dynamics [5].

The data visualization challenge is to support the combination of qualitative or heuristic decisions that must be made in conjunction with quantitative data driven decisions. These can be categorized as knowledge-driven versus data-driven decisions. How the network of decision-makers collaboratively use data, information, and shared knowledge is paramount.

Progress on visually linking qualitative knowledge with quantitative data is still lacking but can be enabled by machine learning tools that find and semantically link knowledge and data. In complex and uncertain situations, the flexibility of most data visualization tools to create the "story" that is needed to move forward falls short, and decision makers must explore data in more qualitative frameworks. The challenge is to situationally master the combination of tools and visualization forms that visualize data and information to collect, transfer and communicate shared knowledge. The goal of this research is to build linkages between qualitative and quantitative visualization methods to aid decision making. This is discussed further in section II.

II. CONTEXT: COMPLEXITY IN SOCIAL SYSTEMS

Although all human and social systems can be described generally as complex adaptive systems, they undergo periods of stability and disruption driven by internal and external drivers of change. It is important to understand the drivers of this situational complexity and choose appropriate analytical constructs to assess and implement change. Geraldi and Albrecht [5] provided a useful categorization of complexity from the complex project management domain ascribing complexity across three dimensions: Complexity of Fact, Complexity of Faith, and Complexity of Interaction.

A. *Dimensions of Complexity*

Complexity of Fact is a measure of the number of entities and their interdependence as an issue of interdependent information. Given large complexity of fact, it is difficult to obtain and use information rapidly enough to support decision making. Data modelers search for available higher-level abstractions or simplifications to base their data for decisions. In this dimension, there exists a fundamental problem of abstraction – one needs to visualize the whole of the project and represent information in patterns that are embedded in the whole. Visualization frameworks that maintain the holistic perspective while allowing access to detailed information are necessary.

Complexity of Faith relates to program situational uncertainty, often associated with the newness of the problem being solved or methods used to solve it. Complexity of Faith implies a need for learning. In periods of high uncertainty, decisions rely more on shared knowledge than on availability of data and information. Decision makers and their visualization methods and tools in these periods must encourage facilitation, knowledge transfer, and more abstract conceptualization of decision alternatives.

Complexity of Interactions exist at interfaces between different systems and domains. These include people, disciplines, locations, external stakeholders, and social and political factors. In complex situations, it is important to frame program interactions in a larger enterprise architecture framework. Understanding interactions drives the need for facilitation and conceptualization methods and tools.

To manage complexity, one must develop strategies and tools that support 1) exchange and visualization of information across social networks, 2) exchange and visualization of knowledge between decision agents, and 3) evolutionary planning that includes cycles of learning. The presence of all three of these strategies imply that project learning be data-driven, so visualization methods that support access to both information and knowledge must be used. These methods are discussed on literature related to systems thinking and the complexity sciences.

B. *Modeling Complexity using Enterprise Architecture*

Sociotechnical systems analysis is a specific methodology that supports modeling of multiple factors across all layers of a complex situation, enterprise or societal construct using sets of tools derived from system science and system modeling. The methods recognize that factors arise from the interaction of many and diverse enterprises that can be defined by their entities, relationships, established processes, pursued strategies, and emergent phenomena. The sociotechnical systems analysis attempts to capture the combined conceptual, data, and analytical modeling artifacts necessary to completely describe the problem [6] [7].

With respect to social situations, the method produces a set of artifacts that describe the system context and boundaries, system entities and relationships, primary construct variables, potential causal variables, and phenomena of interest. This is the system meta-model. The process is conducted such that insight can be fed into dynamic computer models. The sociotechnical systems analysis produces artifacts that communicate the abstractions and aggregation of behaviors across different scales, helping to explicitly document both the assumed and modeled variables. At the core are entities and their relationships, which can be organized into associated databases and warehouses. The entity-relationship model can be created, modified, and refined over periods of short- and long-term study. Standardized coding of the data entities then makes relevant data elements accessible to researchers and analysts.

The conceptual model representations produced by the sociotechnical systems analysis serve as a bridge between the qualitative aspects of the problem (system meta-model) and the quantitative analysis approach (executable meta-model). This is the purpose of the framework shown previously in Figure 1. In the long-term, we expect that advances in machine learning and semantic graphs can bring the system meta-model (data constructs and conceptual models) and executable meta-model (collected data and algorithms) into the same visualization toolsets. The bridge between the two meta-models is a conceptual model that uses semantic relationships to specify the analytical models. This process of deconstructing complexity is tightly linked to mindsets and tools from the domain of systems thinking.

C. Modeling Complexity of Gray Zone Warfare

Russia's use of "Gray-Zone" warfare is an example of intentional complexity as used to hide or ambiguate purposeful actions leading to objectives that would prepare or position a state for possible armed conflict. Figure 2 depicts the set of factors used in Gray Zone conflict.

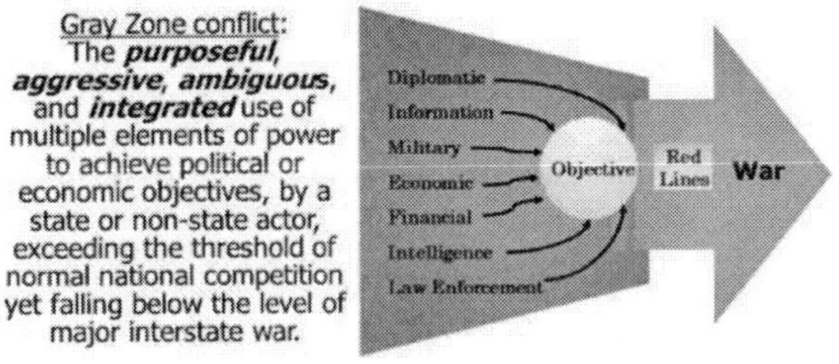

Figure 2. Multiple Objectives used in Gray Zone conflict.

All three types of complexity are exhibited in Gray Zone conflict. Complexity of Fact is exhibited in the almost infinite number of actions and related events that a nation state might pursue. For a data analyst, finding the right abstractions to represent as evidence of such conflict is a continual challenge, as well as ensuring those abstractions are relevant to the current time or predictive of continuing events. The relationship between different objectives - such as diplomatic exchanges, troop movements, and economic sanctions - must be considered holistically. Care must be taken against presenting individual constructs, such as diplomatic exchanges, as a single indicator of state objectives. A conceptual model that shows the relationship between all objectives is important but often ignored by data analysts and even policy makers.

Likewise, Complexity of Faith and Complexity of Interaction are reflected in the pursuit of multiple simultaneous objectives in dynamic combinations. In Gray Zone conflict this is intended to create uncertainty in the adversary and the relationship between an action and the adversary's response – dynamic interaction – is the intent of the strategy. Again, a conceptual model in important before data analysis is relied upon. In section IV a conceptual modeling tool called a "Systemigram" is used to visualize knowledge about Russia's strategies in the country of Moldova.

III. Systems and Complexity Thinking in Data Analytics Design

McDermott and Freeman describe three systems thinking characteristics and competencies that are essential to managing complexity. These are *sensemaking*, *adaptive and computational thinking*, and a *design mindset*. Each of these competencies use data-driven activities that encourage visualizing the relationships between project uncertainties and the underlying project activities [1].

Sensemaking is a collaborative process that involves collection of knowledge, visually describing or modeling a problem or solution in the wider context and learning by doing. *Adaptive and computational thinking* is the ability to situationally adjust a team's thinking and related activities by employing analytics and simulation methods that make sense of large amounts of data (or to understand when data is lacking). Evolution of strategy and planning is a process of iterative design. Building a *design mindset* moves the entrained thinking of the team away from continued use of available data, methods and tools to a participatory team process of understanding and selecting new data, methods and tools. In complex situations, one should strategically design and redesign data analytic measures in response to new insights and understanding of the situation. Computational thinking then relates existing data constructs (generally performance measures) to new constructs selected to guide future evaluation and prediction. The challenge in data visualization is to begin automating these relationships.

Systems thinking encourages modeling or mapping the program and external context together in order to visualize the internal and external interactions that drive project execution. Conceptual models are developed by experts who have the capacity to develop objectively multiple views of a system and its context based on background research and discussions at expert meetings. Conceptual modeling as a visualization strategy is thus a core aspect of any data analytic activity that involves complexity and uncertainty.

The foundation of sensemaking is visualization. Visual modeling is used to frame the program and situation within the enterprise system that is addressing it.

A. System & Complexity Thinking in Data Analytics Design

Boulton, Allen, and Bowman describe the social networks in a design strategy as a "learning multi-agent model" – networks of individual agents who act according to their experience and their beliefs, but ideally aligned around common goals. Inducing change in complex systems requires self-organization around new shared beliefs [8]. A core concern of human social analytics is discovering, measuring, and informing those beliefs. However, creation of new shared beliefs is a knowledge transfer activity across individual agents.

Snowden [9] in his work on complexity and the "Cynefin" framework recognized knowledge exchange in the form of a "learning multi-agent model." Snowden's work suggests that a data artifact may relate to a team's knowledge, but it is the continual flow of new knowledge and artifacts that must be managed in complex situations. Knowledge exchange requires both content and a context. The content can only be exchanged if the context can be shared (language, education, experience, culture, etc.). Visualization tools that address both changing content and changing context are essential.

Data visualization tools and strategies are part of that knowledge exchange but can work against it – they represent the situation only in the context of the tool and existing data, and force information exchange over knowledge transfer. Visualizing a future path of execution, in complexity and uncertainty, requires representation of information in a metamodel framework that tells a story.

This gives us frameworks to evaluate two types of visualization, those that focus on data and information transfer and associated execution, and those that focus knowledge transfer and associated strategy development. Both have application in complex situations. Having a basis for and learning when to apply each type is the key to design of successful human/social analytics. In section IV we demonstrate how these can come together in a data analytic analysis.

Knowledge visualization will often use text-based content in a form that emphasizes relationships or patterns. While information visualization is typically used to explore large amounts of abstract data, knowledge visualization is more used to aid in communication of abstract knowledge. The visual models provide the conceptual language for shared context that is required for knowledge flow. Knowledge visualization tools tend to support the sensemaking process, helping the observer to fill in additional insights based on patterns in the underlying information and data.

The purpose is to properly conceptualize, structure, relate, and validate the relationships in the complex situations from factual data and information to the higher levels of abstraction or aggregation needed to relate meaning and knowledge. This is key to the abstraction of "Fact" to "Faith." Narrative conceptual modeling forms are used to express emergence, relating to evolving situations in the domain or enterprise. In our research we have settled on a conceptual modeling tool called a "systemigram" which blends narrative and diagram. The next section provides an example.

IV. Case Study: Interactive Conceptual and Data Analytic Modeling and Visualization

In the case study, we used a combination of scenario analysis and systems thinking methods, such as creating narratives, taxonomies, and accompanying visual diagrams, to build data analytic models that searched for evidence of Russian Gray Zone conflict in the country of Moldova. The Russian objectives, strategies and tactics are identified by scenario development. This leads to a set of conceptual models, and we identified methods to bridge them to computational models via data mining.

In order to visualize the problem space of gray zone warfare in Moldova, the conceptual model of the system was produced using the systemigram tool that describes the many actors, interactions, processes, resources, and feedback loops present in the Russia-Moldova interaction. Systemigrams are a qualitative model of system behavior that is useful for human reasoning about the dynamics of complex systems [10]. A systemigram serves to illustrate the relationships and flows that exist within a system in its specific context. Figure 3 shows the full systemigram diagram.

The term systemigram is derived from the phrase and portmanteau "systemic diagram." Consisting of both narrative and diagram, systemigrams are a type of conceptual modeling tool closely related to concept maps – or "maps of learning." These maps explore complex situations through the perspective of those embedded in the system or those who are affected by a specific challenge occurring within the system [10].

The systemigram models are developed by experts who have the capacity to develop objectively multiple views of a system based on background research and discussions at expert meetings. To frame such a model, a context for analysis was provided, then tested against the context of Russia's perspective of gray zone warfare in Moldova. Central questions of interest are developed to derive system boundaries and ontology structure to support informing the computational model development.

However, they are not quantitative models that are able to make predictions. In order to enable to the tools of inferential statistics and machine learning to bear on these systemigrams, they must be transformed into quantitative models. This required further addressing and defining ontological and semantic challenges to effectively model the semantics, and identifying the transformations that exist and occur between qualitative and quantitative approaches. In this phase, the team used exploration of the Global Database of Events Language and Tone (GDELT) events and established coding, as defined by the broader research on Russia-EU aggression, to find evidence that either confirm or deny Western perceptions of gray-zone operations and tactics, established by real event chains. This creates a model that links a series of events to sets of tactics, which together, form a perceived strategy.

GDELT includes events reported in the global media coded with many pieces of extracted data. The primary information used in this project is the Date/Time, Location, Actors, and Cameo Event Code [11]. The Actors are the entities (people, government agencies, corporations) that engage in behaviors and the CAMEO codes are a systematic representation of the behaviors on a scale from 1, Make Public Statements, to 20, Unconventional Mass Violence. These codes are extracted from the news articles to enable researchers to study the dynamics of the global system of large-scale human behavior. These machine learning techniques will be specifically adapted to take as input the occurrences and frequencies of coded diplomatic events as related to gray zone conflict.

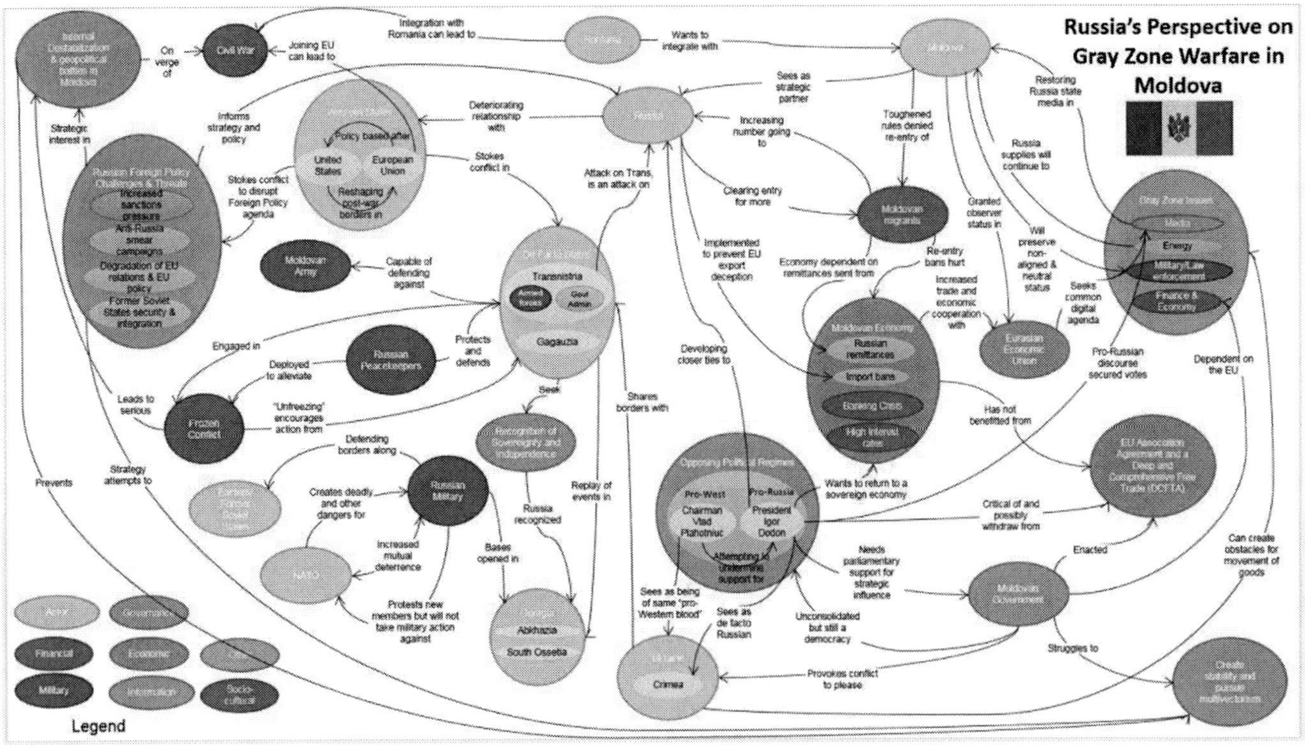

Figure 3. Systemigram Diagram of Russia's Perspective on Gray Zone Warfare in Moldova.

Covariates such as Consult, Make Public Statements, Appeal, Express Intent, Threaten, Dis- approve, Approve, and Demand, along with control variables intended to proxy each dyadic member's socioeconomic, demographic, and geopolitical characteristics (including discretizations and dyad-level combinations thereof), are used to predict the occurrences and frequency of specific outcome events. These are categorized categorized as: Engage in Diplomatic Cooperation, Engage in Material Cooperation, Yield, Investigate, Coerce, Assault, Fight, Reject, Exhibit Military Posture, Reduce Relations, and Provide Aid. By mapping the GDELT events to systemigram nodes, we are able to represent the world at any particular time in terms of the nodes of the systemigrams. Each systemigram node represents a predicate on the GDELT event records and we count how many records match the predicate for each node in the systemigram. An example is shown in Figure 4. At this point, relating the systemigram nodes and links to GDELT event codes is a manual process. However, additional research is exploring how to automate or partially automate this linkage.

This yields two quantitative models from the systemigram. The first is a model based on the representation of a window of time as a multivariate state space. Each systemigram node is a variable and the window of time is represented as a number of events in each variable within that window. These counts are represented in Table 1. Once the system is represented as a multivariate time series it can be modeled with any appropriate time series technique. For example, this representation lends itself to a Kalman filter approach tracking changes in the true system in the presence of noisy observations. We then took bilateral relations data from the Moldova, Russia relationship as well as some surrounding actors and build both models. Since the Kalman filter approach can only generate windowed data, we will compare both models in terms of their ability to forecast at the windowed level. Comparisons will take the form of quality of fit assessment and visual representations of the dynamics of the system. In Table 1, the numbers on the top row represent individual system concepts that are represented by a node 1 + node 2 + link tuple. The numbers in column 1 are year/month date codes. Each data item represents an individual event in the GDELT database for that concept in a given year/month.

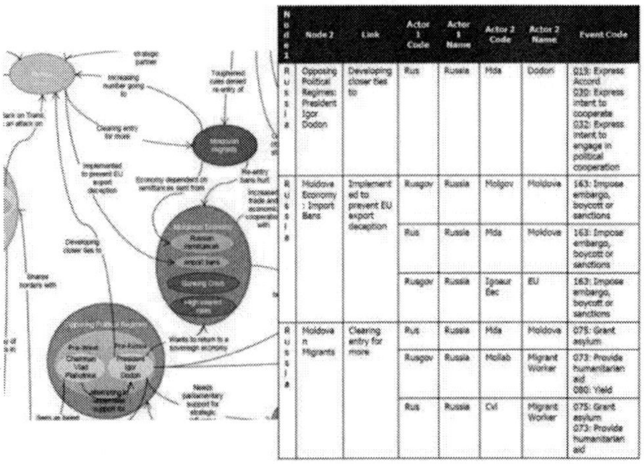

Node 1	Node 2	Link	Actor 1 Code	Actor 1 Name	Actor 2 Code	Actor 2 Name	Event Code
Russia	Opposing Political Regimes: President Igor Dodon	Developing closer ties to	Rus	Russia	Mda	Dodon	013: Express Accord 030: Express intent to cooperate 032: Express intent to engage in political cooperation
Russia	Moldova Economy: Import Bans	Implemented to prevent EU export deception	Rusgov	Russia	Mdgov	Moldova	163: Impose embargo, boycott or sanctions
			Rus	Russia	Mda	Moldova	163: Impose embargo, boycott or sanctions
			Rusgov	Russia	Igoeur Bec	EU	163: Impose embargo, boycott or sanctions
Russia	Moldovan Migrants	Clearing entry for more	Rus	Russia	Mda	Moldova	075: Grant asylum
			Rusgov	Russia	Mdlab	Migrant Worker	073: Provide humanitarian aid 080: Yield
			Rus	Russia	Cvl	Migrant Worker	075: Grant asylum 073: Provide humanitarian aid

Figure 4. Relating systemigram nodes and links to GDELT codes.

TABLE 1. EVOLUTION OF SELECTED MOLDOVA SYSTEM CONCEPTS OVER THE TIME BETWEEN 12/2016-5/2018

Month	0	1	2	3	5	6	7	8	9	13
201612	25	6	44	13	2	50	43	2515	5437	54
201701	49	58	37	58	6	231	115	7856	9861	182
201702	24	57	25	18	2	317	161	6909	10616	122
201703	44	49	35	37	1	244	173	6558	11034	176
201704	19	20	10	31	4	177	112	5318	10403	172
201705	28	29	11	24		170	82	5900	7729	122
201707	44	72	39	80		171	202	6452	11060	676
201708	44	63	23	53		113	97	3303	6540	346
201709	51	60	15	26		221	120	3504	6625	142
201710	18	34	6	11	1	173	82	2577	4048	34
201711	13	34	6	26	3	165	123	3620	7635	76
201712	25	12	22	7	2	199	106	4956	8776	8
201801	12	16	10	10	4	183	119	3888	5548	64
201802	15	15	20	16		146	152	4850	6646	42
201803	10	4	17	11		296	186	6193	10409	50
201804	10	8	19	8	1	193	120	4513	8186	80

Concept 5 and concept 13 displayed the most obvious correlation of concept to events. Both of these concepts are shown in the full systemigram in Figure 3 as node (Russian Peacekeepers) link (deployed to alleviate) node (Frozen Conflict). These are periods of Russian troop withdrawals from Moldova. In 07/2017 and 12/2017 Russian troops were withdrawn from Syria which was picked up as a local maximum (676) and minimum (9) of the GDELT queries associated with concept 13. Concept 3, node (Russian Foreign Policy) link (Strategy attempts to) node (Create stability and pursue multivectorism) was also found to correlate with signals from the other two concepts and thus provide strategic analysts and planners with confirmatory signals of Russian objectives. We also see that some events with large coverage and a persistent presence such as node (Western States: United States) link (Stokes conflict to disrupt foreign policy agenda) node (Russian Foreign Policy Challenges and Threats), and this node to link (Informs strategy and policy) to node (Russia) follow a long term cyclical trend rising and falling together without significant spikes or crashes in concepts 8 and 9. These events form the background environment which is important to shaping the understanding of polities and decision-makers, and quantified systemigrams can help us understand these entities for foresight.

V. CONCLUSIONS

This paper presented a framework to bridge qualitative and quantitative models and associated visualization of data with knowledge. Few efforts have been made to translate emerging research in these approaches into user-friendly and interactive visual tools that can aid in both hypotheses' generation, strategic forecasting, and scenario assessment. To create a holistic approach and toolset, this research draws on theories and frameworks from multiple disciplines including systems thinking, complexity thinking, and complex project management. Qualitative methods promote the development of conceptual models to aid in structuring and understanding real world systems and problems, in this context, applied to Russia's application and perspective of gray zone conflict in Moldova. However, qualitative models are difficult to directly measure or validate. Thus, building off the conceptual models developed using the systemigram tool and identifying methods to bridge them to computational models via data mining provided insight into the system to inform further research and development of more quantitative models. The techniques presented here can be adapted to near-real-time detection of hot-spots and anomalies or used as a basis for post-hoc quantitative analysis.

The conversion of qualitative to quantitative models requires the construction of detailed mappings into coding spaces. These mappings are useful because they enable database systems to calculate measurements for each concept in the soft system model. This approach allows segmentation of the data by arbitrary filters on the actors involved and time spans covered, thus allowing researchers to compare these effects on various subsets of the corpus and draw conclusions about how these effects differ across regions, times, and combinatorial pairings of country- level characteristics for more foresightful strategy development.

REFERENCES

[1] T. McDermott and D. Freeman, "Systems Thinking in the Systems Engineering Process, New Methods and Tools," in M. Frank, S. Kordova, H. Shaked (Eds.), Systems Thinking: Foundation, Uses and Challenges, Nova 2016.

[2] J. Ernst, "What is metamodeling, and what is it good for". Retrieved from http://infogrid.org/trac/wiki/Reference/WhatIsMetaModeling. November 2015.

[3] M. Nadolski and J. Fairbanks, "Complex Systems Analysis of Hybrid Warfare," 17th Annual Conference of Systems Engineering Research (CSER), Washington, DC, 2019.

[4] Nadolski, Molly. A Sociotechnical Modeling Framework for Complex Systems Analysis of Gray Zone Warfare. Conflicts in the Gray Zone: A Challenge to Adapt. Budapest, Hungary, 2017.

[5] J. G. Geraldi and G. Adlbrecht, "On faith, fact and interaction in projects," Project Management Journal, 38 (1), pp. 32-43, 2007.

[6] W. B. Rouse & D. Bodner, Multi-level modeling of complex socio-technical systems – phase 1, A013 - final technical report, SERC-2013-TR-020-2, Systems Engineering Research Center.

[7] W. B. Rouse & M. Pennock, Multi-level modeling of socio-technical systems a013 - final technical report, SERC-2013-TR-020-3, Systems Engineering Research Center.

[8] Boulton, J., Allen, P., & Bowman, C. 2015. Embracing complexity: strategic perspectives for an age of turbulence. Oxford University Press.

[9] Snowden, D. 2002. Complex acts of knowing: paradox and descriptive self-awareness. Journal of Knowledge Management, 6 (2), 100-111. May 2002.

[10] Sauser, B., & Boardman, J. (2013). Systemic thinking: Building maps for worlds of systems. Chichester: Wiley-Blackwell.

[11] Conflict and Mediation Event Observations Event and Actor Codebook [Scholarly project]. (2012, March). GDELT Project. Retrieved from http://data.gdeltproject.org/documentation/CAMEO.Manual.1.1b3.pdf

Data for Healthy Decisions: Computation for Passive Monitoring of Medium-Risk Individuals at Home

Dennis J. Folds
Lowell Scientific Enterprises
Carrollton, Georgia USA

email: dennis.folds@gmail.com

Abstract— **Many senior adults living independently are at some risk of severe health problems, and have adult caregivers who do not live with them. There is a need for positive indicators of well being to be available to those caregivers. Technology that requires the senior adult to actively perform tasks, such as filling out logs or hooking up sensors, may not be effective, due to the burden on the individual leading to non-compliance. What is needed is technology that is largely passive, installed unobtrusively in the home, that can generate the data needed for calculating indicators of well being. Such data is useful to remote caregivers as well as to medical professionals. One example of such a system, a prototype used to passively monitor and compute nocturnal trips to the bathroom, is presented. Data were collected from 7 senior adults living alone over a four-week period. Computational challenges were significant. Effectiveness of such technology requires social acceptance, ease of use, data security, and calculation of reliable, actionable metrics.**

Keywords- Computational social science; social analytics, independent living.

I. Introduction

Increasing life expectancy across the developed and developing world results in significant increases in the sheer number of senior adults, and in many countries, of the percentage of the population that are seniors. The quality of life experienced by seniors is directly impacted by the adequacy and efficacy of the health care they receive. There are tradeoffs between the common desire for seniors to continue to live independently, versus the need to monitor and manage risk factors related to health.

Senior adults tend to value their ability to continue to live independently, either in their long-occupied home, or in a newer domicile. Independent living is a strong contributor to Subject Well Being (SWB) in senior adults, and higher levels of SWB are associated with better health outcomes [1].

Individuals who live alone – even if in a close community – may be at particular risk for maladies that are associated with general trends of decline. Poor sleep, poor medication adherence, and poor nutrition are examples of trends that are associated with increased risk of a multitude of health problems that may require treatment. The problem is likely worse when living conditions are more isolated.

Many senior adults continue to live quite active lifestyles, especially in the earlier years of that period labeled as "elderly". These individuals may be considered low risk. Some develop acute conditions that require close medical monitoring for a period of time, while others develop chronic illnesses or other chronic conditions that require medical monitoring on a continuing basis. These individuals may be considered high risk. For such individuals, whether on temporary or long-term basis, it is reasonable to expect that the devices and procedures used for medical monitoring may be somewhat intrusive, and may require active participation by the individual being monitored.

In the present paper, a third group of senior adults is of primary interest. These are perhaps well described as "medium risk", in that they have no particular health issues that require ongoing monitoring, but are experiencing some general trends that are predictive of increasing probabilities of various health problems. An increased risk of falling is an obvious concern, especially for people who live alone. Undetected rapid growth of certain skin features, such as moles or warts, is another. This list of examples can go on and on; the challenge is to find ways to help monitor general indicators in a way that can help the individual, and care givers (e.g., an adult child), make good decisions about (a) medical interventions that may be needed, and (b) whether continued independent living is wise.

One example of a general indicator of risk is gait speed. Imagine two senior adults walking in the park. One may walk confidently, at a pace unchanged since middle age. The second may walk hesitantly, with a much slower pace and somewhat irregular gait. This second person not only has a higher risk of falling, but also has a higher risk of cognitive decline, disability, and other maladies [2]. Thus, monitoring gait speed could help with a general assessment of a person's level of risk.

A second general trend, and the one of particular interest in the present paper, is the number of nocturnal (nighttime) trips to the bathroom to void the bladder. Falls are but one risk during nocturnal trips to the bathroom. Frequent nighttime urination, known as nocturia, is common in older adults. Up to three fifths of the senior adult population void at least twice during the night [3]. In this context, a nocturnal void means the person awakes from sleep, goes to the bathroom and voids the bladder, and returns to bed and to sleep. In addition to a potential fall, these frequent trips directly reduce sleep quality, which in turn is a general predictor of increased risk. Perhaps more importantly, nocturia can also be an indicator of other serious health conditions (including chronic kidney disease and congestive heart failure), and may indicate a general neurological decline in which the brain's ability to control the kidneys at night (to produce more concentrated urine) is lessening.

In Section 2 below, an example of a passive monitoring system focused on monitoring indicators of nocturia is presented. The example system is a prototype kit of sensors used in an exploratory study [4], aimed at identifying key challenges for this type of monitoring. Results from that study are summarized in Section 3. Discussion of the technical challenges, ease of use issues, and computational methods appears in Section 4. In Section 5, the key attributes of a passive monitoring system that would achieve the goals of unobtrusively monitoring medium-risk individuals at home are described.

II. Example

The kit used in the exploratory study featured Commercial Off The Shelf (COTS), prototype, and custom components, specifically chosen to unobtrusively measure indicators of nocturnal trips to the toilet. The kit was placed in the homes of eight research participants for a period of four weeks. The data were used to develop the computational algorithms necessary to automatically compute the number of trips to the bathroom each night, and to compile that data by individual in a summary form suitable to share with a caregiver.

The kit consisted of the following components:

- A COTS sleep tracker called Beddit, which is installed under the sheet and measures bed presence along with various physiological parameters used to infer sleep state.
- A prototype sensor called SmartMat, which primarily consists of a pressure sensitive film affixed to the underside of a mat. We placed the mat in front of the toilet in the homes of the participants.
- The Misfit Shine, a COTS activity tracker worn on the wrist that detects steps and sleep, among other things.
- A custom built proximity detector that we dubbed the Ping Presence Sensor (PPS), which used ultrasound to detect a person sitting on, or standing in front of, the toilet.

These components permitted redundant measures of sleep and proximity to the toilet, and single measures of steps and bed presence. With ideal data, it should have been possible to parse for the following sequence: bed presence, sleep, bed departure, steps, toilet proximity, steps, bed presence, and sleep. The number of times this sequence occurred each night was the measurement of interest in the study.

III. Results

Given that the components used in this kit were a mixture of COTS, prototype, and custom components, it was not surprising that there were numerous instances of lost or corrupted data. The Beddit bed presence sensor generally worked well, but did not reliably sense bed presence or sleep state when the participant was in a position that was partially off the sensor. This was a bigger problem with participants who slept in a queen sized bed. The SmartMat exhibited a data loss problem when it temporarily lost data connectivity – a problem not seen in preliminary pilot testing – and required a power cycle to resume proper data collection. The PPS was dependent on a direct line of sight between the sensor and the person seated on (or standing in front of) the toilet. There were instances of the other objects also being placed on the back of the toilet, partially blocking the direct line of sight, and hence corrupting the data from this sensor.

A different set of challenges emerged with the Misfit Shine activity tracker. The data were reliably collected and stored on the device, but the device did not reliably synch with the IPod that was paired with it. The path to get the data off the device required the IPod to retrieve the data and then upload it to a cloud-based service. The research technicians were able to manually trigger the synch operation during the last home visit; little data were lost. Nevertheless. these data were not available for use in computing day-to-day results as the study progressed. Another issue was that the default data provided by the device was simply a summary of the total number of steps for a day (midnight to midnight). Time-stamped step data would have been better, for use in algorithms to help distinguish the cases of interest (simple trips to the toilet) from other cases in which the person left the bed and performed some other action (e.g., going to the kitchen), as well as going to the toilet. Rectifying this problem would have required interaction with the engineers for the device and access to a special device configuration not normally used with consumers. Consequently, it was not possible to use the time-stamped step data in our algorithms.

Usable data sets were obtained from seven of the eight participants. The kit placed in the home of the eighth participant repeatedly malfunctioned, and the participant had difficulty performing the required tasks. A set of algorithms were developed to align the data from the four sources, and to identify patterns that fit the profile of interest. For each of the seven participants, there were a few nights that had data amenable to straightforward parsing. More generally, though, the data for a given participant on a given night tended to have data missing or corrupted from at least one of the four components of the kit.

A general observation on the computing challenges is that the two COTS products provided data that were easier to integrate, whereas the prototype and custom components provided data that were more challenging. The COTS product data had reliable time stamps, but required some post-processing to combine data from two days (midnight to midnight) into a single night. The data from the prototype and custom components were also time-stamped, but there appeared to be some drift or inaccuracy in the time base, as there were many instances in which the time stamp of the toilet proximity event differed between the two components, and in some cases, was logged as earlier than the bed exit event.

The pervasive challenge was that the incomplete data did not provide a solid basis for computing reliable counts of the number of trips to the toilet during the night. In some instances, it was possible to manually inspect the data and spot an anomaly that, if corrected, could result in apparently correct data. Thus it is possible to include case-by-case anomaly corrections into the algorithms, but this required manual detection (and understanding) of the anomaly.

IV. Discussion

This section contains a description of the research results related to technical feasibility of the technology, ease of use by the participants, and the computing challenges that were encountered during the execution of the study.

A. Technical Feasibility

The example described above demonstrates that it is technically feasible to collect certain data of interest for medium risk individuals in a home setting, without imposing undue burdens on the person to perform required tasks, such as starting or stopping a device, manually transferring data, or keeping logs. A combination of consumer products (especially from the burgeoning personal fitness sector) and custom-designed components can yield a combined data set that supports calculation of the measures of interest.

Although feasible, there are significant technical challenges ahead. Power management, especially for devices powered by batteries, will be a challenge. In the example study, the Beddit sensor was powered through an electrical plug, and the other three devices ran off batteries. The Misfit Shine required regular recharging (preferably daily.) The SmartMat and the PPS had batteries that were sufficient for the four-week study, but would have required replacement for a longer deployment period.

The network connectivity of the devices was also a technical challenge. The Beddit and the Misfit Shine relied on transferring data through a mobile device (tablet or phone) to a cloud-based service, and thus required an internet connection that could be accessed by the device. The SmartMat also required its own data connection through WiFi, and did not automatically reconnect in certain conditions after interruption.

B. Ease of Use

The two commercial products required some minimal interaction from the participants, but were generally typical of products in the commercial fitness tracking market. Usability concerns will be greater when using such products with some senior adults – those less familiar with mobile devices in general, and with common actions, such as pairing and synching.

The other two components were generally easy to use and required little active cooperation from the research participants. Their effectiveness, though, required the participant to leave them in place and to leave them configured as intended. In a longer term deployment, laundering the SmartMat would be an issue. Neither of these two components provided any direct signal to the participant if they had malfunctioned or were not configured correctly.

C. Computing Challenges

The computing challenges were significant. If commercial products are to be used, it is desirable to get their data in relatively raw form (e.g., time stamped step data rather than daily summaries). Summary data for the midnight-to-midnight day will have limitations on its usefulness to compute the measures of interest. Partial redundancy on certain measures led to higher confidence when both agreed, and allowed computation of a measure of interest when one was absent. Cases in which they disagreed, however, led to anomalies that had to be manually corrected.

The algorithms themselves were relatively straightforward to develop for the subset of data that were intact. Applying a time-stamp correction in the form of an offset solved some data problems, and this process could probably be automated. Many of the other anomalies, however, required manual inspection and speculation to resolve. For example, in one instance the SmartMat showed proximity to the toilet when the PPS did not, and the Beddit indicated the participant was in the bed. The proximity signal persisted for many minutes. We speculated that the participant's pet had probably laid down on the mat for that period of time, and manually discarded it.

In the example study, participant eligibility required that they live alone, normally sleep in the same bed each night, and normally use the same toilet during the night. The computational challenges will increase significantly with more than one occupant, especially if they sleep in the same bed. With more than one occupant, however, there may be less need for passive monitoring.

V. Key Attributes

This section presents a description of the key attributes of systems that will provide the capability to monitor medium-risk individuals in the home, unobtrusively.

A. Ease of Use for the Intended Population

Ideally, the technology used for this type of monitoring should only require consent for the equipment to be installed in the home. Realistically, though, it may require some user actions, such as replacing batteries. Initial actions, such as entering network credentials, could be performed by a technician or another caregiver. Day to day activities, including donning and doffing a device, charging and synching a device, or updating a device, should be as non-intrusive as possible, and should be commensurate with the types of actions already familiar to the individual.

It is important that such technology not be reliant on active participation and cooperation, such as entering data or completing logs. It is also important that normal activities, such as house cleaning, be minimally impacted by the presence of the technology.

B. Data Security and Privacy Protection

Given that the intended use of technology of interest in this research is to promote independent living for senior adults as long as they wish, and that it wise to do so, it is vitally important that the senior adult not feel like the technology is too intrusive on their privacy. It is important that the data be provided, securely, to only those people acceptable to the senior adult. Further, it is essential that the data are positively associated with the senior adult, not inadvertently collected from guests or other non-occupants in the home temporarily (e.g., service providers).

The reliable availability of the data to the caregiver is also important. If the caregiver, living elsewhere, is to use these data to help monitor well being of the senior adult, prolonged periods of unavailable data will be counterproductive. Instances in which the data have become unavailable should be flagged for correction.

C. Actionable Metrics

Most importantly, the technology of interest should provide to the decision maker clear data on specific instances and general trends so that a decision can be made. Primary decisions of interest are (a) whether a specific follow-up, such as a home visit, is needed, (b) whether a medical intervention, such as a doctor's appointment or trip to a clinic is needed, and (c) whether continued independent living is wise. In many cases there is access to graduated levels of care before residency in a skilled nursing facility is warranted. The graduated levels may include daily visits related to medication and meals, assistance with transportation and general community mobility, and taking measurements (such as blood pressure) directly.

Development of suitable metrics will require a focused research program. The example used in the present paper concentrated on integrating measures of sleep and activity, to produce a simple count of the number of trips to the bathroom during the night. Such data from a single night is not the basis for a decision. Data over weeks and months are needed to establish whether the person routinely awakens to void the bladder more than once per night. Long term data is also needed to establish whether the frequency of the nighttime voids is increasing.

In developing these metrics, it is important to develop positive indicators of well being, as well as indicators of potential concerns. That is, it will be useful to caregivers outside the home if they can see results showing that the person being monitored exhibits such attributes as (a) gets plenty of uninterrupted sleep, (b) is taking their medication appropriately, (c) has good nutrition, (d) has a good gait, (e) has a healthy appearance of the face and skin, and (f) has plenty of social interactions. Such measures, along with others that might be added, are predictive that the senior adult is doing well.

D. Positive Socialization

One can imagine two different socialization paths for passive monitoring technology. There is a negative path, in which the technology is seen as invasive of privacy and denigrating to dignity. On the other hand, there is a positive path, in which the technology is seen as supportive, wise, useful as a precaution, and an enabler of independent living.

Positive socialization will not occur in a vacuum. Introduction of technology that measures the activities described in the present paper is easily labeled as "spying" or other pejorative terms. The current trends in fitness and activity tracking may provide a path for positive socialization. These trends include presentation of feedback to the person on a daily basis, along with a summary of recent (and sometimes long-term) trends, comparing the person's data with data from peers, and sharing data among a designated group.

Current trends across healthcare providers and public health services reveal growing interest in using mobile devices (e.g., smartphones) and the Internet of Things (IoT) to help monitor at-risk individuals, groups and regions. For example, monitoring for spread of infectious diseases in areas of concern can possibly be accomplished more efficiently using specialized sensors that scan populated areas for indicators of interest (e.g., high fever), and combine that data with data from other sources, to more quickly detect spread of serious disease [5]. The hybrid crowdsensing paradigm [6], applied to healthcare, may result in greater familiarity with using general surveillance of people in public places, along with specialized sensors intentionally carried by individuals. This greater familiarity may help facilitate easier acceptance of similar technologies deployed in private residences.

Indeed, there is general interest in leveraging the IoT to improve healthcare for senior adults, across the spectrum of early warning systems (enabled by artificial intelligence), assisted living, and mobile health [7]. IoT data obtained from home appliances, utilities, and smart home technologies may enable the types of algorithms of interest in the present paper to be developed and used to monitor individuals at all levels of risk.

Ultimately, positive socialization will require that the senior adult feel more confident as they continue to live independently, as well as increasing the confidence of caregivers who monitor the metrics remotely. If the technology can improve the SWB of the senior adult, perhaps it will also help promote better health and quality of life outcomes for this segment of the population.

VI. Conclusions and Future Work

It is clear from the results that the goal of monitoring individuals at the medium-risk level, unobtrusively, is attainable. The challenges, however, require deliberate design and engineering to ensure that the burden of making this technology work does not fall on the individual to be monitored. Supporting technologies, such as batteries and wireless communications, are improving at an impressive pace. They will be required for the technology of interest to become successful. Future research should focus on improving the reliability and interoperability of the key component technologies, making it easier to integrate multiple sources of information into an unambiguous chronology of events. Future work is also needed on developing complementary sensors that could provide additional, confirmatory sources of information. One example, investigated in the current effort but not included due to lack of maturity, is technology to monitor water usage in the home. Actions such as flushing the toilet may have a unique signature that, in principle, can be monitored by sensors attached to water lines in the home. Monitoring electrical circuit loads can also provide information about activities such as laundry, cooking, and light housework. Use of mobile communications devices can provide information about community mobility and social interconnectedness. Still further information may come from a variety of sources (such as home appliances) associated with the IoT. Collectively, an array of such technologies can be useful in monitoring medium-risk individuals performing a variety of activities of interest. By combining information about bed presence, sleep, walking (including gait speed), using the toilet, using water and electricity in the home, mobility outside the home, and communications patterns, it may be possible to compute indices of well-being across a wide spectrum of activities that are vital to the physical and mental health of senior adults.

REFERENCES

[1] E. Diener and M. Chan, "Happy people live longer: Subjective well-being contributes to health and longevity," Applied Psych: Health and Well-Being, vol. 3, no. 1, pp. 1-43, 2011, https://doi.org/10.1111/j.1758-0854.2010.01045.x.

[2] G. Abellan Van Kan, et al. "Gait speed at usual pace as a predictor of adverse outcomes in community," J Nutr Health Aging, vol. 13, pp. 881-889, 2009, https://doi.org/10.1007/s12603-009-0246-z

[3] J. R. Bosch and J. P. Weiss, "The prevalence and causes of nocturia" J of Urology, vol. 184, no. 2, pp. 440-446, 2010.

[4] D. Folds, J. Ray, T. Johnson, and B. Ake, "Data to healthy decisions (D2HD)," GTRI IRAD Report, 2015, Atlanta, GA: Georgia Tech Research Institute.

[5] T. Edoh, "Risk prevention of spreading emerging infectious diseases using a hybrid crowdsensing paradigm, optical sensors, and smartphone. Journal of Medical Systems, vol. 42, no. 5, article 91, 2018, http://doi.org/10.1007/s10916-018-0937-2.

[6] M. Avvenuti, S. Bellomo, S. Cresc, M/ La Polla, and M. Tesconi, "Hybrid Crowdsensing: A Novel Paradigm to Combine the Strengths of Opportunistic and Participatory Crowdsensing," WWW 2017 Companion, April 3-7, 2017, Perth, Australia. ACM 978-1-4503-4914-7/17/04. http://dx.doi.org/10.1145/3041021.3051155.

[7] [7] B. Farahania, F. Firouzib, V. Changc, M. Badaroglud, N. Constante, and K. Mankodiyae, Towards fog-driven IoT eHealth: Promises and challenges of IoT in medicine and healthcare," Future Generation Computer Systems, vol. 78, part 2, pp. 659-676, 2018, https://doi.org/10.1016/j.future.2017.04.036.

Understanding Societal Well-Being Through the Eyes of the News World Media

Vasiliki Voukelatou
Scuola Normale Superiore and
Institute of Information Science and
Technologies (ISTI)-CNR
56126-56127, Pisa, Italy
Email: vasiliki.voukelatou@sns.it

Luca Pappalardo
Institute of Information Science and
Technologies (ISTI)-CNR
56127, Pisa, Italy
Email: luca.pappalardo@isti.cnr.it

Fosca Giannotti
Institute of Information Science and
Technologies (ISTI)-CNR
56127, Pisa, Italy
Email: fosca.giannotti@isti.cnr.it

***Abstract*—Societal well-being is an important value for people's lives and it contributes considerably to the societal progress. It has been traditionally captured with surveys and during the last decades innovative approaches have been applied for its measurement. Global Peace Index is an indicator, which measures well-being in terms of peace and safety. This study suggests the potential measurement of this index through a novel automatic methodology.**

***Keywords*–GDELT; Well-being; Global Peace Index; Big Data**

I. INTRODUCTION

Defining well-being has been always considered a challenge. Therefore, researchers have expressed its nature by focusing on the dimensions of well-being, rather than on definition[1]. In fact, well-being encompasses a set of health, socio-economic (such as unemployment) and political dimensions (such as peace and safety) [2], [3], [4]. Therefore, monitoring it is one of the main concerns of policy-makers. In fact, when a new policy is applied or an unexpected event occurs, what policy-makers focus on is eventual consequences on humans' well-being.

Researchers have traditionally considered Gross Domestic Product (GDP) as a good indicator of well-being in society. The reason for which it has been considered as a suitable indicator for measuring well-being is that it is strongly linked with the standard of living indicators [5]. However, GDP has been criticized as a weak indicator of well-being and therefore a misleading tool for public policies [6]. In fact, Stiglitz Commission [7] in 2009 observed that there could be used other statistical tools, complementary to GDP, for the well-being measurement. Following this direction, researchers have created various indexes, for the measurement of well-being, for many purposes and for capturing a variety of its dimensions [6]. Some important examples are the Human Development Index (HDI), created by the United Nations Development Programme (UNDP) [8], the Better Life Index (BLI), created by the Organisation for Economic Co-operation and Development (OECD) [4] and the Sustainable Well-Being Index (Benessere Equo Sostenibile-BES), created by Italian National Statistics Istitute (ISTAT) [9].

Traditionally, well-being and territorial socio-economic development are measured through surveys of household income and consumption [10]. Nevertheless, surveys are usually very costly, making it difficult for many developing countries to update their estimates frequently. During the last decades, with the proliferation of technology, researchers are inclined to use more innovative and cost-effective approaches complementing the traditional measurement of well-being. In fact, over the last years, researchers have frequently used Big Data sources, which seem to offer new opportunities to study the well-being dimensions and to circumvent the limitations carried from traditional methodologies. For this research purpose, several data sources have been used, with the most important ones being Twitter (see e.g. [11], [12]), Call Detail Record data (CDRs) (see e.g. [13], [14], GPS and transportation data (see e.g. [15], [16], [17]), and a variety of approaches have been applied, such as sentiment analysis, face recognition, network analysis and others.

II. METHODOLOGY AND RESULTS

For the purposes of the current study, nowcasting well-being is the main task to be realized. In particular, well-being is explored in terms of safety, which is one of the well-being dimensions, as defined by OECD [4], and in terms of peace, which is one of the sustainable development goals, as defined by United Nations [18]. *Global Peace Index (GPI)* [19], created by the Institute for Economics and Peace, captures the peacefulness of continents and ranks 163 independent states and territories . GPI is traditionally measured by institutional surveys and governmental data. Therefore, an innovative data source is suggested, which could capture the GPI score automatically, complementing the traditional methodology.

GDELT[20], yet a barely explored data source, is validated whether it could satisfy the aforementioned needs. It is a publicly available event database supported by Google Jigsaw. contains data based on international English-language news, such as AfricaNews, Agence France Presse, Associated Press, Associated Press Online, Associated Press Worldstream, BBC Monitoring, Christian Science Monitor, Facts on File, Foreign Broadcast Information Service, The New York Times, United Press International and The Washington Post etc. In particular, Tabari system extracts the events from each article and stores them in an expanded version of the dyadic CAMEO format, a conflict and mediation event taxonomy [21]. Examples of identified events are protests, conflicts, peace appeals, terrorist attacks, violence, etc. Additional software identifies the location of each event, with a similar approach used to map wikipedia [22], and the tone, using the tonal algorithm from Shook et al. [23]). Multiple references to the same event across one or more articles from the same newswire are collapsed into a single event record, but are not deduplicated across newswires. Data are updated daily and historical data, since 1979, are also provided (see Leetaru et al. [24] for more details on GDELT).

the study presented here, the measurement of GPI is by the creation of new variables extracted from 0 GDELT event . In particular, official GPI variables are recreated by mapping them with GDELT data, which provide similar information. For instance, "Number of jailed population per 100,000 people" official GPI variable is recreated by "Arrest, detain; legal or extrajudicial arrests, detentions, or imprisonments" and "Threaten with repression" GDELT event categories and is simply called "jailed" for convenience. After a careful mapping, 9 new variables are extracted from the GDELT event database, as a count of events associated with at a country and year level, normalized to the total number of events, at a country and year level.

order to evaluate the new variables on their relationship with the GPI official score, correlation analysis is conducted. Preliminary analysis is done without distinguishing between countries and years. Results show noticeable correlations between the created GDELT variables and the official GPI score. particular, the simply called "conventional weapons" variable and GPI, as well as "impact of terrorism" variable and GPI show Pearson's correlation coefficients r=0.41 and r=0.35 respectively.

III. DISCUSSION AND FUTURE STEPS

The next step of the study is the creation of odel, that given the variables created, will nowcast/predict the official GPI score a country and year level. The model will be built with the new variables and, potentially, with the Scale ranking data provided by GDELT, capturing the potential impact each event might have on the stability of a country. model is expected to provide a GPI trend pattern similar to the one provided by the official model. Such a result would contribute to the official GPI yearly study, since GDELT data are updated daily, making it possible to provide policy researchers with GPI variations throughout the year. In addition, in case of a new instability in a country, such a model could provide predictions for the variations of the GPI score of the country for the upcoming year.

REFERENCES

[1] R. Dodge, A. P. Daly, J. Huyton, and L. D. Sanders, "The challenge of defining wellbeing," International journal of wellbeing, vol. 2, no. 3, 2012.

[2] B. Rapporto, "Il benessere equo e sostenibile in italia," 2015.

[3] W. H. Organization, World health statistics 2016: monitoring health for the SDGs sustainable development goals. World Health Organization, 2016.

[4] O. for Economic Co-operation and Development, How's life?: measuring well-being. Oecd Paris, 2011.

[5] C. M. Reinhart and V. R. Reinhart, "After the fall," National Bureau of Economic Research, Tech. Rep., 2010.

[6] M. Fleurbaey, "Beyond gdp: The quest for a measure of social welfare," Journal of Economic literature, vol. 47, no. 4, 2009, pp. 1029–75.

[7] J. E. Stiglitz, A. Sen, and J.-P. Fitoussi, "Report by the commission on the measurement of economic performance and social progress," 2017.

[8] S. Anand and A. Sen, "Human development index: Methodology and measurement," 1994.

[9] C. Istat, "Il benessere equo e sostenibile in italia," Roma, Istat, 2013.

[10] A. Deaton, The analysis of household surveys: a microeconometric approach to development policy. The World Bank, 1997.

[11] J. C. Eichstaedt, H. A. Schwartz, M. L. Kern, G. Park, D. R. Labarthe, R. M. Merchant, S. Jha, M. Agrawal, L. A. Dziurzynski, M. Sap et al., "Psychological language on twitter predicts county-level heart disease mortality," Psychological science, vol. 26, no. 2, 2015, pp. 159–169.

[12] L. Dong, S. Chen, Y. Cheng, Z. Wu, C. Li, and H. Wu, "Measuring economic activity in china with mobile big data," EPJ Data Science, vol. 6, no. 1, 2017, p. 29.

[13] P. Sundsøy, J. Bjelland, B.-A. Reme, E. Jahani, E. Wetter, and L. Bengtsson, "Towards real-time prediction of unemployment and profession," in International Conference on Social Informatics. Springer, 2017, pp. 14–23.

[14] F. Finger, T. Genolet, L. Mari, G. C. de Magny, N. M. Manga, A. Rinaldo, and E. Bertuzzo, "Mobile phone data highlights the role of mass gatherings in the spreading of cholera outbreaks," Proceedings of the National Academy of Sciences, vol. 113, no. 23, 2016, pp. 6421–6426.

[15] C. Smith, D. Quercia, and L. Capra, "Finger on the pulse: identifying deprivation using transit flow analysis," in Proceedings of the 2013 conference on Computer supported cooperative work. ACM, 2013, pp. 683–692.

[16] A. I. Robinson, F. Carnes, and N. M. Oreskovic, "Spatial analysis of crime incidence and adolescent physical activity," Preventive medicine, vol. 85, 2016, pp. 74–77.

[17] B. Ariel and H. Partridge, "Predictable policing: Measuring the crime control benefits of hotspots policing at bus stops," Journal of Quantitative Criminology, vol. 33, no. 4, 2017, pp. 809–833.

[18] G. Assembly, "Sustainable development goals," SDGs), Transforming our world: the, vol. 2030, 2015.

[19] The Institute for Economics and Peace, "VISION of HUMANITY," http://visionofhumanity.org//, 2017, (Online; accessed 05-June-2010).

[20] Kalev Leetaru, "The GDELT Project," https://www.gdeltproject.org/, 2013, (Online; accessed 05-June-2010).

[21] D. J. Gerner, P. A. Schrodt, O. Yilmaz, and R. Abu-Jabr, "Conflict and mediation event observations (cameo): A new event data framework for the analysis of foreign policy interactions," International Studies Association, New Orleans, 2002.

[22] D.-L. Magazine, "Fulltext geocoding versus spatial metadata for large text archives: Towards a geographically enriched wikipedia," D-Lib Magazine, vol. 18, no. 9/10, 2012.

[23] E. Shook, K. Leetaru, G. Cao, A. Padmanabhan, and S. Wang, "Happy or not: Generating topic-based emotional heatmaps for culturomics using cybergis," in 2012 IEEE 8th International Conference on E-Science. IEEE, 2012, pp. 1–6.

[24] K. Leetaru and P. A. Schrodt, "Gdelt: Global data on events, location, and tone, 1979–2012," in ISA annual convention, vol. 2, no. 4. Citeseer, 2013, pp. 1–49.

A Survey on Studying the Social Networks of Students

Akrati Saxena

Department of Computer Science, School of Computing
National University of Singapore, Singapore
Email: akrati@comp.nus.edu.sg

Pratishtha Saxena

Department of Computer Science and Engineering
Center for Advanced Studies, Lucknow, India

Harita Reddy

Department of Computer Science and Engineering
National Institute of Technology Karnataka, India

Ralucca Gera

Department of Applied Mathematics,
Associate Provost for Graduate Education,
Teaching and Learning Commons
Naval Postgraduate School, Monterey, CA
Email: rgera@nps.edu

***Abstract*—Do studies show that physical and online students' social networks support education? Analyzing interactions between students in schools and universities can provide a wealth of information. Studies on students' social networks can help us understand their behavioral dynamics, the correlation between their friendships and academic performance, community and group formation, information diffusion, and so on. Educational goals and holistic development of students with various academic abilities and backgrounds can be achieved by incorporating the findings attained by the studies in terms of knowledge propagation in classroom and spread of delinquent behaviors. Moreover, we use Social Network Analysis (SNA) to identify isolated students, ascertain the group study culture, analyze the spreading of various habits like smoking, drinking, and so on. In this paper, we present a review of the research showing how analysis of students' social networks can help us identify how improved educational methods can be used to make learning more inclusive at both school and university levels and achieve holistic development of students through expansion of their social networks, as well as control the spread of delinquent behaviors.**

Keywords–Students' Social Networks; Education; Team Work; Collaborative Learning; Adolescent Behavior

I. INTRODUCTION

Social networks of students, both physical and online, have been used to understand various phenomena, such as the correlation between the social network position of students and their academic performance, information diffusion in a classroom, collaborative learning and teamwork among students and the emergence of homophily in classrooms [1]. Through the analysis of such students' networks, there can be a progress in the understanding of effectiveness of collaborative learning environments to achieve pedagogical goals [2] [3] [4], [5]. Existing research studies the relationship between network dynamics and students' academic and social behaviors. Educators can use this research to ascertain whether enough collaborative learning among students exists, whether there are isolated students who are deprived of help from their peers, and whether there is an effective information flow among the students in a classroom [6] [7].

Identifying central students in educational social networks helps in discovering the influential students who spread the information across the network [8]. Using homophily and community detection in such networks, we may also identify the tightly-knit groups of the students that support each other [7] [9] [10]. Dynamic network models explain the evolution of social networks and aid in understanding students' changing behaviors as a social network's links can lead to the development of positive and negative behaviors among the students [11]. These studies help in understanding the spread of various habits such as smoking, drinking and drugs among students [12] [13] [14].

For the analysis of learning environments, a commonly used method to actively create social network datasets is asking students to nominate their friends, gurus (students from whom they seek help), and adversaries, through filling out questionnaires [15]. Also, passive data collection tools like Moodle [16] and other collaborative learning systems [2] [3] are used, where connections are discovered through students' interactions on online platforms. In both methods, various types of students' social networks can be created, including friendship networks, collaboration networks (where the interaction between the students constitute the collaboration), help-seeking networks (where the students have links with peers whom they ask for academic help), and so on.

With these collection methods in mind, several software programs are currently used for analyzing social networks. UCINET [17] supports various network analysis techniques including transformation, connectivity measurement, centrality and subgroup identification. The R Package RSiena implements the SIENA method [18] and is popularly used to study the relationship between the network and behavior dynamics through stochastic actor based models. The SNAPP tool [6] is used to view the real time social network of students based on their online interactions, helping instructors identify the community structures, as well as students who are isolated from others. Gephi [19] is another popular open source software that uses 3D rendering for real-time complex networks and supports multi-task modeling. NetworkX [20] is an easy to use Python package that supports a number of graph algorithms.

Having outlined the most commonly used software programs for SNA, we now present a structured review of studies that have used such tools to analyze offline and online social networks of students. The motivations behind the survey are:

- Educators are moving away from the traditional teaching methods and are introducing innovative ways to improve learning experience. A good understanding of students' social network structure can help designing effective educational techniques for inclusive learning.
- A comprehensive review of the existing methods that use SNA to evaluate students' learning and behavior can provide a thorough understanding of the state-of-the-art in the field of networks and education.

Our key contributions through this survey include the systematic partitioning of the work in the area of networks and education into six key fields, highlighting certain limitations in the existing work and suggesting areas for future research.

Section II reviews the existing work under six subsections discussing the use of SNA to study the (A) effectiveness of collaborative learning methods employed by educators, (B) teamwork among student groups, (C) relationship between individual student performance and network structure, (D) extent of knowledge dissemination among students and development of networks for peer support, (E) existence of homophily and communities among students and (F) relationship between network structure, and student habits like smoking and drinking. Section III concludes the survey along with outlining the limitations of existing work and various future directions.

II. ANALYSIS OF STUDENT SOCIAL NETWORKS

Social Network Analysis (SNA) can be a good tool in studying the relationships between students forming a collaborative network, between groups of students, as well as individuals themselves as part of a larger network. Analyzing the network structure indicates not only the extent of learner's benefit from the interactions among the students, but also shows the importance of a particular actor or group in supporting learning in the learning environments modeled by networks. We now discuss the six main aspects related to education that the analysis of students' networks highlights.

A. The Effectiveness of Collaborative Learning Environments

Early research applying SNA to the field of education studied the interactions in a learning environment furnished by Computer-Supported Collaborative Learning (CSCL). These CSCL environments are learning environments that leverage technology to facilitate learning through computer supported interactions between students such as online discussion forums and collaborative writing. Analyzing these students' networks helps in evaluating the students' participation in learning achieved through CSCL. For example, university CSCL log files have been used to determine whether each student plays an effective role in the process of learning [2]. Researchers also created a network structure in which edges capture the number of sent and received messages between pairs of students on the learning platform. Through the study of betweenness centrality and Stephenson-Zelen information measure [17], it can be determined if the communication in the CSCL environment is centralized only around the instructor [2]. By evaluating whether the interactions in a CSCL environment are instructor-centric, one can perform timely intervention to achieve the goal of more student-student interactions. This evaluation is achieved by measuring (1) the level of activity based on nodes' degree, (2) the position of students in information exchange network through betweenness and closeness centrality measures, and (3) identification of roles of university students [5] [21]. Having fewer student-student interactions implies a poor collaborative environment, and an intervention helps in the emergence of certain students with high betweenness centrality who relay information between the students across the network [5].

Students are a part of different types of networks based on different collaborative activities such as discussion, doubt solving and information sharing. The usage of Basic Support for Co-operative Work (BSCW) software [22] for CSCL shows that doubt solving is the most decentralized activity, whereas the network based on sharing of information has few actors with very high centrality thus implying that information sharing depends a lot on few highly active participants [3]. It is also of interest to researchers to understand if the formation of collaborative networks in a CSCL community depends on the already existing friendship ties. Formation of such ties can be studied using change propensity and degree centrality [4]. The change propensity measures the extent to which an individual adds more links in her ego network. Students with high centrality in the network of pre-existing ties have a low change in propensity in the CSCL network, whereas peripheral students in the CSCL network tend to show a greater willingness to form connections over time [4].

An important aspect to understand is whether students start playing a major role in sharing knowledge with the progress of a CSCL based course. The More Knowledgeable Other (MKO) in a CSCL learning environment is the actor with highest knowledge that everyone engages with for guidance [23]. Initially, only the instructor starts as an MKO [24]. Later, the students start becoming more influential in sharing information with their peers. As expected, such an emergence of peer MKOs happens due to increase in the knowledge of the students as the course proceeds and knowledge spreads.

Online Threaded Discussions (OTDs) are often used to enhance peer interactions in university courses. Threads enable students to post their comments asynchronously on a particular topic of discussion and respond to other students' comments. Such discussions can be modeled through directed networks. As expected, high achieving students tend to be the bridges across these discussion groups [25]. Proper usage of OTDs leads to an increase in the number of students joining the interactions, increase in the number of connections, and a decrease in the average of the closeness centrality of all the students [26]. Decrease in the average closeness centrality indicates lesser delay in information sharing in the network. Meerkat-ED helps to dynamically view students' interactions and identify the central students in each topic's discussion [27] [28].

Apart from the above discussed collaborative learning methods, researchers have studied the effectiveness of several other online collaborative learning environments, such as Co-operative Open Learning (COOL) [29], Peer Assisted Learning (PAL) [30], online blogging groups [31], and so on. The use of collaborative learning methods like OTDs successfully increases student interactions. However, it is possible that the students show high participation only when such learning methodologies are introduced for the first time, and may lose interest with repeated usage. Also, the success of such collaborative environments not only depends on characteristics of the social network but also on the motivation and academic abilities of individual students. This is shown in one particular higher education scenario in which even after the adoption of PALs, an individual's academic performance was observed to be comparatively more dependent upon the individual's previous performance than the characteristics of the social network [30], highlighting that the usage of PALs may not have been effective in benefiting students through social interactions.

We have discussed how SNA is used to check if collaborative learning methods are able to achieve significant participation of students in the process of learning. More participation implies students ask questions, get their doubts clarified, explain their views and understand other students' views about the topic [32]. We now discuss how the study of network structure helps us evaluate teamwork among students.

B. Studies on the Teamwork Among Students

Teamwork is essential among students for performing various activities like group projects, group discussions, or just for sport. Moreover, teams help building long-term connections to possibly support life-long learning. Friendship and communication networks of university students are mostly formed within their teams and high levels of communication within the teams are positively correlated with the team effectiveness, measured by positive outcome [15]. Apart from high levels of communication, good team results also depend on balanced communication within a team, measured on the basis of contribution index of each team member, where the contribution index is an indicator of balance in the number of sent and received emails for each individual student within the team [33] [34]. As expected, adversarial relationships within teams are the cause for lesser team satisfaction. One unexpected observation indicates that more workload sharing in a team results in lesser grades. This observation may be explained by the intuition that many successful teams often have a few bright and hard working students who take up most of the workload [15].

Measures such as cohesion (ratio of the number of mutually positive relationships to the total number of possible relationships), group conflict (ratio of mutually negative relationships to the total number of possible relationships), and degree centrality have been used to understand students' interactions in networks. In particular, based on four types of relationships – advice, leadership, social and obligation – research shows that cohesion and centrality are the most important predicting factors for team performance [35]. The edges in the above constructed networks are weighted, with $+1$ indicating a positive relationship and -1 indicating a negative one – it is challenging to capture negative relationships as students may not be willing to reveal such information. To resolve this, the students were presented a questionnaire with only positively stated questions, in which they were just asked to rank their teammates. The lowest ranked student was considered to be having a negative relationship.

The teaching behavior and course structure also impact the evolution of groups and social network formation among students. Based on a study on two sections of undergraduate engineering classes, a less structured class leads to connected groups and some students who are disconnected from others, whereas a more structured class creates a more even distribution of interactions [36]. Disconnected students do not interact with their classmates even when teamwork is required. Based on SNA's significance in identifying connected and disconnected groups of students, the instructors can use these results to identify the disconnected students, in order to encourage them to participate in teamwork and to improve the inclusiveness in the projects.

Working in teams helps students in accomplishing course tasks, getting doubts clarified and involving in discussions, thus achieving deeper level of understanding that individual students cannot achieve alone just by attending the course [37]. Teams should have students who play the role of a broker to transfer knowledge between various groups, thus giving the teams access to new and different ideas, information and opinions. An SNA based methodology for forming teams dynamically on Massive Open Online Courses (MOOCs) for achieving tasks assigned in the courses helps in enhancing students' participation, thus reducing attrition from MOOCs through active engagement of students [37].

Thus, the level and balance of communication within team, team cohesion, presence of brokers, and absence of disconnected students helps in determining teams' success, both in terms of team grades and the student engagement achieved within the team. In the next section, we change the granularity level to discuss the relationship between an individuals' academic performance and their position in the social network.

C. Academic Performance versus Social Networks

Analyzing the correlation between students' academic performance and their position in the social network provides interesting insights into the social aspects that make high achieving students different from others. Researchers have focused on studying the relationship of a student's centrality in the network with her academic performance. The centrality in communication networks is a positive indicator of the academic performance of engineering and management students compared to friendship or behavioral networks, and centrality in adversarial networks is negatively correlated with student satisfaction [15] [38]. Advice networks created using data obtained from graduate students in a management course suggest that centrality in advice networks is also a strong indicator of students' academic performance [39]. More fine-grained dimensions like the exchange of learning materials, informal communication, and formal study teamwork show that students' centrality in the study environment in university affects both their learning and employability [40].

A factor that has to be considered while analyzing whether a particular network metric predicts students' academic status is the reciprocal effect, i.e., it is possible that a student with good academics might participate more actively in the network, thus obtaining high centrality values. Hence, it is important to understand the changes in time-varying networks as analyzing a static network may lead to misleading conclusions. The impact of a students' performance on the social network dynamics has been studied through both cross-sectional and temporal networks [41] [42]. High-performing college students tend to establish persistent ties from the beginning of the course itself with other highly performing students. This often leads to the formation of a 'rich' or 'high academic performance' club due to their willingness to collaborate and learn. Thus, academic achievements are a good predictor of the social ties among students having similar academic performance. Also, the students taking advanced coursework often have large ego networks and more interactions in the network [43].

These days, Massive Open Online Courses (MOOCs) are becoming popular and useful resources for education. Such platforms also enable students enrolled in a course to interact via collaborative discussions. Correlation and regression analysis to study the relationships between various social characteristics and the students' online course performance indicate that Eigenvector centrality is one of the most useful predictors for academic achievement, with high-performing students taking up central positions in the network [44]. The studied social characteristics include degree centrality, closeness centrality, betweenness centrality, Eigenvector centrality, PageRank, clustering and hubs.

Spectral clustering on network created on the basis of student participation on university Moodle suggests that similarity in students' behavior is positively correlated with similarity in grades but surprisingly, fails to support the hypothesis that higher centrality causes better performance [16]. Analysis of triads and transitivity in student social networks recorded at different times in an introductory biology course, i.e., the network created during their first exam and the network during the second exam showed that the overall number of complete triads indicated the build-up of more study groups in the classroom and increase in the density of the network [45]. Apart from this, there is a significant correlation between performance in the second exam and the students' betweenness and degree centralities. Existing methods can be used to estimate the centrality rank of a student in a class without computing the centrality value of all students [46] [47] [48].

Students are a part of both offline and online social networks, though these networks are often overlapping. Online communication includes communication through mobile and messenger texting, and emails. There is a significant relation between the closeness centrality of the online and offline networks. The offline closeness centrality is significantly correlated with the students' academic performance; however, the correlation is not much in the case of online closeness centrality [49]. The study of online social networks comes with its limitations as the structure and properties of online social networking data are different from the offline collected data, and a rigorous analysis of the data is required while applying the metrics proposed by sociologists and anthropologists [50].

Hence, these studies show that high-achieving students tend to have central position in the network and establish persistent ties with their classmates. Next, we discuss the role of social network in knowledge dissemination and providing peer help to students.

D. Knowledge Dissemination and Peer Support

Knowledge diffusion is the process by which knowledge spreads over a network. Knowledge can be effectively diffused in students' networks when there is (1) good presence of leaders, (2) optimal network density and (3) existence of subgroups with adequate inter-subgroup connections in a classroom [8]. Degree and betweenness centrality in networks based on emotional, counseling and intelligence relationships between students are used to determine the presence of leaders, and cohesion is used to identify the extent of inter-group diffusion in a university cohort [8]. Bridge students, i.e., the students that constitute the connecting nodes between different groups in a classroom should take up more active roles to improve the diffusion between different groups. As expected, the bridge students are found to be academically outstanding students [8].

Giving collaboration-demanding assignments to students can lead to the development of an information network that is useful for them throughout their studies. It results in increasing network density, decreasing average geodesic distance, and increasing average degree centrality of students with the progress of a university course [51]. The use of student activities requiring intense collaboration also improves information diffusion efficiency and network inclusiveness. The risk of collapse of the collaborative network is also alleviated due to the absence of cutpoint in the evolved network [51].

Seeking help from peers is often a good way to learn and clarify doubts, especially in advanced courses at the university level. Students who are central in the network constructed on the basis of $getting\ information$ from peers benefit and learn the most due to gaining of knowledge from others [52]. An important question is who the students consult for any help among their peers- their close friends or high-performing students. Though the formation of project groups by university students is highly dependant on the students' pre-existing friendships, among the members of a particular group most students connect to peers who have good knowledge about that subject for help [53]. Implementation of an online discussion forum makes it easier for graduate students to seek help by strengthening their social networks. Apart from fueling students' participation in solving problems, such a forum also leads to the expansion of the ego networks of students [54].

The relationships between students change due to some special events, but they are stabilized over time [55]. Similar behavior is observed on Twitter microblogging scenario where the rate of development of connections stabilizes as students start exhibiting more selectivity in forming ties with other students [56]. Application of Stochastic Actor-Based Models (SABMs) for probabilistic analysis shows that high-achieving students obtain more incoming connections with the passage of time implying that high-scoring students gain more attention from their peers, possibly due to the need to seek help in studies.

In this section, we have discussed how the network structure plays an important role in determining the dissemination of knowledge and making it easier to seek help, and how such ideal networks can evolve through collaborative activities. In the next section, we will discuss how SNA is used to study the subcultures in a classroom and the existence of homophily.

E. Study on Subcultures and Homophily Among Students

The tendency of humans to form relationships with people having similar traits is known as homophily [1]. There is an existence of homophilic connections among high school students, with denser connections among students having similar attributes, such as academic performance, gender, and if they also work while studying [7]. Several other longitudinal network data analysis on academic and friendship networks have shown that students mostly form connections with the similarly achieving and same-gender students both for friendship and academic consultation, thus indicating a strong academic and gender-based homophily [10].

Do students adapt to the academic performance of their friend circle or try to seek out similarly achieving friends? The observed similarity in academics of friends can be a result of either selection or due to adaptation. Students tend to reorganize their ego networks and form friendships with students having similar academic performance rather than changing their academic performance based on their current set of friends, thus indicating the development of strong homophily. This observation is made through the use of Pearson correlation measure between students' GPA and the average of their direct friends' GPA [9]. Girls exhibit more selection phenomenon, which can be explained by the general observation that girls tend to form groups for study far more than boys, thus making academic achievement a major predictor in their friendships [57].

Students can be similar in terms of more than one attribute. However, most studies evaluate different dimensions (of similarities like gender, race, etc.) in a disjoint fashion. For a complete understanding of the impact of homophily on the evolution of the network or other way around, the studies should be performed using multidimensional attributes. A multidimensional homophily study on adolescent networks shows that the connections between individuals having more than one similar attribute might not evolve further [58]. This is explained with the idea that students may usually try to make friends with people who have different thoughts and knowledge, thus seeking variety in their friends' circle.

How does SNA help in identifying the sense of community in students? Degree and closeness centrality are positive indicators of the sense of community in a student whereas betweenness centrality shows a negative correlation. This conclusion is obtained from the evaluation of relationships in evolving students' social networks and the feeling of community (social and learning) in those students using Classroom Community Scale (CCS) [59] [60]. However, this study only considers communication through online discussions.

Homophily based groups are helpful for students to feel inclusiveness, but at the same time, they have several drawbacks. The poorly performing students might form groups among them and it may lead to an inverse effect on their academic performance, therefore institutions and teachers should focus on the disruption of such groups and formation of more versatile groups. Strong homophily in a classroom is also an indicator of segregation based on racial or ethnic terms; development of inter-group ties can help develop better inter-racial and ethnic relations among students [61]. Research shows that strong homophily in a classroom can be overcome by creating more connections between separated groups based on performance or legislation. For example, one study has shown that minority groups can have better inter-ethnic relations by performing better in academics. That is because by performing well the minority students tend to get more attention and therefore more friends and lesser adversaries from the majority groups [61]. SNA has also been used to study the impact of affirmative actions, such as reserving seats for underrepresented community students, motivating more women to study sciences and technologies, organizing events to bridge the gap of two communities, etc [62]. A mathematical analysis of the seat reservation system for backward class students in Indian academic system showed that such affirmative actions reduce the gap of backward and upper-class students with time [62]. This work is based on a very basic mathematical modeling of the network and needs to be extended by considering more real-life parameters. The survey included in the research also showed that the opinion of upper class students changes about backward class students once they meet more of such students [62].

In this section, we discussed how SNA is helpful in studying the community, groups, and subculture formation among students based on similar attributes like race and gender. Another important factor that influences the evolution of ties is similar habits. In the next section, we will discuss the impact of the behavior of friends on a person and friendship formation based on behavioral attributes.

F. Studies on Adolescent Behavior

Friendships can influence a student's behavior in several ways, ranging from improving academic performance to getting an antisocial behavior. Students tend to have connections with peers having similar behavior, including aggressive behavior [63]. For the majority of adolescents, increase in individual importance in the social network leads to increased aggression, except for very highly central students who do not need to resort to aggression to improve their social standing, with the social standing measured through betweenness centrality [64]. A rise in the average aggression of friends also leads to a rise in the aggression of an adolescent [64]. There is a significant impact of friends' delinquent behavior on an adolescent and this impact is beyond that of the impact of school involvement. Study of structural characteristics of the network and behavioral dynamics model explains such a correlation between changing behaviors of adolescent students and their changing network connections [11].

Students acquire several habits and behaviors through the influence of their friends. Such relationships between network dynamics and behavioral changes are often studied through SABMs [69]. Students modify their smoking habits to match their friends, thus corroborating that influence from their network increases smoking among youth. This is observed through the study of dynamic networks based on three measures: smoking alter, smoking ego, and smoking similarity among students [13]. Similar methods are used to study the impact of social networks on alcohol consumption by the youth. Adolescents often select friends with similar drinking behavior and start consuming alcohol if a large number of friends already have the habit of consuming alcohol; alcohol onset can be seen as a diffusion process in the students' network [14] [65]. Moreover, adolescents often get attracted to drinkers and try to be friends with them due to the teenage culture of giving high status to drinkers as shown through the SABMs analysis [66]. The selection of friends is also heavily influenced by levels of marijuana use based on the study performed in two schools [70]. However, the phenomenon of non-users trying marijuana for the first time because of their friends' influence is observed only in one of the schools. Such

TABLE I. COMMONLY USED NETWORK SCIENCE CONCEPTS TO ANALYZE STUDENTS' NETWORKS

Network Concept	Applications
Degree Centrality	Find centrally positioned high performing students [39] [45], willingness of students to add more ties in CSCL environment [4] team performance [35], development of information network [51], sense of community in students [59]
Closeness Centrality	Find students with good academic performance [49], delay in information sharing in network [26], sense of community in students [59]
Betweenness Centrality	Determine if the communication is centralized around the instructor in a CSCL environment [2], students who relay information across the network [5], students who perform well in exams [45], the presence of leaders [8], increase in aggression [64]
Stephenson and Zelen Centrality	Find centrally positioned high performing students in communication networks [15], determine if the communication is centralized around the instructor in a CSCL environment [2]
Eigenvector Centrality	Find centrally positioned high-performing students [44]
Cohesion	Predict performance of student teams [35], find the extent of inter-group information diffusion [8]
Network Density	Find if knowledge is effectively diffused in classroom [8], development of information network due to collaborative assignments [45] [51]
Strongly Connected Components	Study the improved flow of information due to decrease in the number of components through the use of threaded discussions [26]
Triads	Study the formation of study groups in a classroom [45]
Bridges	Find students who can play an important role in improving information diffusion in classroom, and are usually academically outstanding [8]
Geodesic Distance	Study the development of information network and how information diffusion improves [8]
Stochastic Actor Based Model	Study the phenomenon of influence and selection of friends in terms of smoking [13] and drinking [14] [65] [66] habits, physical activity levels [67], academic achievements [42] and junk food consumption [68] among students
Homophily	Evaluate the tendency of students with similar attributes forming friendship ties with each other [7] [10] [58], racial and ethnic segregation in classroom [61]

analyses can help in identifying schools where youth drug interventions are required to prevent potential marijuana use.

In understanding adolescents' health, students gradually adjust to obtain a Body Mass Index (BMI) and physical activity levels similar to that of their friends, as shown by SABMs in a study of the relationship between longitudinal adolescent friendship networks and their physical activity [67]. The converse is also true, i.e., there is a tendency of students to connect with students having similar BMI and physical activity levels, based on homophily as discussed in the previous section. Moreover, apart from a few personal attributes, an adolescent's junk food consumption is also largely influenced by her friendship network [68]. Such SABM based studies can be used to understand student behavior and intervene in case of disorders faced by them. Based on these findings, educational institutions may design appropriate policies and activities to overcome these patterns, making the students aware of this data and motivating a better decision while choosing friends.

Another research problem is the correlation between students' networks and the prevalence of cheating. Empirical evidence suggests that formation of tightly knit groups or *cliques* among students, and weak ties with the faculty is positively correlated with the adoption of unethical behavior [71] [72]. Friendship networks can be used to design effective seating arrangement strategies for exams to prevent cheating. Optimized solutions for lattice-based student placement layouts, with less lattice links matching with actual friendship network links can be obtained through the use of genetic algorithms [73].

The section elaborated on the relationship between dynamics of network ties and adolescent behavior including aggression, smoking, and consumption of alcohol, marijuana and junk food. We now conclude our review and elucidate the possible directions of research in future.

III. Conclusion and Future Directions

Analysis of networks of students constructed on the basis of different types of relationships helps us understand students' behavior, information diffusion, and acquisition of various habits like smoking and drinking based on network structure. Research shows the correlation between the academic performance of the students and their position in the network. These observations can be used to design correcting behaviour, alternate teaching methods, group activities, and policies that impact students. A limitation of the studies carried out on students' networks is that generalization drawn from the observations on small groups of students may not always be correct. Another issue is that self-reporting on adversarial relationships, and habits like smoking and drinking may not give accurate information as it is subject to students' bias and hesitation. There is also a need to increase the frequency of evaluation of students' networks using the different frameworks. Evaluation should also be done a significant amount of time after the introduction of new learning methodologies to check if students' participation remains persistent.

Currently, there is little research that studies combined teacher-student social networks. These mixed networks may provide more information than what only students' or teachers' social networks provide individually. Such combined networks can be explored for studying the long-lasting teachers' impact on the students, and their influence in the formation of groups among students. We can also determine students who are not well-connected to the faculty and encourage them to interact more. Also, real-life scenario based case studies need to be conducted to evaluate teacher-student networks in terms of prevalence of unethical practices among students like cheating.

Student segregation based on racial, ethnic or class homophily is detrimental in nature. Future research can compare the changes in homophily in students' networks over time at different universities that have different amount of diversity and that have different or no programs for encouraging intermingling. This can help in identifying the best methods for disrupting segregation in higher education.

Another network science based learning tool is CHUNK learning methodology that takes into consideration the different learning abilities and skills of students, and uses network-based approach to represent content and suggest learning modules to students [74]. Such tools can complement existing collaborative learning techniques to furnish a personalized learning experience and enable all students to participate proactively in learning.

Analysis methods should be easy to implement in real life scenarios, with lesser time spent by students like in filling questionnaires. Certain studies use rigorous questionnaires and surveys which are time-taking to implement on a regular basis in universities or schools. We suggest that future research should focus on automatic data collection using online platforms like Moodle and discussion forums, which have already been utilized by some studies, along with integration of student ties on online social networking sites. Software should be developed to analyze networks constructed from the data to examine student participation and identify disconnected students so that the faculty can identify appropriate corrective steps. We believe that teachers should be able to use the SNA tools easily to continuously monitor the students' social networks to bring awareness to possible appropriate interventions that improve the interactions and knowledge diffusion in a classroom. We promote social network analysis as a tool to complement easily observable behavior, but not to replace the observations captured through human teacher-student or student-student interactions.

ACKNOWLEDGMENTS

Ralucca Gera would like to thank the DoD for partially funding this work.

REFERENCES

[1] M. McPherson, L. Smith-Lovin, and J. M. Cook, "Birds of a feather: Homophily in social networks," Annual review of sociology, vol. 27, no. 1, 2001, pp. 415–444.

[2] K. Nurmela, E. Lehtinen, and T. Palonen, "Evaluating cscl log files by social network analysis," in Proceedings of the 1999 conference on Computer support for collaborative learning. International Society of the Learning Sciences, 1999, p. 54.

[3] A. Martınez, Y. Dimitriadis, B. Rubia, E. Gómez, and P. De La Fuente, "Combining qualitative evaluation and social network analysis for the study of classroom social interactions," Computers & Education, vol. 41, no. 4, 2003, pp. 353–368.

[4] H. Cho, G. Gay, B. Davidson, and A. Ingraffea, "Social networks, communication styles, and learning performance in a cscl community," Computers & education, vol. 49, no. 2, 2007, pp. 309–329.

[5] M. Saqr, U. Fors, M. Tedre, and J. Nouri, "How social network analysis can be used to monitor online collaborative learning and guide an informed intervention," PloS one, vol. 13, no. 3, 2018, p. e0194777.

[6] S. Dawson, A. Bakharia, and E. Heathcote, "Snapp: Realising the affordances of real-time sna within networked learning environments," in Proceedings of the 7th International Conference on Networked Learning. Lancaster University, 2010, pp. 125–133.

[7] M. G. R. Ortiz, J. R. C. Hoyos, and M. G. R. López, "The social networks of academic performance in a student context of poverty in mexico," Social networks, vol. 26, no. 2, 2004, pp. 175–188.

[8] H. Xia, R. Wang, and S. Hu, "Social networks analysis of the knowledge diffusion among university students," in 2009 Second International Symposium on Knowledge Acquisition and Modeling, vol. 2, Nov 2009, pp. 343–346.

[9] I. Smirnov and S. Thurner, "Formation of homophily in academic performance: students prefer to change their friends rather than performance," PLOS ONE, vol. 12, no. 8, 2016.

[10] J. Brouwer, A. Flache, E. Jansen, A. Hofman, and C. Steglich, "Emergent achievement segregation in freshmen learning community networks," Higher Education, vol. 76, no. 3, 2018, pp. 483–500.

[11] W. Burk, M. Kerr, and H. Stattin, "The co-evolution of early adolescent friendship networks, school involvement, and delinquent behaviors," Revue franaise de sociologie, vol. 49(3), 2008, pp. 499–522.

[12] C. Steglich, T. A. Snijders, and P. West, "Applying siena," Methodology, vol. 2, no. 1, 2006, pp. 48–56.

[13] C. M. Lakon, C. Wang, C. T. Butts, R. Jose, D. S. Timberlake, and J. R. Hipp, "A dynamic model of adolescent friendship networks, parental influences, and smoking," Journal of youth and adolescence, vol. 44, no. 9, 2015, pp. 1767–1786.

[14] W. Burk, H. van der Vorst, M. Kerr, and H. Stattin, "Alcohol use and friendship dynamics: Selection and socialization in early-, middle-, and late-adolescent peer networks," Journal of studies on alcohol and drugs, vol. 73, 01 2012, pp. 89–98.

[15] T. Baldwin, M. Bedell, and J. Johnson, "The social fabric of a team-based mba program: Network effects on student satisfaction and performance," The Academy of Management Journal, vol. 40, 12 1997, pp. 1369–1397.

[16] G. Obadi, P. Drázdilová, J. Martinovic, K. Slaninová, and V. Snásel, "Finding patterns of students' behavior in synthetic social networks," in Proceedings of the International Conference on Advances in Social Networks Analysis and Mining. IEEE/ACM, 2010, pp. 411–413.

[17] S. P. Borgatti, M. G. Everett, and L. C. Freeman, "Ucinet," Encyclopedia of Social Network Analysis and Mining, 2014, pp. 2261–2267.

[18] R. Ruth, T. A. Snijders, Z. Boda, A. Vrs, and P. Preciado, Manual for SIENA version 4.0. Oxford: University of Oxford, Department of Statistics, 2017.

[19] M. Bastian, S. Heymann, and M. Jacomy, "Gephi: an open source software for exploring and manipulating networks," in Proceedings of the Third International Conference on Weblogs and Social Media. AAAI, 2009, pp. 361–362.

[20] A. Hagberg, P. Swart, and D. S Chult, "Exploring network structure, dynamics, and function using networkx," Los Alamos National Lab.(LANL), Los Alamos, NM (United States), Tech. Rep., 2008.

[21] J.-A. Marcos-García, A. Martínez-Monés, and Y. Dimitriadis, "Despro: A method based on roles to provide collaboration analysis support adapted to the participants in cscl situations," Computers & Education, vol. 82, 2015, pp. 335–353.

[22] GMD-FIT. Basic support for cooperative work 3.3.1. [Online]. Available: http://bscw.gmd.de

[23] L. S. Vygotsky, Mind in society: The development of higher psychological processes. Harvard University Press, 1980.

[24] B. Sundararajan, "Emergence of the most knowledgeable other (mko): Social network analysis of chat and bulletin board conversations in a cscl system," Electronic Journal of E-Learning, vol. 8, no. 2, 2010, pp. 191–208.

[25] J.-H. Kang, J. Kim, and E. Shaw, "A network analysis of student groups in threaded discussions," in International Conference on Intelligent Tutoring Systems. Springer, 2010, pp. 359–361.

[26] R. C. Rodrguez-Hidalgo, C. Zhu, F. Questier, and A. M. Torres Alfonso, "Using social network analysis for analysing online threaded discussions," International Journal of Learning, Teaching and Educational Research, vol. 10, 04 2015, pp. 128–146.

[27] R. Rabbany. Meerkat-ed. [Online]. Available: http://www.reirab.com/MeerkatED/index.html

[28] R. Rabbany, M. Takaffoli, and O. Zaane, "Social network analysis and mining to support the assessment of on-line student participation," Sigkdd Explorations, vol. 13, 05 2012, pp. 20–29.

[29] C. Helm, "Effects of social learning networks on student academic achievement and pro-social behavior in accounting," Journal of Educational Research, vol. 9, 01 2017, pp. 52–76.

[30] M. AbdelSalam, M. El Tantawi, A. Al-Ansari, A. AlAgl, and F. Al-Harbi, "Informal peer-assisted learning groups did not lead to better performance of saudi dental students," Medical Principles and Practice, vol. 26, no. 4, 2017, pp. 337–342.

[31] A. Jimoyiannis, P. Tsiotakis, and D. Roussinos, "Social network analysis of students participation and presence in a community of educational blogging," ITSE, vol. 10, 02 2013, pp. 15–30.

[32] A. Soller, A. Lesgold, F. Linton, and B. Goodman, "What makes peer interaction effective? modeling effective communication in an intelligent cscl," in In the Proceedings of the fall symposium: Psychological models of communication in collaborative systems. AAAI, 1999, pp. 116–123.

[33] P. A. Gloor, M. Paasivaara, D. Schoder, and P. Willems, "Finding collaborative innovation networks through correlating performance with social network structure," International Journal of Production Research, vol. 46, no. 5, 2008, pp. 1357–1371.

[34] P. A. Gloor, R. Laubacher, S. B. Dynes, and Y. Zhao, "Visualization of communication patterns in collaborative innovation networks-analysis

of some w3c working groups," in Proceedings of the twelfth international conference on Information and knowledge management. ACM, 2003, pp. 56–60.

[35] H.-L. Yang and J.-H. Tang, "Team structure and team performance in is development: a social network perspective," Information & management, vol. 41, no. 3, 2004, pp. 335–349.

[36] A. Hernandez and V. Uddameri, "Heard it through the grapevine - social network analysis of a hydrology class," Journal of Contemporary Water Research & Education, vol. 158, 08 2016, pp. 85–97.

[37] T. Sinha, "Together we stand, together we fall, together we win: Dynamic team formation in massive open online courses," in The Fifth International Conference on the Applications of Digital Information and Web Technologies (ICADIWT 2014). IEEE, 2014, pp. 107–112.

[38] Y. Mastoory, S. Rajaee Harandi, and N. Abdolvand, "The effects of communication networks on students academic performance: The synthetic approach of social network analysis and data mining for education," International Journal on Integrating Technology in Education, vol. 5, 12 2016, pp. 23–34.

[39] H.-L. Yang and J.-H. Tang, "Effects of social network on students' performance: a web-based forum study in taiwan," Journal of Asynchronous Learning Networks, vol. 7, no. 3, 2003, pp. 93–107.

[40] B. Divjak and P. Peharda, "Social network analysis of study environment," Journal of information and organizational sciences, vol. 34, no. 1, 2010, pp. 67–80.

[41] L. M. Vaquero and M. Cebrian, "The rich club phenomenon in the classroom," Scientific reports, vol. 3, 2013, p. 1174.

[42] J. Flashman, "Academic achievement and its impact on friend dynamics," Sociology of Education, vol. 85, 01 2012, pp. 61–80.

[43] C. Barber and J. W. Wasson, "A comparison of adolescents friendship networks by advanced coursework participation status," Gifted Child Quarterly, vol. 59, no. 1, 2015, pp. 23–37.

[44] Z. Liu, L. Kang, Z. Su, S. Liu, and J. Sun, "Investigate the relationship between learners social characteristics and academic achievements," in Journal of Physics: Conference Series, vol. 1113, no. 1. IOP Publishing, 2018, p. 012021.

[45] D. Z. Grunspan, B. L. Wiggins, and S. M. Goodreau, "Understanding classrooms through social network analysis: A primer for social network analysis in education research," CBE Life Sciences Education, vol. 13, no. 2, 2014, pp. 167–178.

[46] A. Saxena, R. Gera, and S. Iyengar, "Observe locally rank globally," in Proceedings of the 2017 IEEE/ACM International Conference on Advances in Social Networks Analysis and Mining 2017. ACM, 2017, pp. 139–144.

[47] A. Saxena and S. Iyengar, "Global rank estimation," arXiv preprint arXiv:1710.11341, 2017.

[48] A. Saxena, R. Gera, and S. Iyengar, "Fast estimation of closeness centrality ranking," in Proceedings of the 2017 IEEE/ACM International Conference on Advances in Social Networks Analysis and Mining 2017. ACM, 2017, pp. 80–85.

[49] X. Zhang, V. Venkatesh, and B.-y. Huang, "Students interactions and course performance: Impacts of online and offline networks," in In the Proceedings of International Conference on Information Systems. AIS, 2008, p. 215.

[50] J. Howison, A. Wiggins, and K. Crowston, "Validity issues in the use of social network analysis for the study of online communities," Journal of the Association for Information Systems, vol. 12, no. 12, 2011, pp. 767–797.

[51] G. Han, O. McCubbins, and T. Paulsen, "Using social network analysis to measure student collaboration in an undergraduate capstone course," NACTA Journal, vol. 60, no. 2, 2016, pp. 176–182.

[52] J. Hommes, B. Rienties, W. de Grave, G. Bos, L. Schuwirth, and A. Scherpbier, "Visualising the invisible: a network approach to reveal the informal social side of student learning," Advances in Health Sciences Education, vol. 17, no. 5, 2012, pp. 743–757.

[53] M. Nurminen, P. Heino, and P. Ihantola, "Friends and gurus: do students ask for help from those they know or those who would know," in Proceedings of the 17th Koli Calling International Conference on Computing Education Research. ACM, 2017, pp. 80–87.

[54] P.-Y. Chao, K. R. Lai, C.-C. Liu, and H.-M. Lin, "Strengthening social networks in online discussion forums to facilitate help seeking for solving problems," Educational Technology & Society, vol. 21, 2018, pp. 39–50.

[55] Y. Imamverdiyev, H. Z. Asl, N. Janani, S. Siami, N. Babapoor, S. Nezhadseifi, B. Sami, S. Faraji, D. Pilevar, M. Bazel et al., "A longitudinal study on degree centrality changes in a group of students," in In the Proceedings of 4th International Conference on Application of Information and Communication Technologies. IEEE, 2010, pp. 1–3.

[56] K. Stepanyan, K. Borau, and C. Ullrich, "A social network analysis perspective on student interaction within the twitter microblogging environment," in 2010 10th IEEE International Conference on Advanced Learning Technologies, July 2010, pp. 70–72.

[57] D. Kretschmer, L. Leszczensky, and S. Pink, "Selection and influence processes in academic achievementmore pronounced for girls?" Social Networks, vol. 52, 2018, pp. 251–260.

[58] P. Block and T. Grund, "Multidimensional homophily in friendship networks," Network science, (Cambridge University Press), vol. 2, 08 2014, pp. 189–212.

[59] S. Dawson, "A study of the relationship between student social networks and sense of community," Educational Technology & Society, vol. 11, no. 3, 2008, pp. 224–238.

[60] A. P. Rovai, "Building sense of community at a distance," International Review of Research in Open and Distance Learning, vol. 4, no. 1, 2002, pp. 1–9.

[61] T. Hajdu, G. Kertesi, and G. Kézdi, "High-achieving minority students can have more friends and fewer adversaries - evidence from hungary," Budapest Working Papers on the Labour Market BWP, 2015.

[62] A. Saxena, J. Singh Saini, Y. Gupta, A. Parasuram, S. Iyengar et al., "Social network analysis of the caste-based reservation system in india," arXiv preprint arXiv:1512.03184, 2015.

[63] R. B. Cairns, B. D. Cairns, H. J. Neckerman, S. Gest, and J.-L. Gariepy, "Social networks and aggressive behavior: Peer support or peer rejection?" Developmental Psychology, vol. 24, 11 1988, pp. 815–823.

[64] R. Faris and D. Felmlee, "Status struggles: Network centrality and gender segregation in same-and cross-gender aggression," American Sociological Review, vol. 76, no. 1, 2011, pp. 48–73.

[65] J. M. Light, C. C. Greenan, J. C. Rusby, K. M. Nies, and T. A. B. Snijders, "Onset to first alcohol use in early adolescence: A network diffusion model." Journal of research on adolescence : the official journal of the Society for Research on Adolescence, vol. 23, no. 3, 2013, pp. 487–499.

[66] D. Osgood, D. T Ragan, L. Wallace, S. Gest, M. Feinberg, and J. Moody, "Peers and the emergence of alcohol use: Influence and selection processes in adolescent friendship networks," Journal of Research on Adolescence, vol. 23, no. 3, 2013, pp. 500–512.

[67] S. D. Simpkins, D. R. Schaefer, C. D. Price, and A. E. Vest, "Adolescent friendships, bmi, and physical activity: untangling selection and influence through longitudinal social network analysis," Journal of Research on Adolescence, vol. 23, no. 3, 2013, pp. 537–549.

[68] K. de la Haye, G. Robins, P. Mohr, and C. Wilson, "Adolescents' intake of junk food: Processes and mechanisms driving consumption similarities among friends," Journal of Research on Adolescence, vol. 23, no. 3, 2013, pp. 524–536.

[69] T. A. Snijders, G. G. Van de Bunt, and C. E. Steglich, "Introduction to stochastic actor-based models for network dynamics," Social networks, vol. 32, no. 1, 2010, pp. 44–60.

[70] K. de la Haye, H. D Green, D. Kennedy, M. Pollard, and J. Tucker, "Selection and influence mechanisms associated with marijuana initiation and use in adolescent friendship networks," Journal of Research on Adolescence, vol. 23, no. 3, 2013, pp. 474–486.

[71] D. J. Brass, K. D. Butterfield, and B. C. Skaggs, "Relationships and unethical behavior: A social network perspective," Academy of management review, vol. 23, no. 1, 1998, pp. 14–31.

[72] P. A. Hutton, "Understanding student cheating and what educators can do about it," College Teaching, vol. 54, no. 1, 2006, pp. 171–176.

[73] A. Topîrceanu, "Breaking up friendships in exams: A case study for minimizing student cheating in higher education using social network analysis," Computers & Education, vol. 115, 2017, pp. 171–187.

[74] R. Gera, M. Isenhour, D. Bartolf, and S. Tick, "CHUNK:Curated Heuristic Using a Network of Knowledge," in The Fifth International Conference on Human and Social Analytics. HUSO, July 2019.

A Recommender Model for the Personalized Adaptive CHUNK Learning System

Daniel O. Diaz
Department of Operations Research,
Naval Postgraduate School,
Monterey, CA

Ralucca Gera
Department of Applied Mathematics,
Associate Provost for Graduate Education,
Teaching and Learning Commons,
Naval Postgraduate School, Monterey, CA
Email: rgera@nps.edu

Paul C. Keeley
Department of Information Sciences,
Naval Postgraduate School,
Monterey, CA

Matthew T. Miller
Department of Operations Research,
Naval Postgraduate School,
Monterey, CA

Nickos Leondaridis-Mena
Department of Operations Research,
Naval Postgraduate School,
Monterey, CA

***Abstract*—Recommender systems attempt to influence one's behavior based on explicit and implicit information provided by the users of the system. Users who take part in e-commerce or watch cat videos online will be familiar with this concept. Different algorithms exist that determine what objects or concepts to recommend to users, but every one of them has the similar goal of providing a *good* recommendation. In this context, *good* means that the recommendation will be user relevant suggesting accurate topics, and will influence the user's behavior. Additionally, a good recommendation system is adaptive, consistently seeking feedback from the user. Feedback is then used to make the next recommendation better. In this work, we develop a recommendation methodology for an existing personalized learning system, where both content and teaching methodology options are presented to the user. Our methodology provides solutions to both the user and the network coldstart problems, where little up-front information is available in order to make good recommendations. Using real system data, we show how our method recommends the most relevant learning topics and styles and incorporates user feedback to improve future recommendations.**

***Index Terms*—Education; Chunk Learning; Adaptive Learning**

I. Introduction and Motivation

The Internet changed the world in many ways. Globally, it transformed the way people conduct banking, commerce, communication, and even warfare. The field of education is no exception, yet lagging behind other fields. Educational websites like Khan Academy [1], Chegg [2], and Coursera [3] allow people to personalize their educational path and interfaces at all levels of learning. These websites provide students a way to broaden their learning at their own pace, in a linear fashion similar to a text book, broadcasting the same information to everyone. Factors that once limited one's learning, such as the personality or the delivery method of an instructor, can be reduced by personalizing the learning experience using a network of knowledge, and we seek it in this work.

One such network is CHUNK Learning [4], a website that provides "a modular real-time and adaptive teaching-learning method for enhanced and personalized education which enables the student to heuristically discover and learn based on personal background and interests" [4]. The CHUNK acronym is from the Curated Heuristic Using a Network of Knowledge. The CHUNK Learningsystem allows users to explore topics via a Graphical User Interface (GUI), and choose topics and teaching methods matching their *personal* interests. Figure 1 shows the CHUNK's user interface as of March 2019.

Each red bubble, called a CHUNK, represents a topic, and within each topic are various learning modules called CHUNKlets. The content of CHUNKlets is uploaded by instructors, and users can graphically explore connected topics and view content as a network rather than linear fashion. This mimics more of a map of the world view for learning, rather than back to back linear chapters learning.

While the visualization is helpful to get a global view of the network of knowledge, the website only provides an initial set of topic recommendations based on keywords in the user's profile. In the current work, we explore to improve this selection of topics by adding an adaptive mechanism to generate future, more tailored recommendations, other than users being directed on what topic to learn. We seek to incorporate a recommendation system within CHUNK that recommends relevant topics to each learner based on profile information about the learner. This will better align with the goal of CHUNK Learning system to support life long learners whose new knowledge builds on and relates to the previous learner's skills and knowledge. Throughout the paper, "user" and "learner" are used interchangeably.

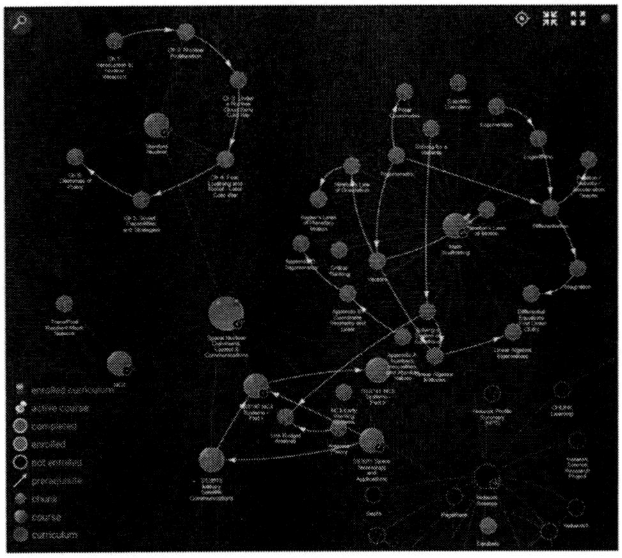

Fig. 1: CHUNK GUI. The main view that users see when initially logging on to the system.

The structure of the paper is as follows. We begin with establishing the needed definitions and the problem statements in Section II followed by an overview of the related work in Section III. We then introduce the methodology for computing similarity between the users in this environment and the methodology for recommendations in Section IV. We present the experimental setup in Section V, followed by the results and interpretation in Section VI. We conclude and present further direction in Sections VII and VIII.

II. Definitions and Problem Statement

The CHUNK GUI learning system presents a network view of a variety of different courses, each of which has a collection of public-facing 30-60 minute modules called "CHUNKs" (shown in Figure 1). Each CHUNK represents a different topic, much like a section in a textbook. At a more granular level, each CHUNK is composed of a varied number of components called "CHUNKlets", with each CHUNKlet presenting a different explanation on the same topic. The goal of presenting these different views is to personalize a learner's experience in exploring a topic, based on learner's interests, learning styles and previous knowledge. Furthermore, a CHUNKlet may belong to one or more CHUNKs, depending on the CHUNKlet's applicability to topics of those CHUNKs.

The CHUNK Learning system also carries a user profile for each learner. This is populated with data on courses the user has explored, as well as information about the user's preferred learning method, existing skills, and topics of interest. The data captured in the user profile is used to present the user with a map of all the CHUNKs associated with that registered course. The edges of the network capture natural progressions through the topics based on prerequisites at the topic level, thus allowing users to move around the network with a global view of how the topics build on each other.

Once the user chooses a CHUNK to study, the user is presented with a selection of associated CHUNKlets. These CHUNKlets could be videos, slide shows, research papers, code, websites, or various other methods of facilitating information, with four purposes in mind: (1) a "Why" CHUNKlet motivating the topic, (2) a "How" CHUNKlet showing how subject matter experts use the topic in real life, (3) a "Methodology" CHUNKlet as lectures or activities teaching a skill, and finally (4) an "Assessment" CHUNK as a set of knowledge assessments for the topic of interest of the particular CHUNK.

The intended audience is made up primarily of two groups–what we term as the "exploratory learners" and the "directed learners." Directed learners are students who are directed to some course(s) or CHUNK(s) within the system–perhaps by an instructor to refresh or re-mediate them on a particular topic. Exploratory learners are students who are interacting with the system in a more open-ended fashion–perhaps to learn about a topic related to something they are studying or perhaps to familiarize themselves with an unrelated discipline. These two categories are not mutually exclusive–in fact, a desired outcome of our proposed recommendation system is that directed learners become exploratory learners as a result of meaningful, serendipitous recommendations. Both, directed and exploratory learners, have choices on how to progress through the CHUNKs associated with a course. Yet exploratory learners may choose a sequence of CHUNKs that are associated with many different courses.

In this paper, we examine the **user cold-start** problem for both types of users: How best to match a new user to material that fits his or her interests and learning style; particularly when we assume little to no knowledge of the user's actual preferences. We assume that the profile information provided by the average user is incomplete, and it will be updated as the learner progresses through the CHUNKs, making it easier to suggest CHUNKs at that point. In particular, we assume that the directed learners will provide the least amount of information, since we also assume that their motivation to provide information is the lowest.

The second aspect we research in this effort is the **network cold-start** problem: With little user data on-hand, how do we best acquire useful information over time to identify emergent connections and apply collaborative filter methods? Putting in another way, how does the network improve its recommendations and internal connections through implicit or explicit feedback?

III. Related Work

Technology Enhanced Learning (TEL) develops and tests technical innovations that will support and enhance learning practices based on technology. Such an introduction to TEL and recommender systems (RS) building on the educational information retrieval supporting life long learning can be found in [5], [6]. There is a large group of TELs and papers [7] on TEL are regularly presented at Social Information Retrieval for Technology Enhanced Learning (SIRTEL) and expanded on topics presented at SIRTEL such as [8], [9] Through these means "interesting conclusions, the main ones being that:

- There is a large number of RS that have been deployed (or that are currently under deployment) in TEL settings;
- The information retrieval goals that TEL recommenders try to achieve are often different to the ones identified in other systems (e.g. product recommenders);
- There is a need to identify the particularities of TEL recommender systems, in order to elaborate on methods for their systematic design, development and evaluation" [5].

Further work have extended these topics to introduce a "paradigm for building intelligent systems that can better predict and anticipate the needs of users, and act more efficiently in response to their behavior" and summarized in several surveys [10], [11] as well as a summary of Mobile multimedia recommendation in smart communities [12].

A survey of educational RS that appear in the literature show various approaches to solving both of the cold-start problems identified above [13], [14], as well as summaries of requirements for such systems [15], [16]. These include the application of ontologies, rulesets and content-maps to filter, interactive tagging and sort responses to queries, with the goal of guiding a learner through a topic in a progressive fashion. User profiles are frequently generated in an explicit, manual fashion, similar to the existing CHUNK method; however, unlike the current CHUNK implementation, many of the systems described actually expand or augment user profile data following interactions with the system.

Typical of many examples are educational RS which use several of the techniques outlined above in a multi-round fashion to attack both the network and user cold-start problems. Albatayneh at al [17] incorporate semantic indexing and negative feedback to both determine a user's level of knowledge and recommend content in a logical, progressive manner. However, the use case (curating and recommending posts on an e-learning forum) has a much higher level of user interaction than we expect for CHUNK. This type of context-aware RS is akin to that described in [18], which seeks to identify users' strengths and weaknesses using the common Knowledge, Skills and Abilities paradigm. We see this as a well-suited approach to a highly structured learning environment (such as primary education), but we believe it would need constraint relaxation to provide a good fit for the exploratory learner model that we apply to CHUNK. Applying a more strictly ontological approach, another multi-round RS is developed by [19], which first matches content with user queries, then rates and selects offerings based on an ontological mapping of topical material paired with an adaptive knowledge of user mastery. In this case, an ontological map provides the structure needed to overcome the network cold-start problem, while the feedback gained through assessments is used to develop and update user profiles.

In the current work, we present a hybrid networked approach to overcome the cold-start problems identified above. We view users and content as nodes on a network, and we combine elements of content-mapping with syntactic sorting to determine a user's initial location on this network. We incorporate feedback and learning objective completion to update the user's location in the network of knowledge and then provide the user with recommendations to help guide him/her through the network.

IV. Methodology

In our modelling, we strip the CHUNK network of any ontological structure. Therefore, when we save the data, CHUNKs are not connected to each other via a topic umbrella or any prerequisite relationship. This allows the user to be unfettered in his or her path through the network. In contrast to the existing network, we create a strongly connected network of CHUNKs, where each CHUNK can be reached from every other CHUNK. For visualization and comparison purposes, we compute a similarity value between each pair of CHUNKs and display our new network in Figure 2. Note the logical grouping of CHUNKs into communities based on CHUNK title. While the ontological structure of the network is absent, a natural structure occurs based on similarity values. The methodology for computing this similarity value will be described in this section.

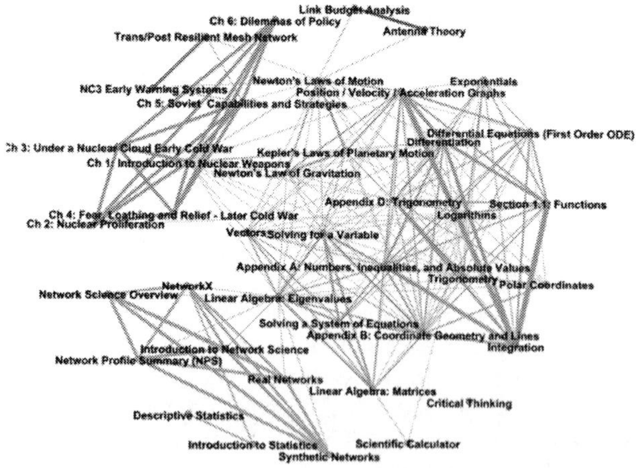

Fig. 2: CHUNK network using syntactical closeness and arranging by modularity class.

In order to make relevant recommendations, our recommendation system relies on computing similarity values between pairwise CHUNKlets, the user and each CHUNK, and subsequently between the user and each CHUNKlet. To compute the similarity value, we use the cosine distance between two vectors in a $1 \times k$-dimensional space or a $1 \times \ell$-dimensional space, where k and l are the cardinalities of the network's CHUNK or CHUNKlet keyword sets, respectively. The CHUNKs and/or CHUNKlets (across all CHUNKlet types) with the highest similarity value relative to the user are recommended first. Before providing a methodology for computing this similarity value, we outline system information and structure requirements:

1) Initial System Inputs. The system resides in an information database, where each entity (CHUNK, CHUNKlet, and user) is identified with a profile(s). This profile has a unique identifier, a set of keywords, and, in the case of a CHUNK-CHUNKlet, a parent-child relationship. System administrators decide on CHUNK titles, and instructors upload CHUNKlets. When CHUNKlet upload occurs, the instructor must do four things: define the parent-child relationship between the CHUNKlet being uploaded and the CHUNK that it is assigned, categorize the CHUNKlet with one of the four categories "Why", "What, "Methodology", or "Assessment", assign to the CHUNKlet content keywords, and assign to the CHUNKlet learning method keywords (Video, PowerPoint, etc.).
2) User Profile Vectors. Two profile vectors will be built for each user: one based on content keywords that will be used for computing similarity values between the user and each CHUNK, and one based on learning method keywords that will be used for computing similarity values between the user and CHUNKlet. The first will be a $1 \times k$-dimensional vector, where k is the cardinality of the network's content keyword set, and the second will be a $1 \times \ell$-dimensional vector, ℓ being the cardinality of the set comprising learning methods keywords. The system populates the user's vectors when the user initially creates his or her profile. It is a binary vector, where a one represents the user's interest in that keyword, and a zero represents no feedback or negative feedback in that keyword. The manner in which the system obtains these keywords from the user during initial profile build is left to the current system administrators.
3) CHUNKlet Profile Vectors. CHUNKlets have two profile vectors: a $1 \times k$-dimensional content keyword vector and a $1 \times \ell$-dimensional learning method keyword vector. They are populated when the instructor uploads the CHUNKlet into the CHUNK Learning system based on that instructor's input.
4) CHUNK Profile Vector. Similar to the user's content keyword vector, the CHUNK's keyword vector is $1 \times k$-dimensional, but it is not a binary vector, rather it is the sum of the vectors of its CHUNKlets. That is, the value associated with each keyword position in the vector will be based on the parent-child relationship between each CHUNK and CHUNKlet. The keywords associated with the CHUNKlet that the instructor tagged during upload will aggregate within the CHUNK, and this aggregated number will be the value for the keyword's position within the vector. Therefore, unlike the user's initial content keyword vector of ones or zeros, the CHUNK's keyword vector is not limited to a binary value.

Figure 3 shows a possible data structure representation of these vectors. The top row is the user, and the rows beneath the user represent CHUNKs. The column titles are the keywords.

	absolut	aerospac	aircraft	algebra	analysi	angl	architectur	area	astronaut	aviat	...
Nickos	0	0	0	0	0	0	0	0	0	0	...
f13deca2-27f8-4c59-9499-64a73b81b6e8	0	0	0	0	1	2	1	0	0	1	...
79dc2521-3b1f-4062-8675-1823f73a7bdd	0	0	0	5	0	0	0	0	0	0	...
11fa0110-d428-4eea-bccf-6d81d6d43c35	0	3	1	0	0	0	0	0	1	0	...

Fig. 3: CHUNK data. Possible keyword data structure representation.

Now that the system has its requisite information and appropriate vector lengths, we can compute the cosine distance between vectors and provide as recommendations the CHUNKles with the highest cosine distance value. We do this in a two-round process.

Recommendation Round. Using the standard linear algebra cosine distance formula, we compute the distance between the user's keyword vector and all CHUNK keyword vectors. CHUNKs are then ranked from highest to lowest similarity value, and the first ranked CHUNK is recommended first. The user can accept or reject the CHUNK that is recommended, but we focus here on users that will always accept the first recommendation. Once the user accesses the CHUNK, another cosine distance is calculated between the user's learning method vector and all CHUNKlets associated with the current CHUNK. The closest m CHUNKlets for each CHUNKlet type are recommended in decreasing order, where m represents the desired number of CHUNKlets shown based on system administrators' input.

User Feedback Round. During this round, the user completes CHUNKlets within the current CHUNK. Implicit feedback, such as the length of videos watched, may be captured during this phase, but we do not focus on those possibilities here, rather capture it in the future work section. Our focus is on explicit feedback, which will be captured at the completion of each CHUNKlet and CHUNK.

In the CHUNKlet case, the user will be presented with a choice of rating the CHUNKlet as either a "like" or a "dislike". The user's learning method profile vector will then be adjusted by multiplying a scalar value to the vector entry associated with the CHUNKlet type, expanded upon later in this section.

In the CHUNK case, the user will be presented with the same "dislike" or "like" question regarding the CHUNK as a whole, but if the user indicates positive feedback, a second feedback question will be asked. To support an adaptive CHUNK Learning system, this feedback round presents the user with the top three keywords (based on frequency) associated with the CHUNK and asks the user for either positive or negative feedback for each of the three keywords. The feedback collected will then impact the keywords attached to the CHUNK.

Lastly, to make the profiles adaptive, the user's profile vector will then be adjusted by multiplying a scalar value to the keyword(s) position in his or her content keyword vector. Additionally, if the user indicates positive feedback on any of the three keywords shown at the end of the CHUNK, and that keyword is not already represented in the user's keyword vector, a "1" value will be added to the user's keyword vector before the scalar is applied. This enables the user to prolong his or her exploration in the CHUNK Learning network by making it possible for related CHUNKs to be suggested to the user.

We set the "like" scalar value to 1.05 and the "dislike" scalar value to 0.01. These values can be adjusted depending on system administrator preference. Because of these updates, we refer to the CHUNK Learning system as having "dynamic profiles", since each user's profile adjusts according to explicit feedback.

Upon completion of a CHUNK, that CHUNK's similarity value to the user profile will be assigned the value zero. This is to prevent the user from being recommended a CHUNK that has already been completed.

The process then repeats. It should be noted that our methodology is applicable to both directed and exploratory learners. For the directed learner case, users may take a different path through the network than a purely exploratory learner might, but they can still use and benefit from the feedback mechanisms built into the system particularly in respect to the learning methods presented over time.

V. Experimental Set Up

Using the CHUNK data available as of January 2019, we conduct two distinct experiments in order to compare the exploratory performance of our RS against the performance of the current CHUNK Learning system.

The first experiment looks at network discovery using both systems. For this simulation, three users are created with unique profiles containing distinct sets of keywords. As a base case, one more profile is created that did not have any keywords. Each user starts the exploratory process by taking the CHUNK named "Vectors". To model our RS, we apply the similarity methodology to the user's profile in order to model the shift in paths from user to user. To differentiate the impact of user feedback, each user provides positive feedback on the CHUNK taken at each iteration. The user's profile is then updated with the top three keywords in each CHUNK profile studied, if the keywords are not already present in the profile. To model the existing CHUNK Learning system, because the user's profile does not change, feedback is not applied, and the user profile gains no new keywords. The model runs through twenty iterations and records the CHUNK taken as well as the similarity value between the user and that CHUNK during each iteration. We then visualize and analyze the simulation output using Gephi.

The second experiment is designed to demonstrate our system's ability to adjust CHUNKlet type recommendations based on user feedback. Because the current CHUNK Learning system does not apply a profile updating step, this experiment is only applicable to our new RS. Due to the infancy of the network, there was a lack of data when each CHUNKlet breaks down into each of the four categories for recommendations. It would be difficult to assess the true performance of the feedback mechanism on sparse data. Therefore, for this simulation we build only one user whose initial profile shows affinity for only one learning style, represented by its CHUNKlet type. We then simulate the user going through fourteen CHUNKlet recommendations, where the user's feedback to each CHUNKlet varies. At each recommendation, we record the CHUNKlet type as well as the "likeability" that the user has with each CHUNKlet type. We analyze the output data using Python.

VI. Results and Analysis

We begin by analyzing the network discovery data based on the different exploratory paths taken by a user with a dynamic profile as compared to a user with a static profile. Figure 4 shows the path that a user with a dynamic profile. The width of the edges is proportional to the similarity of the user to that CHUNKlet, represented by the red lines forming the path the user takes.

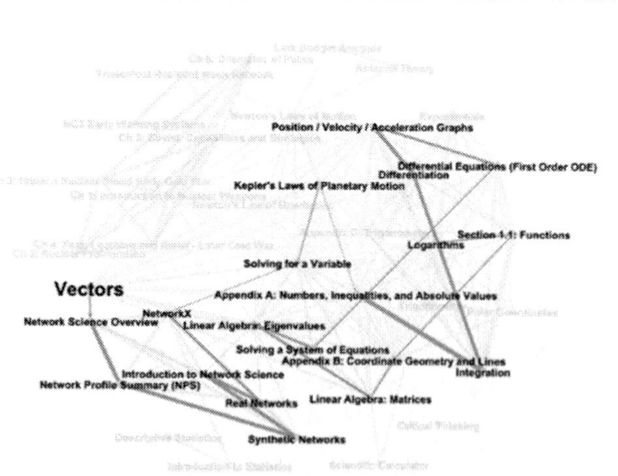

Fig. 4: Exploratory path based on a dynamic profile.

Figure 5 shows a user's path with a static profile. In this case, the red lines end when the user's similarity values relative to the remaining CHUNKs drop to zero. Because the user's profile is not updated at the end of each CHUNK, the user cannot acquire new keywords. At this point, the user's next CHUNK is chosen at random, since no relevant recommendation can be given, and the remainder of his or her path is denoted by green lines.

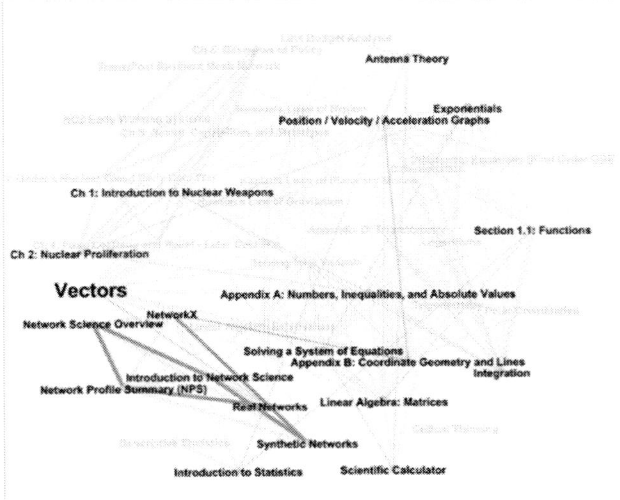

Fig. 5: Exploratory path based on a static profile.

From Figure 4 and Figure 5, we see that updating a user's profile at the end of each CHUNK prolongs the user's relevant exploratory path through the network. Since our network's construct does not incorporate prerequisites or any ontological structure, it is important that the user's profile be updated in order to provide both a logical and meaningful progression of CHUNKs.

We next demonstrate network discovery by showing different paths taken by unique users. Figure 6 and Figure 7 outline paths taken by users whose initial set of keywords showed an interest in Physics and Space, respectively. Since no randomness was used in any steps, the different paths taken by each user demonstrate that our recommendation system provides unique recommendations based on user input. The accuracy and relevancy of these recommendations is, of course, dependent on the system's data. However, by noting the different CHUNKs that are recommended to each of the users, we see that the system points users in directions that appear appropriate and relevant.

We have graphically demonstrated that our recommendation system positively impacts network discovery based on profile updates as well as differences in initial user profile input. Next we present results on how the similarity value between the user and the CHUNKs, as well as the user and the CHUNKlet learning methods, changes over time based on user feedback, given a dynamically updating profile.

Figure 8 shows the change in similarity values between a user with a Nuclear and Space centered profile, and four of the nine most similar initial CHUNKs to the user. Five of the nine CHUNKs were removed in order to keep the chart readable. From Figure 8, we see that the CHUNK with the highest similarity value relative to the other CHUNKs is chosen before the others. This is a simple observation that

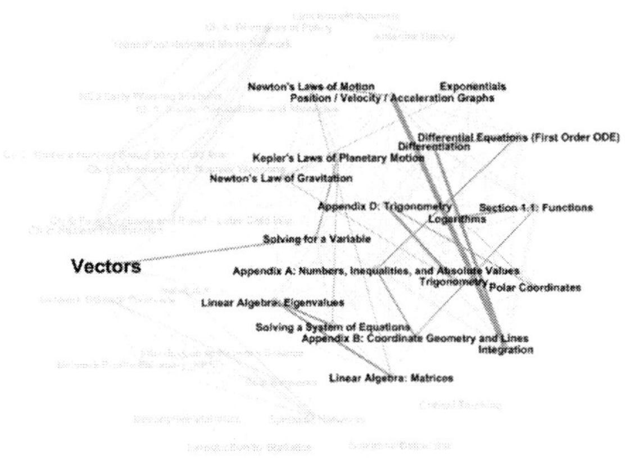

Fig. 6: Path for a student interested in Physics.

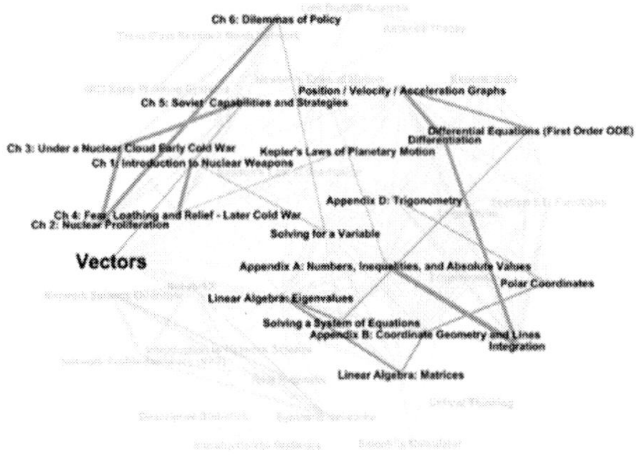

Fig. 7: Path for a student interested in Space.

should not come as a surprise based on our methodology. Once the CHUNK with the highest similarity value has been "completed', its similarity value decreases to zero and that CHUNK is no longer considered for recommendation. Thus the next CHUNK chosen has the next highest similarity, and lower than the one of the just completed CHUNK.

Two noteworthy observations are: (1) The similarity value between the user and a group of similar CHUNKs decreases as that user completes each CHUNK in that group. While we did not explore the underlying reason behind this behavior, our hypothesis is that as the user gains keywords, he or she is becoming more of an "expert' and less of a "generalist', bringing the similarity value down as the user progresses through the network. (2) Based on the dynamic nature of the user's profile, our system recommended the CHUNK "Kepler's Law", which started with a similarity value of zero, after nine iterations of CHUNK completions. This further demonstrates that the use of a dynamically updating profile enables the user to prolong his or her exploratory learning experience.

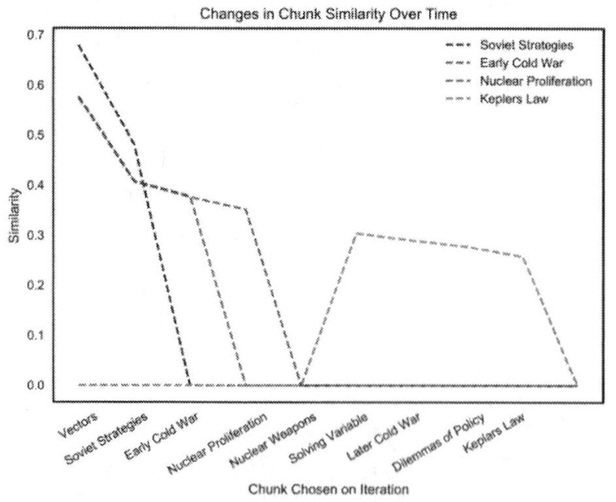

Fig. 8: Changes to CHUNK similarity values as a user completes CHUNKs.

In addition to observing changes in CHUNK similarity values over time, seeing the result of CHUNKlet feedback is also important in order to demonstrate to the reader the recommendation system's ability to adapt to each user in a unique way, as well as how adjusting system parameters can influence system behavior. Figure 9 shows CHUNKlet recommendations over the course of fourteen CHUNKlet completions.

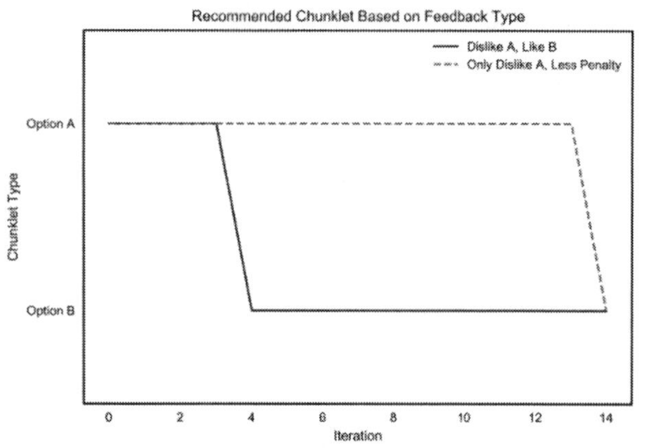

Fig. 9: CHUNKlet recommendations over time based on different user feedback.

To demonstrate the adaptability of our feedback mechanism, in our second experiment we repeatedly show the user the same two CHUNKlet options- Option A and Option B. Each option represents a different learning style. Option A represents a CHUNKlet labeled as a video while CHUNKlet B represents a CHUNKlet labeled as a PowerPoint. In both cases, our user initially indicates that they prefer videos on their user profile. However, as soon as they are shown a video CHUNKlet, they realize they dislike videos. When the user signals that they dislike videos, we apply the 'dislike' penalty scalar to their user profile. To demonstrate the effect of the penalty value, we display two lines. The red line represents a penalty of .5 while the blue line represents a penalty of .01. As shown in Figure 9, the user repeatedly dislikes videos until the system randomly selects them a CHUNKlet containing a PowerPoint. Once they see a PowerPoint, the user signals that they do in fact prefer this style of learning.

While not groundbreaking, the second experiment demonstrates how the severity of the penalty correlates to how quick the system adapts and responds to user behavior. A 'dislike' penalty scalar of 0 immediately removes keywords from the user profile while higher penalty values introduce a lag. The penalty offers the system administrators another layer of flexibility in how they choose to control the feedback loop.

VII. Conclusions

In this work, we describe a method for providing relevant and personalized topic recommendations as applied to the CHUNK Learning system. By storing topic and method keyword counts in vectors, we are able to compute a simple similarity value between the user of the CHUNK Learning system and each CHUNK as well as each CHUNKlet. Those CHUNKlets with the highest similarity values are then recommended first, to include the CHUNKs they are part of. Secondly, user feedback provides a method for dynamically updating the similarity calculation in order to promote the most relevant information to the user throughout his or her use of the CHUNK Learning system. Through multiple simulations, we have demonstrated that this methodology provides unique and accurate recommendations to the user based on his or her profile and feedback.

While our simulations show proof of concept, time and data limitations only allowed for simple feedback behaviors and a limited number of user profile builds. In future, one can perform sensitivity analysis on our methodology.

VIII. Further Directions

Our team barely scraped the surface on providing a comprehensive recommendation system for CHUNK, rather we looked to test the possibility of an adaptive system. Below are numerous suggestions for follow-on research:

1) Feedback Method. Our feedback mechanism only allows the user to either "like" or "dislike" a CHUNK, CHUNKlet, or keyword. However, various other feedback methods exist that are not necessarily binary in nature, which may provide more relevant or accurate recommendations than our binary response. For example, user interactions with CHUNKlets could be tracked using metrics such as video/module completion to get implicit feedback on content or learning method relevancy. Alternatively, the exercises and knowledge checks already included as CHUNK assessments could

tagged down to the individual question level with supporting content keywords. If a user is struggling with questions associated with one of these supporting areas, those keywords could be added to his or her profile to generate future recommendations.

2) Keyword Updates. We implement a way for the user to explore the CHUNK network by dynamically updating the user's profile based on keyword feedback at CHUNK completion. These keywords are chosen based on overall count in the CHUNK. Choosing these keywords in this manner, however, may not be the best way of ultimately providing the user with the most opportunities to explore the various topics in the network. It may indeed be a limiting factor depending on the sparsity of the data or the current similarity of the CHUNK to the user. Instead of choosing the top three keywords by count, the system could calculate all of the possible similarity values based on all $\binom{n}{3}$ combinations of keywords and then providing the combination that supports the best exploratory option. Many other possibilities can be devised. On the topic of keyword collection, manual methods would soon prove cumbersome, especially when videos are concerned. We recommend an automatic keyword scraper instead.
3) Collaborative Filtering/Recommendations. At the time of this work, the CHUNK Learning system was in its infancy. Once the system has time to incorporate many users and CHUNKlets, it will be possible to incorporate collaborative filtering and recommendations.
4) Exploiting social tagging in the TELs much like it has been done for the Web 2.0 recommender system [20].

ACKNOWLEDGMENTS

The authors would like to thank the DoD for partially funding this work.

REFERENCES

[1] "Khan academy," https://www.khanacademy.org/, Mar. 2019.
[2] "Chegg," https://www.chegg.com/, Mar. 2019.
[3] "Coursera," https://www.coursera.org/, Mar. 2019.
[4] R. Gera, M. Isenhour, D. Bartolf, and S. Tick, "CHUNK:Curated Heuristic Using a Network of Knowledge," in The Fifth International Conference on Human and Social Analytics. HUSO, July 2019.
[5] N. Manouselis, H. Drachsler, R. Vuorikari, H. Hummel, and R. Koper, "Recommender systems in technology enhanced learning," in Recommender systems handbook. Springer, 2011, pp. 387–415.
[6] O. C. Santos, J. G. Boticario, S. Baldiris, G. Moreno, D. Huerva, and R. Fabregat, "Recommender systems for lifelong learning inclusive scenarios," in Workshop on recommender systems, 2008, p. 45.
[7] H. Drachsler, K. Verbert, O. C. Santos, and N. Manouselis, "Panorama of recommender systems to support learning," in Recommender systems handbook. Springer, 2015, pp. 421–451.
[8] H. Drachsler, H. Hummel, and R. Koper, "Identifying the goal, user model and conditions of recommender systems for formal and informal learning," 2008.
[9] R. Vuorikari and R. Koper, "Ecology of social search for learning resources," Campus-Wide Information Systems, vol. 26, no. 4, pp. 272–286, 2009.
[10] K. Verbert, N. Manouselis, X. Ochoa, M. Wolpers, H. Drachsler, I. Bosnic, and E. Duval, "Context-aware recommender systems for learning: a survey and future challenges," IEEE Transactions on Learning Technologies, vol. 5, no. 4, pp. 318–335, 2012.
[11] M.-Á. Sicilia, E. García-Barriocanal, S. Sánchez-Alonso, and C. Cechinel, "Exploring user-based recommender results in large learning object repositories: the case of merlot," Procedia Computer Science, vol. 1, no. 2, pp. 2859–2864, 2010.
[12] D. Gallego, E. Barra, A. Gordillo, and G. Huecas, "Enhanced recommendations for e-learning authoring tools based on a proactive context-aware recommender," in 2013 IEEE Frontiers in Education Conference (FIE). IEEE, 2013, pp. 1393–1395.
[13] Ricci, Recommender systems handbook, 2nd ed. Springer, 2015.
[14] J. K. Tarus, Z. Niu, and A. Yousif, "A hybrid knowledge-based recommender system for e-learning based on ontology and sequential pattern mining," Future Generation Computer Systems, vol. 72, pp. 37–48, 2017.
[15] H. Drachsler, D. Pecceu, T. Arts, E. Hutten, L. Rutledge, P. Van Rosmalen, H. Hummel, and R. Koper, "Remashed–recommendations for mash-up personal learning environments," in European conference on technology enhanced learning. Springer, 2009, pp. 788–793.
[16] H. Drachsler, H. Hummel, and R. Koper, "Personal recommender systems for learners in lifelong learning: requirements, techniques and model," 2007.
[17] N. A. Albatayneh, K. I. Ghauth, and F.-F. Chua, "Utilizing learners' negative ratings in semantic content-based recommender system for e-learning forum," Educational Technology & Society, vol. 21, no. 1, pp. 112,125, 2018.
[18] J. Underwood, "Metis," in Educational Recommender Systems and Technologies, 2012, pp. 24,42.
[19] A. Ruiz-Iniesta, G. Jiménez-Díaz, and M. Gómez-Albarrán, "A semantically enriched context-aware oer recommendation strategy and its application to a computer science oer repository," IEEE Transactions on Education, vol. 57, no. 4, pp. 255,260, 2014-11.
[20] A. B. B. Martinez, M. R. Lopez, E. C. Montenegro, F. A. M. Fonte, J. C. Burguillo, and A. Peleteiro, "Exploiting social tagging in a web 2.0 recommender system," IEEE Internet Computing, vol. 14, no. 6, pp. 23–30, 2010.

An Adaptive Education Approach Using the Learners' Social Network

Ralucca Gera

Department of Applied Mathematics,
Associate Provost for Graduate Education,
Teaching and Learning Commons,
Naval Postgraduate School, Monterey, CA
Email: rgera@nps.edu

Alex Gutzler,
Ryan Hard,
Bryan McDonough, and
Christian Sorenson

Department of Applied Mathematics,
Naval Postgraduate School, Monterey, CA

***Abstract*—How can the 21st century education system capitalize on online social networks to support formal education? As education transitions away from the traditional brick-and-mortar style, so does the social network that supports learners. Traditional collegiate education lacks the use of an adaptive system through which students can optimize learning, and educators can promote such learning with the assistance of real-time digital feedback. We develop the means through which the Curated Heuristic Using a Network of Knowledge (CHUNK) learning [6] can provide an adaptive learning framework by designing a dynamic social network of students based on social and academic attributes. Learners use a rating system to determine what educational methods are effective or ineffective in assisting their learning, and the CHUNK Learning system exploits this data to provide other learners more effective methods. We explore the impact that users have on each other when they are considered to be similar based on sharing similar interests. We learn that while different modeling methodology can capture the strength of similarity between users, our experiments show that strongly connected groups have a stronger influence on each other than the weakly connected ones.**

***Index Terms*—Education; Chunk Learning; Adaptive Learning**

I. Introduction and Motivation

Collegiate education is based on traditional lecturer-student interactions where the educator has a preset construct of how the course material should be conveyed to the students, usually in the form of a lecture, for a set amount of time, at frequent intervals, weekly or otherwise. Students are expected to learn the course material via the lectures as well as textbooks and other supplementary methods. Students can pose inquiries to the educator regarding the material to improve their understanding. As a basic educational structure this method works, but can inhibit both those who quickly grasp the subject matter and those who struggle, since they are all exposed to the same information at the same pace.

The newly introduced CHUNK Learning personalized educational system [6] can be found at [1]. Also, references need to be listed as [7], [8] accelerates and deepens learning by introducing targeted short modules for the students. This system allows students to learn in ways that are effective for them, whether it be watching videos, reading the book, reading through slides of the material, working example problems, running code, or a combination of those and other methods. Learning through these activities frees up the lecturing time, allowing the educator to teach at a higher level with deeper classroom discussion; whether that be critical thinking about the learned topics, teaching at an accelerated rate, focusing more on hands-on examples of the learned material, etc. Similar studies and systems looked at web-based and mobile learning CHUNKing of knowledge [2], [13], studying languages [11], [12], math [9], and so on.

Students at the collegiate level and above leave behind generic education that is received during primary and secondary schooling, and begin picking and choosing topics that interest them, and applying to where they see themselves in their future. Naturally, social connections form between students in similar curricula as they go through coursework together, as well as those that live together or participate in extracurricular activities together. These connections grow into a social network of those participating in higher education. From this social network, learning styles can be observed and extended to groups of similar students to help them learn quicker and with greater impact. Adding this social network to CHUNK Learning attempts to best assign content within the learning modules to each person, based on what the social network suggests about their interests, their preferred learning methods, and also the learning methods from their friends. Using this educational aid, students have the ability to learn in a way that makes sense to them and lets them take more away from each education opportunity.

The structure of the paper is as follows. The required definitions and the problem statement are explained in Section II followed by an overview of the related work in Section III. We then introduce the methodology for the recommender system in this environment in Section IV. We present the experimental setup in Section V, followed by the results and interpretation in Section VI. We conclude and present further direction in Section VII.

II. Problem Definitions

As the amount digital information grows, teaching and learning methods must be adapted to enhance education, especially at the collegiate level. Many current methods of education cater to either a lowest common denominator, where the instructor starts at square one for each subject to ensure no student gets left behind, or at a static level in which no consideration is given to the skill levels of the students.

In the first case, the advanced students academically degrade since they are not challenged and waste valuable education time not improving their knowledge and skills. In the second case, the advance students are still not engaged, and those below the level of instruction might constantly struggle with the material, must work disproportionately hard to achieve some level of academic success, and possibly never gain any understanding. For both cases, the failure to appropriately challenge, engage and enlighten students results in sub-par education and a lack of innovation. Meanwhile, a challenging academic atmosphere can lead to just several students graduating with a high level of academic success. In order for the academic environment to improve, education must adapt to all students' levels, capitalizing on their strengths and knowledge, and do so quickly.

CHUNK Learning is a pilot system seeking to enhance education through targeting modules to match the user's learning style and knowledge [6]. The CHUNK Learning system has three main components: a learner profile, CHUNKs, and CHUNKlets. Each of them is tagged with keywords based on the topics to be learned, the teaching method, applications, and so on.

The learner profile captures static information from the learner regarding interests and preferred learning styles. The learner enrolls in a course, and then is presented with the courses' modules, called CHUNKs. Each CHUNK is built around a topic, equivalent to a section in a textbook. The CHUNK content is broken down into smaller education materials, called CHUNKlets. The CHUNKlets capture the breaking down of a topic into short and intense educational materials, allowing the learners to be engaged for a short period of time and practice it before continuing to the next CHUNKlet. The CHUNKlets are categorized into four types: "Why", "What", "Methodology", and "Assessment". For each CHUNK, the CHUNKlets within the same category are interchangeable as they present the same topic from different points of view, allowing for personalized education when the most appropriate CHUNKs are suggested to the learner.

The above structure of CHUNK Learning is complemented with capturing feedback from users. After the completion of a CHUNKlet of a CHUNK, each user can rate how useful and engaging the CHUNKlet was on a scale of one to five. Moreover, users can give thumbs up and thumbs down to the CHUNKlet capturing the relevancy of the learned content. These two measures streamlining the learning process by support an up to date learning environment, as older and less useful content be suggested less.

In the current work, we propose a two step process for recommending CHUNKs and CHUNKlets to each user to support personalized education, based on its current structure. First, relevant CHUNKs and CHUNKlets are determined based on the user's academic requirements and goals. Second, for each relevant CHUNK, the relevant CHUNKlets are rated based on the user's learner profile and the social connections they share with other user's in the system. The goal of this process is to maximize the chances that the user engage with CHUNKlets that are both useful and interesting to him/her. Currently, the recommendation of a CHUNKlet is based on the learner profile's keywords. For this research, we complement the process of personalizing the chosen CHUNKlet for each user by creating and utilizing a social network that ranks relevant CHUNKlets for each user.

The newly proposed rating for each CHUNKlet is generated using the learner's profile and how that information links him/her to similar users, building on the CHUNKlet feedback provided from previous learners in the network. This maximizes the chances learners use methods that work for them. The built in rating system is used to affect the ranking the CHUNKlet receives for other related users in the network, with the strength of that effect being determined by the strength of the individual's social connection with other users. Throughout the paper, "user" and "learner" are used interchangeably.

Our CHUNK Learning approach requires indentifying the relevant connections between the users in order to accurately recommend appropriate new CHUNKlets to users; that is to say it relies on the overlaying social network that emerges between the users of the CHUNK Learning system. This paper seeks to determine a method to generate this social network and apply the CHUNK Learning approach in tandem by having the social network assign and modify the score of each CHUNKlet, to be used for recommendations to other users. The social network's nodes are the individual learner profiles and the edges (weighted and undirected) connect nodes with similar attributes. We extract the attributes from each student profile. Examples of such attributes are the current degree, branch of service, and previous degrees, and extracurricular interests.

III. Related Work

A CHUNK Learning type adaptive algorithm has already been explored by Cleven in his thesis [4], on a set of courses at the Naval Postgraduate School. Cleven investigates how to create an adaptive learning algorithm that links the best suited learning modules to each user, based on user-specific profiles and feedback. Cleven's work focuses on connecting users to the modules that most suit their method of learning, with emphasis on adapting to favor modules that cater to previous user feedback. Cleven's work provides a base example that we extrapolate to create a social network between users. The same feedback mechanism that Cleven uses to create an interpersonal adaptive learning software can be extended to spread feedback across connected users, thus generating an interpersonal adaptability, rather using the CHUNK Learning modules instead of the courses offered at the Naval Postgraduate School. This approach presents a different challenge, as the courses are tagged and capture different information than the modules in CHUNK Learning.

Diffusion of Knowledge is a problem that has been investigated over the last several decades. The basic concept is that certain network layouts are optimally suited for fast and efficient spreading of knowledge. Cowan and Jonard [5] investigate how knowledge spreads throughout three basic network configurations. The first is a regular network, and the second is a random network. The final network layout is the Watts-Strogatz small world network model [10]. Cowan and Jonard show that the more closely connected two nodes are, the higher the rate of knowledge transfer. They find that the layout of a Watts-Strogatz network is most suited to optimal diffusion of knowledge throughout a social network. This concept can be extended to creating interpersonal connections in educational software, facilitating faster learning by users.

A recommender systems that builds on Social Media websites creates a framework for user-to-user connections that complements the content network for a wholistic approach. In the case of Facebook, these connections manifest themselves as friend recommendations, targeted advertising, and preferential displays on a user's feed. Chen and Fong analyze the algorithm that Facebook uses to create similarity functions and trust factors between users [3]. The authors explain that Facebook's similarity function is generated by taking comparison factors between multiple attributes of user profiles, and subsequently assigning a weight to each attribute. For example, the function put more weight on the "interested in" attribute than the "sex" attribute. The attribute weights are determined by the algorithm developers, based on what they believe are more important connecting traits. Trust factors form the second layer of connectivity generation. Facebook trust factors are formed based on a tiered system. Each tier has a discrete trust factor based on the relationship level between users. For instance, family members have a much higher trust factor than users with which one is not Facebook friends [3]. Collaborative Filtering is the notion that a network of user preferences act as an effective way to filter future data. In other words, the network collaborates to determine what data is favored. The Facebook collaborative filter is formed by the combination of the two levels of connection: similarity functions and trust factors, which form a system that determines what content appears on a user's Facebook interface. Similar algorithms could also ahve an impact in creating educational recommendations in an adaptive learning software.

In this paper we introduce a collaborative filtering algorithm that presents CHUNK Learning users with modules preferred by similar users. The introduction of this algorithm into CHUNK Learning facilitate a higher diffusion of knowledge throughout the network of learners. Building on the adaptive learning techniques used by Cleven [4], we present an initial social network framework for the CHUNK Learning system.

IV. METHODOLOGY

We create the social network using learner profiles as the nodes, and we use the attributes of those nodes as criteria to create edges. If two nodes have the same attribute, they will be connected by an edge. Attribute selection is limited to a predefined set of options to ensure uniform responses for a given category. This minimizes errors during data entry and ensures rank and designator selections correspond to the selected service. As the network grows, new categories and/or attributes may be added.

For the purposes of this paper, we create a set list of categories and attributes to generate a usable network, as a subset of the CHUNK Learning system's list of attributes. The selected categories have either a drop down list of attributes for single selection or a multiple choice list for attributes which may contain multiple items, such as extracurricular interests and classes. The categories are the following:

1) Rank
2) Service
3) Designator/MOS
4) Masters (Current Curriculum)
5) Major (Previous Degrees)
6) Extracurricular Interests
7) Classes.

Our model focuses on the recommendation of CHUNKlets and assumes CHUNKs have already selected by the user directed for the course he/she is enrolled in, since the CHUNKlets are interchangeable within their category. For the purposes of this research, we limit the model to 11 courses, with each course containing exactly one CHUNK and each CHUNK containing exactly three CHUNKlets. For this reason, the terms "course' and "CHUNK' are interchangeable in our model.

For our analysis, we generate a synthetic social network using MATLAB by creating and connecting fictional users. This allows us to create an environment of users and their initial ratings for each CHUNKlet. Though in reality a user not necessarily complete all CHUNKlets relevant to a particular CHUNK, our model assumes that a user completes and rates all three CHUNKlets relevant to a CHUNK if that user is enrolled in the applicable course. As we introduce new users to the network, we connect them to existing users based on the attributes they select. The MATLAB code also allows us to control the similarity distribution of the users resulting in stronger or weaker connections between the users as similarity is adjusted from high to low.

Using the randomly generated profiles, we create a social network by determining how strongly each user is connected to every other user. First, we weigh how important each category is for determining social connectivity. As an example, current degree may be given a weight of three and past degree may be given a weight of one, indicating connections made using a user's current degree are three times more important than connections made using a user's past degrees. Next, for each category, the category's weight is used to form weighted edges between users if the users share an attribute in that category. Finally, these edges are added together to form the connections in the overall social network, where the weighted edge between each pair of users determines how well-connected they are.

We now explore the effect of the social network on CHUNKlet recommendations. As new users are introduced to the network and connected to existing users, the score of a CHUNKlet is updated for that user and may result in different recommendations. These suggestions for CHUNKlets are based on the highest scored CHUNKlet in that category. Though the method for constructing the edge weights in the social network remains the same, we use three methods for the edge weights to determine CHUNKlet ratings. Let x be a new user, and y, z be existing users in the network.

1) The linear method: the CHUNKlet's rating is proportional to the social edge weights. If the weight of the edge x, y is 5, and the weight of the edge x, z is 10, then user z have twice the impact that user y has on the suggestions presented to x.
2) The exponential method: the impact a user has on CHUNKlet ratings grow exponentially with their social weight.
3) The tier method: in this method, connections between users are split into three tiers according to the social weight connecting them. Highly connected individuals fall into Tier 1, followed by Tier 2, and then Tier 3, as their social weight decreases. All individuals in the same tier have the same impact on CHUNKlet ratings - i.e 6 for the top tier, 3 for the middle, and 1 for the bottom tier.

Each method has potential benefits and drawbacks, which is why we proposed three methods. The tiered approach prevents highly connected users from drowning out less connected users, but could also result in dissimilar users having the same effect as those slightly similar, depending on the bounds of each tier. The exponential method does the opposite, it magnifies the effect highly similar users have on each other. The linear method is the middle ground between tiered and exponential. As more users interact with the CHUNKlets the recommendations become more robust. We present the details in Section V.

V. Experimental Set Up

The goal of our experiments is to determine how adding new users to the CHUNK Learning system affects the CHUNKlets' ratings. In this section, we explain the details of the experiment set up.

A. Overview

To focus our approach, we limit ourselves to one specific CHUNKlet of one specific test learner, and observe how the CHUNKlet score for that test learner changes as new users join the network. To minimize the number of variables, the number of original users, the number of new users added, CHUNKlet ratings, and category weighting factors all are held constant between experiments. The original users rate for the observed CHUNKlet is 1, and the new users rate for the observed CHUNKlet is 5. Additionally, we require all users to enrol in just this one single course.

Between experiments, we change how similar the existing and new users are to the test learner. This changes the structure of the social network, which modifies the impact the existing and new users have on the CHUNKlet score to be recommended to the test learner. For each experiment, we use the social network to change the CHUNKlet rating, based on each of the three methods described in Section IV.

B. Similarity

To support the goal of our experiment to test how varying the strength of the social network affects a CHUNKlet's rating, we first see how the random profile generator is adjusted to create groups of similar or dissimilar people. The generator uses a parameter called "Similarity' which helps determine the probability of different users sharing attributes. Similarity can take a value greater than or equal to one, and though the value does not have a linear relationship with the probability distribution (a Similarity of 2 does not double the likelihood of creating matching users as compared to a Similarity of 1), higher Similarities increase the likelihood of creating users with matching attributes.

We start the process by creating a vector for each node category, listing attributes for that category. For instance, the vector ["Officer', "Civilian', "Enlisted'] corresponds to the category of Rank. When a new user is created, one of these values is selected randomly for that user's Rank. If Similarity is set to a value of 1 for Rank, then the probability of selecting each value is uniformly distributed, so the user has an equal probability (i.e. $1/3$) of being an Officer, a Civilian, or Enlisted. As similarity is made higher, the probability distribution is shifted to favor attributes in the order listed in the vector. For instance, a Similarity of 10 results in the probability of the new user to be Officer, Civilian, and Enlisted to be approximately $0.69, 0.19$, and 0.12, respectively.

The exact method for choosing a vector's index uses Equation 1, where Similarity variable (S) and Vector Length (L) are parameters. The input value is a random number (r) uniformly distributed between 0 and 1. The output value, $I(r)$, corresponds to the chosen index for that vector. Since the output falls in the interval $[0, L]$, the value is then rounded up to the nearest integer to get the actual index selected. Also, since the vectors do not have an index of 0, then $I(r) = 0$ is replaced with $I(r) = 1$.

$$I(r) = r \cdot L \cdot S^{-(1-r)} \tag{1}$$

Figure 1 shows the output of the Equation 1, where $L = 3$ and $S = 10$.

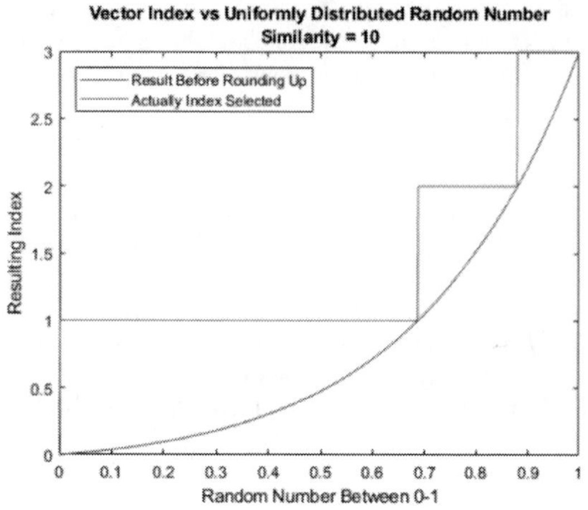

Fig. 1: Chosen Index $I(r)$ vs Random Number r ($L = 3, S = 10$)

Figure 2 shows the probability distribution for selecting a specific index, given $L = 3$and $S = 10$.

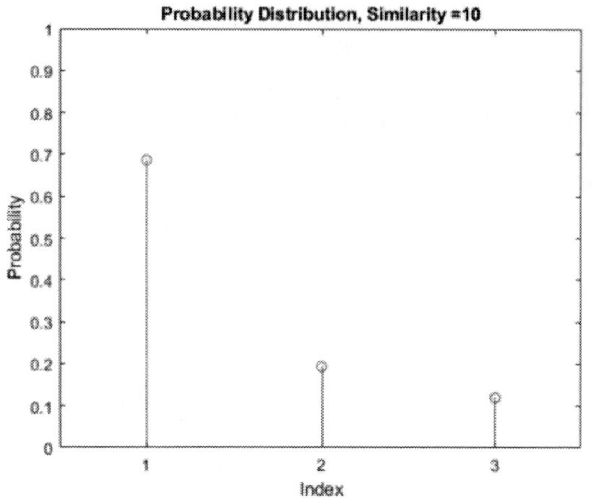

Fig. 2: Index Probability Distribution ($L = 3, S = 10$)

Notice that the probability of selecting index one is much greater than index two or three. Also, the probability of selecting index two is slightly higher than index three. Regardless of the specific values of S and L, lower indices always have a larger probability of being selected than higher indices (except if $S = 1$, in which case the probability is the same for all indices).

C. Experiment Parameters

Each experiment begins with 51 original users that all rate the observed CHUNKlets with a rating of 1. One of the original 51 users is the test learner, and his attributes remain constant between experiments. Note that since we are observing the CHUNKlet's score for the test learner, his ranking does not actual affect the CHUNKlet score (since there are no loops in the social network). The other 50 original users have their similarity to the test learner varied between experiments.

Next, 50 new users are added, one at a time, which all rate the observed CHUNKlet with a rating of 5. The 50 new users have their similarity to the test learner varied between experiments. The observed CHUNKlet score is recorded for each new user added, so a trend of *CHUNKlet score* versus *number of new users* added can be determined.

The available categories for each user profile are Rank, Service, Designator, Current Degree, Previous Degrees, Extra-curricular Interests, and Enrolled Classes. The weight for each category is assigned as $2, 2, 2, 3, 3, 2$, and 1, respectively, and they remain constant between experiments.

The users are selected as *test learner* and *other users* (that come in groups of Similar, Dissimilar, or Realistic people), and are defined as follows:

- The test learner: which remains constant between experiments, always chooses the first (most likely) attribute for each category. For instance, since the Rank vector is ["Officer',"Civilian',"Enlisted'], the test learner is always an officer.
- Similar people use a Similarity value of 9000 for every category (see Section V-B for more details); therefore, there is a high probability each member of this group is similar to other members of the group as well as the test learner.
- Dissimilar people use a Similarity value of 1. This creates an equal chance of choosing any attribute for each category, so the chance that each person in this group is similar to the test learner is completely random.
- Realistic people attempt to better simulate the learner population at the Naval Postgraduate School. Their Rank category is given a Similarity of 100, which gives each person in the group a 0.81 probability of being an officer. Their Service category is given a similarity of 5, which gives each military person in the group a 0.42 probability of being in the Navy. All other categories for this group have a Similarity of 1. The specific probabilities of choosing a index depends on the vector length for that category, Table I shows the probability distribution for a vector length of f5 and Similarities of $5, 100$, and 9000.

TABLE I: INDEX PROBABILITY FOR VARIOUS SIMILARITIES

	Index 1	Index 2	Index 3	Index 4	Index 5
S=5	0.4723	0.1999	0.1363	0.1071	0.0844
S=100	0.7243	0.1177	0.0659	0.0525	0.0396
S=9000	0.8449	0.0661	0.0377	0.0281	0.0232

The first experiment looks at an extreme case where the 50 original people are dissimilar, and the 50 new people are similar. The second experiment uses 50 realistic people as the original group, and 50 similar people are added one at the time. Finally, the third experiment uses 50 realistic people as the original group, and 50 dissimilar are added one at the time. Table II, below, summarizes the experiment groupings.

TABLE II: EXPERIMENT GROUP TYPES

	Original People	New People
Exp 1	Dissimilar	Similar
Exp 2	Realistic	Similar
Exp 3	Realistic	Dissimilar

VI. Results and Analysis

We run each of the experiments described in Section V one time, and record the CHUNKlet score for each new person added. For each experiment, the random number generator is reset, so if nothing else changes, the people generated are identical.

The *CHUNKlet score* versus *number of people added* is graphed in Figures 3-5 for each experiment. Each graph contains four lines. The purple line is used to mark the reference value of 3, the score the CHUNKlet would receive if the test user received no input from the social network. The blue, yellow, and red lines correspond to the linear, exponential, and tiered methods of using social weighting, respectively. For more details on these methods, see Section IV. It should be noted that the exponential and tiered methods are very dependent on the equations and parameters used for those methods. These experiments show only one way the tiered and exponential methods could be established.

We now dedicate a subsection to each experiment established by Table II. Each subsection presents the *CHUNKlet score* versus *new people added*, and be followed by a brief analysis of the results. Note that since the original people always rate the CHUNKlet as 1, the CHUNKlet score always starts as 1, with zero new people added. Also, since the new people always rate the CHUNKlet as 5, the CHUNKlet score always increases as new people are added.

A. Experiment 1: 50 Dissimilar & 50 Similar

As expected, due to the high similarity of the new group, the CHUNKlet score quickly becomes closer to 5 than it is to 1. Due to the high social network values in the Similar group, the exponential method has a significantly greater effect on the CHUNKlet score than the other two methods. The exponential method only requires about eight new people to return the CHUNKlet score to the baseline of 3. The linear and tiered methods require between 15 and 20 people, which is still low considering the original group contains 50 people. The final CHUNKlet score for the exponential method is about 4.25, with the linear and tiered methods having a score just under 4.

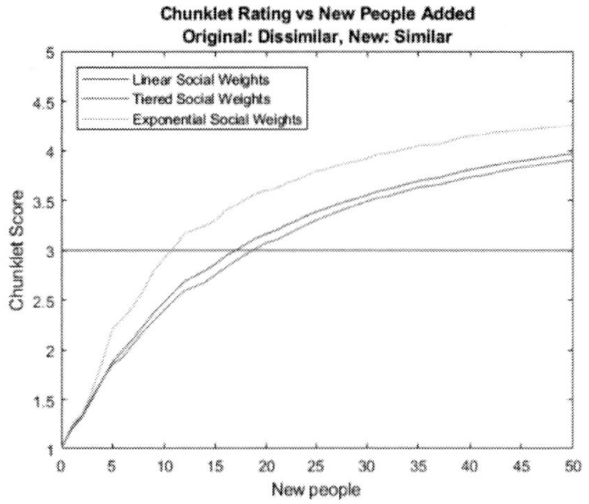

Fig. 3: Experiment 1 Results

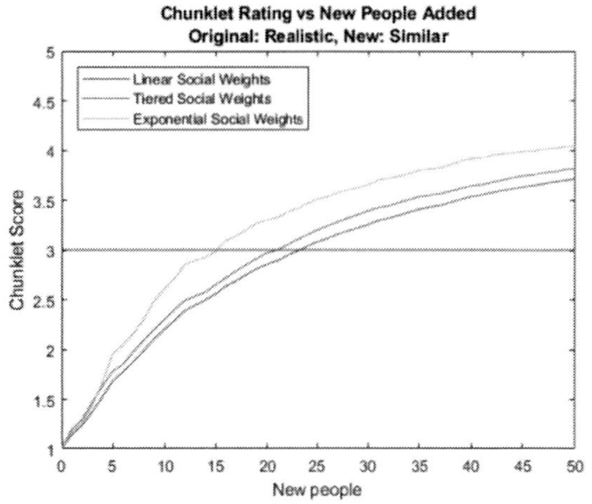

Fig. 4: Experiment 2 Results

B. Experiment 2: 50 Realistic & 50 Similar

As opposed to the first experiment, the original group of people in this experiment are better connected socially. Due to this, the one ratings of the original 50 people carry more weight, so the CHUNKlet score rises slower and reaches a smaller final value. Still, the new people are still better connected than the original people, so the final score is still well above the baseline of 3. The exponential method is still dominant due to the large values in the new group's social network. Of note, the tiered method has a higher final value than the linear method, which is reversed from the first experiment. Since the 50 new people are exactly the same in both experiments, we believe the difference is due to the change in social network for the 50 original people. Therefore, for the parameters used to establish this tiered system, the tiered method appears to carry more weight when the group is Dissimilar than it does when the group is Realistic.

C. Experiment 3: 50 Realistic & 50 Dissimilar

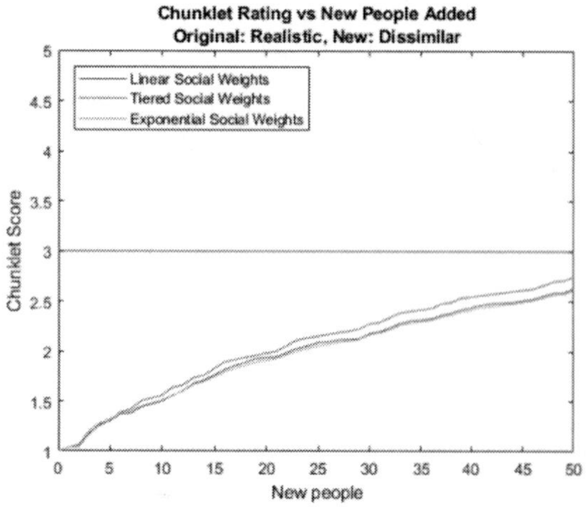

Fig. 5: Experiment 3 Results

The final experiment has a new group which is less connected than the original group. As expected, the CHUNKlet score does not reach the baseline of 3. With no Similar group, the values in the social network are much lower. This appears to cause the exponential method to have a nearly identical effect as the linear method. The tiered method now has the highest final value. This is once again mostly likely due to the relatively smaller effect this tiered system has when dealing with the Realistic populations.

VII. Conclusions and Further Directions

Current teaching methods do not customize the experience to the individual in order to maximize educational gains. The CHUNK Learning system brings attention to this deficiency by assigning material to users that is both relevant to their learning goals as well as compatible with their interests and learning styles. Our method uses the attributes of each CHUNK user profile to establish a social network which helps direct people towards learning materials (CHUNKlets) that are most compatible to their profile.

Our experiments examined how changing the similarity between people in a social network affected CHUNKlet scores. Additionally, three methods for utilizing the social network to affect CHUNKlet scores were examined: linear, exponential, and tiered. No matter which method was used, the experiments always showed that strongly connected groups had a greater effect on CHUNKlets scores than weakly connected groups. This is a validation of our concept, since people that share more of your interests have a greater effect on your recommended learning material.

Another result of the experiments is that the methods used to implement the social network has a variable degree of effect depending on the strength of the connections in the social network. For example, the exponential method appears to have a dominant effect for highly connected social networks, but as the network acquires dissimilar users, the exponential method becomes nearly indistinguishable from the linear method. However, the exact way in which the different methods interact with different social networks is dependent on the equations and parameters that define those methods.

To better understand how a social network affects CHUNKlet scores, an extensive survey is required so that real user data can be collected and used. Only then can the effects of the different social network weighting techniques be analyzed and adjusted. Additionally, user feedback is required to determine if the recommended CHUNKlets are actually well tailored to the individuals based on their social connections. This user feedback can be used to adjust the parameters of the social network, such as the available categories and attributes as well as the weighting factor for each category.

Acknowledgments

The authors would like to thank the DoD for partially funding this work.

References

[1] www.chunklearning.net. www.chunklearning.net.

[2] Peter Brusilovsky. Adaptive hypermedia: From intelligent tutoring systems to web-based education. In International Conference on Intelligent Tutoring Systems, pages 1–7. Springer, 2000.

[3] Wei Chen and Simon Fong. Social network collaborative filtering framework and online trust factors: a case study on facebook. IJWA, 3:17–28, 01 2011.

[4] Jan-Daniel Cleven. A multilayer network approach for real-time adaptive personalized learning, 2018.

[5] Robin Cowan and Nicolas Jonard. Network structure and the diffusion of knowledge. Journal of Economic Dynamics and Control, 28:1557–1575, 06 2004.

[6] Ralucca Gera, Michelle Isenhour, D'Marie Bartolf, and Simona Tick. CHUNK:Curated Heuristic Using a Network of Knowledge. In The Fifth International Conference on Human and Social Analytics. HUSO, July 2019.

[7] DIAO Lin-lin. A survey of chinese english majors' chunk competence [j]. Journal of Pla University of Foreign Languages, 4, 2004.

[8] George A Miller. The magical number seven, plus or minus two: Some limits on our capacity for processing information. Psychological review, 63(2):81, 1956.

[9] Alan H Schoenfeld. Purposes and methods of research in mathematics education. Notices of the AMS, 47(6):641–649, 2000.

[10] Duncan J Watts and Steven H Strogatz. Collective dynamics of 'small-world'networks. nature, 393(6684):440–442, 1998.

[11] GUO Xiao-ying. Prefabricated chunk and college english writing [j]. Journal of Lanzhou Jiaotong University, 2, 2008.

[12] Qian Xujing. A preliminary study on chinese chunk [j]. Journal of Peking University (Philosophy & Social Sciences), 5, 2008.

[13] Chi ZHANG, Gang CHEN, Minjuan WANG, and Huimin WANG. Studying on design of small-chunk learning resources in mobile learning [j]. Open Education Research, 3, 2009.

CHUNK: Curated Heuristic Using a Network of Knowledge

Ralucca Gera[1], Michelle L. Isenhour[2], D'Marie Bartolf[3], Simona Tick[4]
[1]Department of Applied Mathematics, [2]Department of Operations Research, [3]Teaching and Learning Commons
[4]Graduate School of Business and Public Policy
Naval Postgraduate School, Monterey, CA
Corresponding email: rgera@nps.edu

Abstract—**What is the potential of a 21st century education program? In contrast to the standard linear or tree-like educational system of sequential lectures or chapters, we propose the Curated Heuristic Using a Network of Knowledge for Learning (CHUNK Learning) concept, which is designed as a real-time, modular, adaptive teaching-learning method for enhanced and personalized education. CHUNK Learning breaks away from the predictable pattern of traditional education models and provides content delivery that adapts to the capabilities, learning styles, and approaches to problem-solving of every learner. With CHUNK Learning, students are empowered by a student-centered teaching-learning system whose purpose is to make learning efficient, flexible, and respectful of the students' time. Much like a computer game approach, the learner maintains an on-line learning profile which guides the learner through a Network of Knowledge composed of lesson materials joined together by common attributes based on competency or skill levels. Our vision also includes a mix of different delivery methods, to include demos, videos, interactive applications, TED talks, webinars, programming languages (personalized to the skill of the learner), and data manipulations, all delivered through a combination of online and face-to-face experiences.**

Keywords: CHUNK Learning; network of knowledge; education; individualized learning; networks and education.

I. Introduction

Traditional education places all students through the same topics, at the same time, at the same pace, generally teaching to the average student. However, such a system fails to provide every student the appropriate opportunity to learn and engage, leaving some learners struggling, while failing to challenge others. A strength in student-centered learning, as opposed to traditional education, is the opportunity for independence and autonomy that enhances different skills, abilities, and interests learners might have. Unlike most established sciences, new research fields such as Network Science – an emerging field overseeing traditional computer science, operations research, sociology, and other fields – hint at non-traditional methods of education that serve as a starting point for the current effort.

The contrast between our views on the potential of 21st century education and the current educational status quo generates ideas which, we believe, can improve effectiveness of educational programs through enhanced retention, transfer ability and critical thinking linked to learner-centered education. We introduce a vision for an adaptive teaching, flexible learning, and technology-enhanced student-centered education strategy for the 21st century learner that operates in the big data environment [2], [3], [27]. We describe our view on how different teaching and learning tools can be joined into a web or network of knowledge that will individualize learning and leave a persistent impact on the learner's career. We introduce our unique structure and vision for catering to the needs, motivations, and supply of learners with a system that:

- **Offers** intense, short, and focused educational modules
- **Stimulates** interest and demonstrates relevance of topics
- **Integrates** new information with learner's pre-existing knowledge
- **Provides** personalized and individualized education
- **Optimizes** content and methodology delivery to meet the needs of each learner

The structure of the paper is as follows. We present related work in Section II followed by a short overview vision of what the system is becoming in Section III. We then introduces the CHUNK framework in Section IV followed by the science behind CHUNK learning in Section V. We present the Network of knowledge and its components in Sections VI and VII, respectively. Furthermore, we discuss how CHUNK Learning is individualize and personalized in Sections VIII and IX. We conclude with further direction in Section X.

II. Related Work

In the early 90's, education slowly started to incorporate digital resources and use of Internet in the classrooms. By 1999, 80 percent of the schools used these resources in some form [12]. In the same year, studies of the Internet have surfaced and network science research started to bloom [5], [11]. Yet, to this day, we still use the Internet and digital resources primarily as a resource for information or to host distance learning and Massive Open Online Courses (MOOCs). Below, we expand on the richer use of pulling educational information to personalize educational content and to position the learner the way Amazon, Netflix and social media do.

Educational content is generally organized in a hierarchic structure following a textbook or a collection of books. Students enroll in a curriculum that consists of several courses. Each course has themes organized into chapters, and each chapter consists of several sections. In general, the smallest level of educational material relevant for learning is a section, whereas the smallest level a student can choose from is at the course level. Our vision is to consider the data at a more granular level at the tier of topics, where a section could be comprised of one or several topics, possibly captured on transcripts by micro-credits. Moreover, based on design cognition, visualizing the structured representation of concepts and the relations between them as a map allows the learner to generate a deeper, longer lasting learning [20]. Concept mapping allows students to learn in a more meaningful way by elevating their previous experiences and knowledge and relating them to the new concepts for a more complex, longer lasting, more effecting learning [15].

Information theory shows that learners are limited by the amount of information one can receive, process, and remember at the time [19]. Techniques such as "several stimulus dimensions, recording, and various mnemonic devices" along with breaking down the information supports the learning environment. One of these techniques is to present the information in smaller and shorter and interconnected chunks that has been already used for both traditional [16] and for e-learning [31].

A step forward from traditional education is web-based education or e-learning [4], [17], [23], [25]. Particularly, e-learning received more attention in the form of Massive Open Online Courses (MOOCs) [6], [21]. While the digitization of the lectures gives students freedom in interacting with the content whenever they want, all the students are still exposed to the exact same information, presented in a single way, at a single pace.

Recent studies indicate that e-learning efficiency can be dramatically improved if personal prerequisites, skills, and individual learning preferences of students are taken into account [9], [28], often referred to as *personalized learning*. "Personalized learning refers to instruction in which the pace of learning and the instructional approach are optimized for the needs of each learner. Learning objectives, instructional approaches, and instructional content (and its sequencing) may all vary based on learner needs. In addition, learning activities are meaningful and relevant to learners, driven by their interests, and often self-initiated." [26].

A step further from personalized education is the adaptive personalized approach that requires both detailed profiling of the student's personal learning preferences, an extraordinary collection and annotation of educational material, and updating the profile based on the annotation of educational materials [8], [14]. The latter is necessary in order to identify educational material best fitting the student's profile. Network science can provide important tools that help to achieve these goals, as we explore in this thesis.

III. On Becoming a System

We envision a network science approach serving as the foundation for real-time personalized adaptive learning. All curated educational content contained within the content management system must be presentable as a network of knowledge. Building upon this foundation, the learning management system must contain an individualized recommender system which matches learning needs (as stored in student profiles) with educational content and presents each learner with a personalized network of knowledge. Lastly, we envision an adaptive learning environment where student profile data and educational content are continuously updated.

IV. Curated Heuristic Using a Network of Knowledge

The proposed CHUNK Learning is a real-time and Adaptive teaching-learning method for enhanced and personalized education. It provides a Curated way of moving through a Network of Knowledge composed of reusable learning objects joined together by common attributes (i.e., tagged with competency or skill levels), rather than following the standard linear or tree-like system of lectures or chapters. CHUNK Learning thus enables the learner to Heuristically discover or learn based on personal background and interests, which we believe will not only enhance the learner's talents, but will make them a more valuable resource. This system is live at [1].

How do we achieve CHUNK Learning? Our learner's interests determine his/her own learning path through the network of knowledge with individualized learning outcomes. Each student benefits differently from the learning experience based on his/her skills and desires. Simultaneously, the network of knowledge builds on the experiences of the students covertly guiding learners through the educational materials, much like Amazon provides recommendations for buyers. We achieve this by moving away from interdisciplinary teaching that transfers methods from one discipline to another, opting instead for a transdisciplinary teaching approach that crosses the boundaries of many disciplines using a diverse choice of teaching tools and software.

V. The Science behind CHUNK learning: A Motivational Framework

In determining how best to create a platform to support both educators and learners, CHUNK Learning focuses on addressing how to positively affect educational engagement as well as stimulate enthusiasm for self-directed life-long learning. Research supports the need for educators to effectively connect with learners by addressing learner motivation. Pink and Brophy identified the importance of providing relevance and utility of content as students are motivated when they understand why they are being asked to learn material [7], [22]. It is paramount that the learning platform focuses on providing learners the answers to "why should I care about this topic." Additionally, adult learners are more likely to engage in learning when topics have intrinsic value and demonstrate importance within the context of their lives [18]. Providing context for "how will I use this knowledge in my life" ensures learners connect the overall purpose and goals of instruction.

Personalized learning software respects the reality that all learners are unique and in order to maintain proper motivation it is necessary to support their different learning styles and timelines. Utilizing key motivational strategies to include a variety of content delivery methods and styles helps ensure learners generate and maintain a positive attitude [29]. Additionally, recognizing even the most motivated learners, self-directed life-long learners, may experience variables that pose challenges to the pursuit of education, it is necessary to employ strategies that promote learners' control over the delivery of short and intense modules. Respecting learners' time and empowering learning-oriented learners to engage in self-directed study establishes an inclusive invitation to education [18].

CHUNK presents learners materials in a variety of formats supporting multiple pedagogies. This orientation emphasizes: the use of multiple mental and pedagogical representations; the promotion of multiple alternative systems of linkage among knowledge elements; the promotion of schema assembly (as opposed to the retrieval of prepackaged schemas); the centrality of "cases of application" as a vehicle for engendering functional conceptual understanding; and the need for participatory learning, tutorial guidance, and adjunct support for aiding the management of complexity. This approach is geared towards an active construction of new knowledge and critical thinking skills, which is especially learning-enhancing for adult learners who bring a large array of previous experiences and knowledge to their educational journey [30]. Similarities in prior experiences or interests among learners can generate new paths of learning in a network-of-knowledge based system, further deviating from the linear path of the traditional education. We envision an array of assessments of the CHUNK-generated learning and experiences, relative to the traditional, linear educational system, with the paramount goal of enhancing learning outcomes and guiding the continuous shaping of the CHUNK Learning environment.

VI. Educational Material as a Network of Knowledge

We believe using a network science approach to represent the educational material facilitates rapid aggregation and delivery of materials to the student. Therefore, we first transfer all educational material into a *network of knowledge*. In his thesis, Cleven defines network of knowledge as:

> *A **network of knowledge** is the representation of educational material as a (multilayer) network, in which educational content builds nodes that are linked by common attributes in several categories, such as content, prerequisites, instructors, level, etc. Each category of attributes links the nodules in one layer, which provides an ability to filter the entire collection of material with different perspectives.* [10]

We establish the network using metadata attached to the educational material. We envision the backbone of the network as a keyword ontology describing relationships between the content the learners frequently access. However, also included would be other relationships such as content authors, prerequisites, media types, and learning methods.

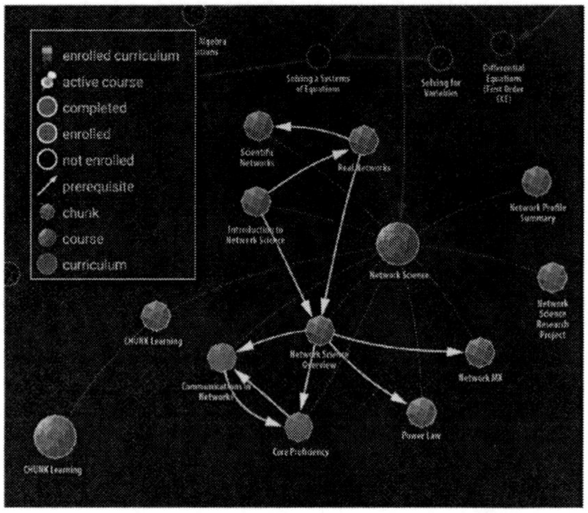

Fig. 1: CHUNK Network of Knowledge.

VII. Why-How-Methodology-Assessment

A baseline template that all CHUNK Learning modules follow in order to provide consistent quality instruction and facilitate learning is an adaptation of Simon's "Why-What-How" [24] format. CHUNK Learning's "Why-How-Methodology-Assessment" format is displayed in Figure 2 and further explained afterwards.

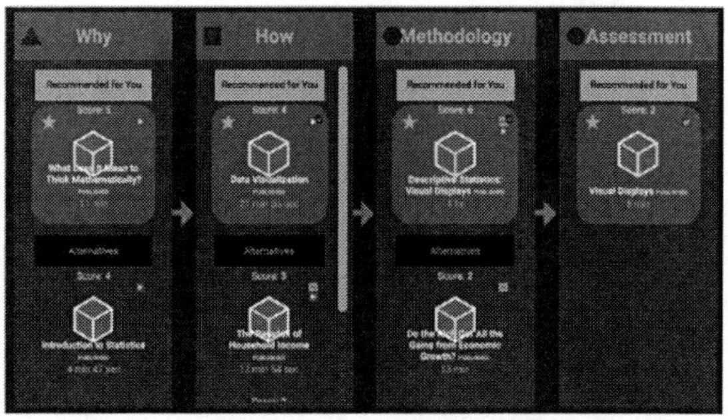

Fig. 2: Why-How-Methodology-Assessment Format.

1) **"Why": Tantalizing the Learner**. Learners open a "Why" CHUNKlet to reveal an enticing one-of-its-kind educational trailer. CHUNK Learning wants to make the student eager to learn, so all CHUNKs begin with a demonstration on **why** learning a particular topic is important. The "why" CHUNLlet demonstrations are

kept short and engaging, and produced in a variety of more informal settings. The 2014 large scale empirical study by Guo, Kim and Rubin found that shorter videos, with enthusiastic speakers, produced in a less formal setting tend to be more impactful for the students' learning experience than more formal, longer videos. [13]. Much like a movie trailer attracts movie-goers to a movie, the "Why" CHUNKlet attracts an exploratory learner to the CHUNK Learning module.

- Why is the topic relevant?
- Why should students learn the topic?

2) **"How": Applications, Real and Relevant** Learners dive into the "How" CHUNKlet to uncover real and relevant applications. Here, students discover the answer to the often-asked question, "When will I ever use this in real life?"
   - How is the topic applied in practice?
   - How does the learner validate what he/she already knows?
   - How are the learning outcomes tested?
   - How is new information, anchored to the learner's interests, incorporated into the module?
   - How can the learner apply the acquired skill/knowledge?
3) **Methodology: A Variety of Delivery Methods** Instructors carefully curate the "Methodology" CHUNKlets, guiding students though a variety of personalized course materials and delivery methods including Massive Open Online Courses (MOOCs) and Creative Commons Licensed resources, as well as instructor-created content. For interactive modules, we envision that instructors will follow the "I do it, We do it, You do it" model.
   - What new information and skills will the module deliver?
   - What activities will the learner be required to perform?
   - What learning outcomes will the learner acquire?
   - What different methodologies could be used to engage with this new knowledge?
4) **Assessment: Competency Based** Learners jump into the "Assessment" CHUNKlet to test knowledge of a topic at any point. Assessments are always available and competency based. Opportunities for remedial learning are always present. Successful completion results in a CHUNK competency credit.
   - Assessment is not personalized, it is rather dictated by a competency based framework designed around learning objectives.

We encourage instructors to complement this basic structure with innovative methods of incorporating information and engaging the learners.

VIII. Individualized System

Due to their various academic and professional backgrounds, learners have unique gaps between current knowledge and required predefined course knowledge standards. Additionally, individuals have different skills, preferred learning modes, and motivation to learn. This challenges educators to expand the one size fits all education method to effectively engage with learners. CHUNK learning provides an interactive learning system that is able to identify unique gaps and then fills those gaps ensuring the same knowledge outcomes are met based on student's uniqueness, such as:

- Preference (topic based for example: social networks, vs brain networks, vs Internet)
- Skills (Fortran, C, C++, Python, R, JMP, Matlab, Excel)
- Education (GED, A.A., A.S., B.A., B.S., M.A., M.S., Ph.D)
- Training (untrained, trained, need practice, refresher)

In CHUNK learning, an author builds the necessary CHUNKs within a course to ensure all learning objectives are met at completion of all course assessments. These CHUNKs are presented to each learner based on the learner profile and the course he/she enrolled in. The CHUNK Learning system provides a pre-test capability by allowing learners to validate an individual CHUNKs by demonstrating competency while bypassing the "why," "how," and "methodology" CHUNKlets, and only completing the "assessment" CHUNKlet. Learners then engage with remaining CHUNKs to satisfy the required learning objectives of he course. The result is an interactive system that identifies and satisfies unique gaps of individual learners.

IX. Personalized System

CHUNK Learning does more than provide a platform for educators to individualize instruction for learners, it allows users to take control of their learning. A recommender system incorporates information from the learner profile:

- Occupational Specialty and Professional Experience
- Learning Methods (exercises, lectures, videos, etc)
- Goals (reinforce something learner knows, expand knowledge, get the gist)
- Interest (depth, breadth, familiarity, practice, gist).

allowing the system to deliver engaging content tailored to users' learning preferences and relevant to their specific interests and realities of their daily lives and futures.

By providing a network-based system CHUNK Learning is able to facilitate an education environment where learners are responsible for their own self-directed learning. Learners' curiosity is ignited as they peruse a wide range of topics, see the connections between them, and determine areas to engage in deep study, utilizing assessments to meet their own learning goals.

X. Conclusions and Further Directions

Traditional education places all the students through the same topics, at the same time, at the same speed, generally teaching to the average student. But such a system leaves some students behind, and fails to challenge others. Traditional education also produces fairly similar skilled graduates, not enhancing the different skills, abilities, and interests learners might have. Unlike most established sciences, new research fields such as Network Science – an emerging field overseeing traditional computer science, operations research, sociology, and other fields – hint at non-traditional methods of education that serve as a starting point for the current proposal.

A personalized, adaptive learning platform. CHUNK Learning breaks away from the predictable pattern of traditional education models and provides content delivery that respects the different capabilities, learning styles, and approaches to problem-solving of every learner. Students are empowered by a system that ensures learning is efficient, flexible, and respectful of their time. Intense and short educational modules broken into smaller bits of information Stimulates interest and applicability of topics through the use of "Why learn" information Integrates new information to learner's pre-existing knowledge through a "How do professionals in your field use this" demonstration that is personalized to each learner's background providing valuable context on how learners can use that knowledge in their fields of expertise Personalized education based on learner's best learning style (both at the instructor level and at topic-to-learn level) Adaptive content and methodology delivery that is optimized for each learner

We thus provide an exploratory environment that promotes curiosity and creativity, collaboration and collegiality as we search for meaningful ways to bring together and curate knowledge for generations to come. This vision also demonstrates the art of possibility in teaching and learning leading to new partnerships with industry, government, and academia to support education. It shows the educator's commitment to providing the best in education that speaks to each learner.

ACKNOWLEDGMENTS

The authors thank the DoD for partially sponsoring the current research.

REFERENCES

[1] Chunk learning. https://www.chunklearning.net. Accessed: 2018-03-16.

[2] e-classroom: The future of education. https://edtechnyc.org/e-classroom-the-future-of-education/. Accessed: 2018-03-16.

[3] Technology trends driving the future of higher education. https://www.youtube.com/watch?v=8FlgXB0eeq4. Accessed: 2018-03-16.

[4] Beverly Abbey. Instructional and cognitive impacts of web-based education. IGI Global, 1999.

[5] Réka Albert, Hawoong Jeong, and Albert-László Barabási. Internet: Diameter of the world-wide web. nature, 401(6749):130, 1999.

[6] Lori Breslow, David E Pritchard, Jennifer DeBoer, Glenda S Stump, Andrew D Ho, and Daniel T Seaton. Studying learning in the worldwide classroom research into edx's first mooc. Research & Practice in Assessment, 8:13–25, 2013.

[7] Jere E Brophy. Teaching. International Academy of Education and the International Bureau of Education, 1999.

[8] Peter Brusilovsky, John Eklund, and Elmar Schwarz. Web-based education for all: a tool for development adaptive courseware. Computer networks and ISDN systems, 30(1-7):291–300, 1998.

[9] Peter Brusilovsky and Christoph Peylo. Adaptive and intelligent web-based educational systems. International Journal of Artificial Intelligence in Education (IJAIED), 13:159–172, 2003.

[10] Jan-Daniel Cleven. A multilayer network approach for real-time adaptive personalized learning, 2018.

[11] Michalis Faloutsos, Petros Faloutsos, and Christos Faloutsos. On power-law relationships of the internet topology. In ACM SIGCOMM computer communication review, volume 29, pages 251–262. ACM, 1999.

[12] Alan Feldman, Cliff Konold, Bob Coulter, and Brian Conroy. Network science, a decade later: The Internet and classroom learning. Routledge, 2000.

[13] Philip J Guo, Juho Kim, and Rob Rubin. How video production affects student engagement: An empirical study of mooc videos. In Proceedings of the first ACM conference on Learning@ scale conference, pages 41–50. ACM, 2014.

[14] Peter A Henning, Florian Heberle, Alexander Streicher, Andrea Zielinski, Christian Swertz, Jürgen Bock, Stefan Zander, et al. Personalized web learning: Merging open educational resources into adaptive courses for higher education. Personalization Approaches in Learning Environments, 55, 2014.

[15] Lilian H Hill. Concept mapping to encourage meaningful student learning. Adult Learning, 16(3-4):7–13, 2005.

[16] DIAO Lin-lin. A survey of chinese english majors' chunk competence [j]. Journal of Pla University of Foreign Languages, 4, 2004.

[17] Colin McCormack and David Jones. Building a web-based education system. John Wiley & Sons, Inc., 1997.

[18] S Merriam. The changing landscape of adult learning theory in comings j, garner b and smith c eds review of adult learning and literacy: connecting research, policy, and practice, 2004.

[19] George A Miller. The magical number seven, plus or minus two: Some limits on our capacity for processing information. Psychological review, 63(2):81, 1956.

[20] Rivka Oxman. Think-maps: teaching design thinking in design education. Design studies, 25(1):63–91, 2004.

[21] Laura Pappano. The year of the mooc. The New York

Times, 2(12):2012, 2012.

[22] Daniel H Pink. Drive: The surprising truth about what motivates us. Penguin, 2011.

[23] José A Ruipérez-Valiente, Pedro J Muñoz-Merino, Derick Leony, and Carlos Delgado Kloos. Alas-ka: A learning analytics extension for better understanding the learning process in the khan academy platform. Computers in Human Behavior, 47:139–148, 2015.

[24] Simon Sinek. Ted talk: How great leaders inspire action. https://www.ted.com/talks/simon_sinek_how_great_leaders_inspire_action. Accessed: 2018-03-16.

[25] Clive Thompson. How khan academy is changing the rules of education. Wired Magazine, 126:1–5, 2011.

[26] U.S. Department of Education. National Education Technology Plan. https://tech.ed.gov/netp/, January 2017.

[27] Daisy Wadhwa. Using artificial intelligence technologies for personalized learning and responsive teaching: A survey (2017).

[28] Daniel S Weld, Eytan Adar, Lydia Chilton, Raphael Hoffmann, Eric Horvitz, Mitchell Koch, James Landay, Christopher H Lin, and Mausam Mausam. Personalized online education—a crowdsourcing challenge. In Workshops at the Twenty-Sixth AAAI Conference on Artificial Intelligence, 2012.

[29] Raymond J Wlodkowski. Enhancing adult motivation to learn: A comprehensive guide for teaching all adults (rev. ed.). San Francisco: Jossey-Basss, 1999.

[30] Susan M Yelich Biniecki and Simone CO Conceição. Using concept maps to engage adult learners in critical analysis. Adult Learning, 27(2):51–59, 2016.

[31] Chi ZHANG, Gang CHEN, Minjuan WANG, and Huimin WANG. Studying on design of small-chunk learning resources in mobile learning [j]. Open Education Research, 3, 2009.

Adaptive Personalized Network Relationships in the CHUNK Learning Environment

Mario Andriulli, Maria Smith, and Shane Smith

Department of Applied Mathematics,
Naval Postgraduate School,
Monterey, CA

Raluca Gera

Department of Applied Mathematics,
Associate Provost for Graduate Education,
Teaching and Learning Commons,
Naval Postgraduate School, Monterey, CA
Email: rgera@nps.edu

Michelle L. Isenhour

Department of Operations Research,
Naval Postgraduate School,
Monterey, CA
Email: mlisenho@nps.edu

***Abstract*—How can learner profiles support personalized online learning? Our current research analyzes a personalized adaptive system for education called CHUNK Learning. The CHUNK Learning system builds on a network of modules, and a learner profile, both tagged with keywords. CHUNK Learning currently utilizes simple keyword relationships to suggest a tailored, personalized, adaptive learning plan guiding the learner through the network of modules. However, supervised machine learning methods may be more suitable to enable the implementation of an iterative algorithm for refined learning plans. In this paper, we investigate the relationship between learner profile and adaptive learning plans. Learners first create a profile in CHUNK Learning which establishes their baseline learning plan. Then, as learners begin to interact with the learning environment, the CHUNK Learning system updates the learning plan based on learner activities (learned, viewed, tested), keyword searches, and content ratings by increasing or reducing the strength of the connection between the learner profile and activities. Additionally, we demonstrate that by connecting all learners within an academic program, we create a stronger bond between learners, which results in a reduced path between activities. We conclude that by reducing the path length between activities, we strengthen connections in the CHUNK Learning environment resulting in a more concise academic plan for learners.**

Keywords*—*education; adaptive learning; learning systems; network theory (graphs); adaptive algorithms.

I. Introduction and Motivation

Institutions design current educational experiences in a manner which presents learning material to students through a very formal and rigid structure. This structure forces all students, regardless of personal academic backgrounds or capabilities, through an academic pipeline where they must complete topics in a sequential order to move forward to the next topic. At the Naval Postgraduate School in Monterey, California, USA, a web-based software application known as CHUNK Learning explores potential methods to relieve some of the rigor of this standard academic environment [1].

The Curated Heuristic Using a Network of Knowledge for Continuum of Learning (CHUNK Learning) environment is an educational platform that draws information from a learner profile to recommend a tailored educational experience for them [1]. The CHUNK Learning environment (Fig. 1) consists of courses, CHUNKs, CHUNKlets, and activities. Courses are generally added by instructors and typically align with a course offered in the academic curriculum. A CHUNK is a topic within a course, equivalent to a section in a textbook. A CHUNK is divided into smaller pieces called CHUNKlets. CHUNKlets are recommended experiences to maximize learning comprehension for each learner, within a particular CHUNK. Finally, activities are the base level of interaction within the CHUNKlets. Activities are the final link to videos, PowerPoint presentations, and other media which may be accessed by the learner. Throughout the paper, "user" and "learner" are used interchangeably.

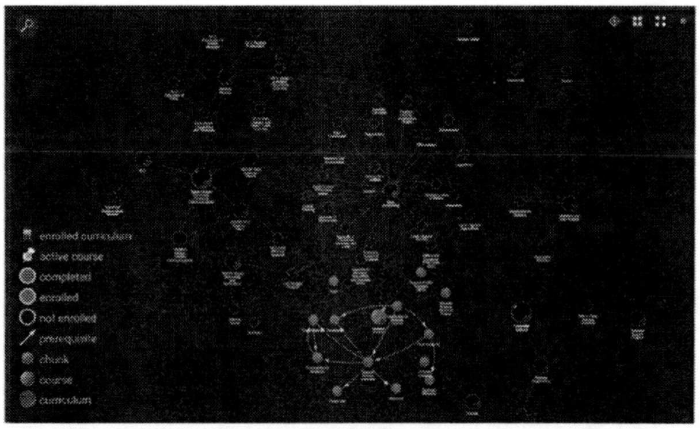

Fig. 1. A Snapshot of the CHUNK Learning Environment.

We desire to implement a web-based program which recommends educational experiences to learners. Our motivation in conducting this research is to analyze links within the learner profile to develop an adaptive network that recommends activities to the learners based on their recent keyword searches, content ratings, and common connections between them. The desired end state is to have refined algorithms in the CHUNK Learning environment to provide recommendations similar to methods currently used in industry. For example, if someone conducts a search engine inquiry regarding a potential product purchase, then commercial services like Amazon will take that information and return not only suggestions for that product, but also additional items which are closely related to the original search [2]. This method has been proven to generate additional revenue in sales, and in our research we would apply the same concept to translate commercial potential into increased academic potential.

To develop the relationship between learners and activities, CHUNK Learning analyzes learner profiles and links activities with the learner based on a simplistic count of keyword matches. Profile information includes information such as military branch of service, course enrollments, prior education, and experience. To conduct our research, we develop a network model linking learners to activities using adaptive keyword weighting based on CHUNK Learning use (viewed, tested, liked) data. As the CHUNK Learning environment does not currently contain this network model, we compare the network relationships for the initial static profile and an adaptive profile to determine overall impacts on the learner's educational experience.

We organize the remainder of this paper as follows. Section II provides an overview of related work. We then establish the definition of our network model and introduce the methodology for comparing and contrasting the existing CHUNK Learning structure to a novel one in Section III. In Section IV, we present the experimental setup, followed by the results and interpretation in Section V. Finally, we conclude and present recommendations for future research in Section VI.

II. Related Work

Existing recent approaches to a personalized adaptive learning methodology include research using web-based services [3]–[6], personalized learning models [7]–[9], the creation of e-learning environments combined with web-based services [10]–[12] and the creation of user interfaces based on user behavior episode identification [13]–[16]. While all methodologies have benefits and limitations, we narrow our focus towards the creation of a user interface based on episode identification, analysis of user feedback, and the creation of an adaptive learner profile.

Prior CHUNK Learning research at the Naval Postgraduate School by MAJ Jan-Daniel Cleven (German Army) introduces a multi-layer network model relating classes to learners through interests [17]. The nodes represent classes and learners in the Operations Research curriculum and the edges represent keyword relationships between the classes and learners. This model incorporates learner feedback by weighting the connection between the nodes. Course syllabi are filtered by metadata tagging to extract the top ten relevant keywords for each course offered, assigned to the nodes. The system uses weighted feedback to provide recommendations for the learner's future coursework. This feedback diminishes the presence of unfavorable courses and brings preferred courses to the top of the recommended list. We are particularly interested in the feedback component of this research and its inclusion in our experiment as a feedback methodology.

Previous research on adaptive user interfaces is of particular interest to our area of study. The approach taken by Jiming Liu, Chi Kuen Wong, and Ka Keung [16] is a design that reacts to different situations and requirements, then records user's behavior. Their approach is based on Episodes Identification and Association (EIA), which recognizes the learner's patterns by tracing the learner's action sequences. The episodes can be thought of as a record of learner behavior used to predict the best educational experience. One of the limitations of this approach is the possibility of losing data due to limitations in the types of recorded events. For example, a user could initiate typing in a search bar, but then select an auto-generated recommendation without recording that search in the action sequence. The goal of their interface is to help learners according to adaptive learning plans. The authors recognized the need to develop learner profiles to enable personalized interactions. Their approach discovers rules that can best describe and predict learner's behavior by finding frequently occurring episodes in the learner's action sequences. They distinguish two types of interface events: text input events and mouse click events. We believe that focusing on both text input events and mouse click events to update an adaptive keyword list will be valuable to improving our network model of an adaptive educational environment.

Another existing approach to personalized learning published by KK Thyagharajan and Ratnamanjar Nayak [5] involves implementing a web-service to ensure the residual validity of learning content. The authors use dynamic methods based on the learner's needs and preferences to fulfill learning objectives. Systems such as Intelligent Tutoring Systems (ITS) [13] and Adaptive Hypermedia (AH) [11] are also possible solutions to personalize the learning experience for the student. Such systems may tailor the educational offerings to the learner's objectives, prior knowledge, learning style, experience, and many other characteristics. The downfall is that these existing systems remain criticized for believing that the embedding of expert knowledge is sufficient for efficient learning to occur. Although beneficial, our model does not include this approach. We do, however, recommend it for consideration in future research.

In our study, we focus on an adaptive network science methodology to propose an improved learner experience in the CHUNK Learning environment. The aim is to improve the educational experience recommendations to the learner through a dynamic profile. The adaptive network studies the effect of a learner feedback loop as well as learner profile updates based on his/her behavior in the CHUNK Learning environment, similar to the study completed by Liu, Wong and Keung [16]. Additionally, we focus on connecting learners based on academic curricula to determine effects to the individual learner in the educational environment.

III. Network Model & Methodology

In this research, we develop a network model for an adaptive, personalized educational environment for CHUNK Learning tailored to enhance each student's educational experience. Our network model includes two elements: nodes and edges. The nodes are learner profiles and activities, while the edges are tuples consisting of keywords from a learner's profile that link him/her to an activity.

Our methodology focuses on comparing and contrasting the existing structure of user-to-activity connections based on static keywords within CHUNK Learning, to a more dynamic structure that updates a keyword list within a learner profile based on his/her CHUNK Learning use. In the existing structure, the learner's profile has a static and adaptive component. The static profile consists of keywords derived from initial data input when each learner establishes his/her initial profile. The keyword tuples in the static profile do not change, unless the learner manually edits the profile. In contrast, the learner's adaptive profile consists of a profile where the keyword tuples dynamically update by capturing data from learner's use of the CHUNK Learning environment. We focus on one adaptive category, activities, which are one level below a CHUNKlet in the CHUNK Learning network, to determine the effectiveness of the keyword relationships. This dynamic network process can be iterated multiple times to further refine the keyword relationships.

The baseline methodology uses the existing structure of the CHUNK Learning curriculum. That is, the nodes in the network are learners and activities. The edges in this network connect learners to activities through keyword matches found in the learner's initial profile. Based on a weighted sum of keywords, the learning system presents the learner with activities that match keywords from their profile. In order to model this network, we develop a small sample of five learner profiles generated with pseudo-random keywords from the available keywords list. We then use this information to generate a network model for the initial static network.

We then modify the simulated learner profiles in such a way as to replicate the effects that an adaptive, personalized education environment may have on a learner. We apply this adaptive concept to generate our second network model, taking into account the new adaptive profile data. The nodes still represent the learners and the activities, and the edges are still the keywords linking the learners to an activity, but now the methodology focuses on an adaptive profile approach. The combination of the initial static profile with randomly updated keyword relationships generates the new adaptive network. Using this method, we expect that edges between activities and learners will evolve based on the learners perceived quality of the available activities. Some activities may become disconnected as lower valued edges diminish, while other activities may gain relevance as they accumulate stronger connections.

In addition to an adaptive learner profile based on keyword updates, we update the adaptive network to include additional edges that connect learners with similar academic curricula in order to analyze the effectiveness of connecting learners sharing similar characteristics within their profiles. These relationships form a completely connected sub-network between learners with similar academic backgrounds. This sub-network shows learners with similar academic curricula having a shared relationship with activities which are prevalent in their academic field. These improved relationships reduce the distance between the learner and content that is relevant to their peers, and additionally, they can be used to pre-compile future learner profiles as new learners begin using the CHUNK Learning system.

Lastly, we analyze the effects that a feedback loop could have on the personalized learning environment. Utilizing the adaptive network model that we create, we use an average learner rating to determine whether or not an activity should be available within the learner environment. We expect our simulation to show the effects of feedback, such as learner activity rating, on the learner's experiences within CHUNK Learning.

Our methodology of comparing and contrasting the effects of two different learning experiences should offer us valuable information on the type of educational environment that is more beneficial to a user.

IV. Experimental Set Up

In order to set up our experiment, we first analyze existing CHUNK Learning data to find data that links learners to activities through keywords. The initial set of keyword relationships from the current database resulted in more than 4200 potential relationships for sources and targets. In order to see the effects on the individual learner, we pare down this available data to create five virtual learner profiles. The decision to create only five learner profiles provides us with a potential advantage. Five is a small number, but still significant in our case, allowing us to visually see changes that we would expect to happen given a larger pool of profiles. We use the sources and targets to generate and investigate a directed network in both R-project [18] and Gephi [19].

We model the five virtual learners with a list of keywords and activities for both the static and adaptive networks. The learners are the same for each network. Only the list of keywords change in the adaptive version. In our static network model, each learner begins with between three to five randomly selected activities each with between one to five keywords for a total of seven to ten total entries. Multiple keywords matching to the same activity provides an integer value for weighted edges.

In order to set up our adaptive profile network simulation, we set some parameters. First, we limit a learner's keyword list to their top eight keywords. Our goal is to strengthen learner connections to activities without creating a network overpopulated with activities due to a long list of keywords.

Also, a long list of keywords could potentially provide too many recommendations to a learner, therefore lessening the benefit of a personalized learning environment. Although the number of keywords is adjustable, we maintain the keyword list to a maximum of eight for our simulation. Another defining parameter is that a learner's established connection to activities is through a minimum of two keywords. The purpose of this parameter is to, once again, strengthen the link between learners and activities. In the static version of the network, these parameters do not exist. There are some edges of weight one, linking a learner to activities by one keyword such as "video". However, the keyword "video", provides no information as to the content most relevant to the learner. Therefore, in order to improve the learner experience, we implement the minimum of two keywords to link a learner to an activity. We update the learner keywords at random to simulate word searches related to their academic activities. We update all learners similarly, each gaining one new keyword. If the learner's keyword list exceeds eight, the simulation removes a keyword from the list at random until the learner profile reaches the number eight. We do not provide a ranking for keywords in our simulation.

We run this experiment in both Gephi and R in order to provide multiple visualizations. As no network visualization is the same, we analyze different things about our two networks by looking at them from different perspectives. We believe that analysis from multiple viewpoints is valuable to this experiment.

After running our initial experiment, we continue working with the adaptive network. The first experiment we conduct connects learners based on their academic curriculum in the adaptive network. Of our five learners, we select two different academic curricula. We assign two learners to the "math" curriculum and two learners to the "operations research" curriculum. We then assign one learner to two curricula as a "double major," in both "math" and "operations research". The experiment connecting learners allows us to analyze a path to an activity that does not exist without the learner-to-learner connection. In addition to path length, the learner connection allows us to analyze the impact of certain learners on the centrality of the overall network.

The last evaluation conducted for this experiment is a feedback simulation. Although we do not create a feedback loop, we want to see possible effects of learner ratings on activities. Therefore, we set a minimum average activity rating within the system. For an activity to be available to a learner, the minimum rating is three. However, sensitivity can be modified to change the weight of feedback at any time. We randomly assign activity ratings to each activity. If an activity has an average rating of less than three, it does not populate the network simulation. We use the results of this simulation to analyze the impacts and effectiveness of a feedback loop in an adaptive, personalized learning environment.

After completing the simulations of our network experiment, we compare and contrast the initial static profile model against the adaptive profile model, without learner connections. Each simulation provides us unique and different information regarding edge weights, number of nodes, number of edges, average out degree, path length, and centralities. We then use this information to analyze our network.

V. Results and Analysis

After completing our experiment by running simulations of our static and adaptive networks in R and Gephi, we review and analyze our results. Our results focus on structural elements, specifically path lengths, path diameters, and network centralities, as well as how suitable a node is for spreading information.

A. *Graph Composition*

The following figures and tables include the results from the incremental changes in our CHUNK Learning environment simulations. Fig. 2 and Table I demonstrate the results from the baseline, static network which models the existing methods of the CHUNK Learning system.

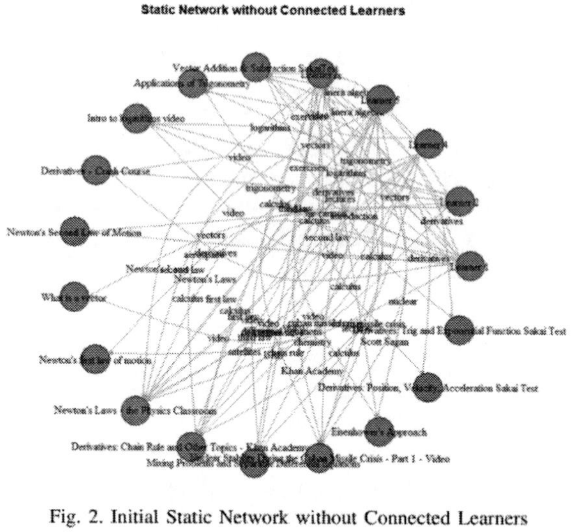

Fig. 2. Initial Static Network without Connected Learners

TABLE I. Static Network Results.

Number of Vertices	19
Number of Edges	59
Average Path Length	3.321
Diameter Length	6

In Fig. 3, learners are connected to activities through a list of keywords and to each other. This model is our baseline, which we use to compare to the adaptive network model simulations. As can be seen in Table II, connecting the learners reduces the average path length between learners and activities immediately.

Fig. 4 is our adaptive profile network simulation. This network shows what would happen if each of our five

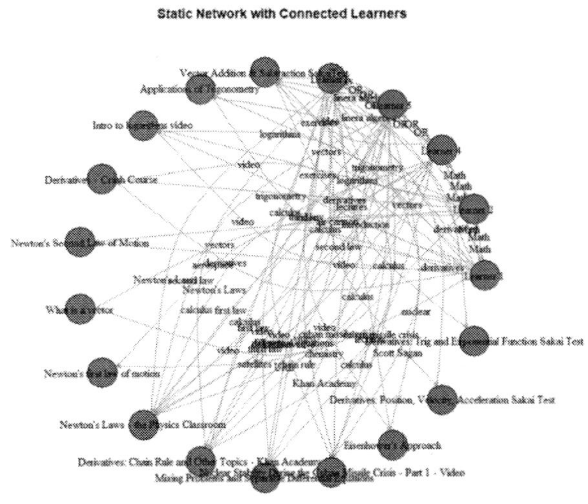

Fig. 3. Initial Static Network with Connected Learners

TABLE II. STATIC NETWORK RESULTS - CONNECTED LEARNERS.

Number of Vertices	19
Number of Edges	71
Average Path Length	2.397
Diameter Length	4

simulated Learners had their keyword lists updated with one new keyword, their keyword lists restricted to eight keywords, and a minimum of two keywords required to link a learner to an activity. Through this change in the simulation, the updated keyword list generated new edges, linking learners to new activities with the addition of one new keyword (Table III). As expected, these new connections increased the total number of nodes in the network. The number of learners did not change, but new activities populated based on their updated keyword lists. We found it valuable to determine if the average out-degree of a learner changed when comparing the static profile to the adaptive profile network. The average out-degree increased by two in the adaptive model. We expected this result as we added the requirement for a minimum of two keywords to connect a learner to an activity. These results tell us that the small changes made have enhanced the educational experience for the learner. The more edges linking a learner to an activity strengthens the learner's experience in this educational environment.

TABLE III. ADAPTIVE NETWORK RESULTS.

Number of Vertices	24
Number of Edges	67
Average Path Length	4.06
Diameter Length	8

Fig. 5 depicts the simulation which connects learners to each other through academic disciplines such as "Mathematics" and "Operations Research." This simulation increased the number of edges in the overall network, and we analyze this a bit further by focusing on path lengths. Fig. 6 and

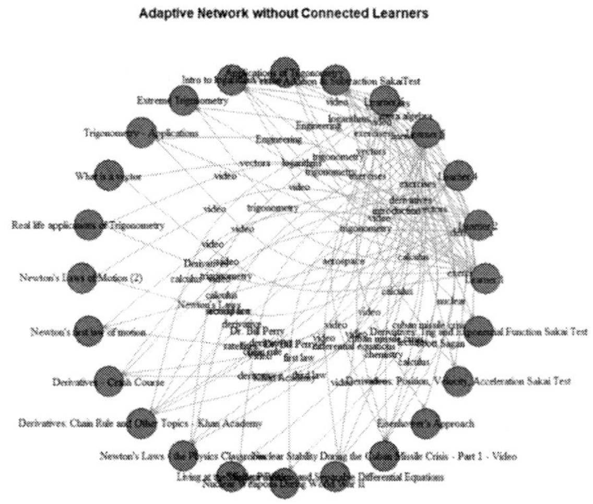

Fig. 4. Adaptive Network without Connected Learners.

Fig. 7 present the results of this analysis and next we discuss the conclusions drawn from our analysis in more detail.

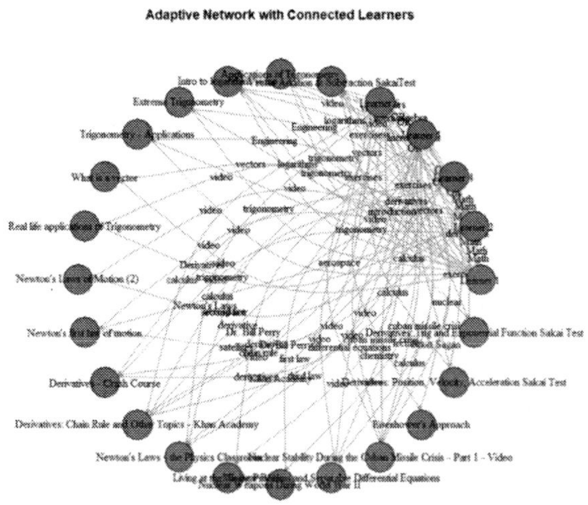

Fig. 5. Adaptive Network with Connected Learners.

TABLE IV. ADAPTIVE NETWORK RESULTS - CONNECTED LEARNERS.

Number of Vertices	24
Number of Edges	79
Average Path Length	2.452
Diameter Length	4

Fig. 6 again shows us the adaptive network without connected learners. This time we highlight the path a user would have to take to arrive at a non-recommended activity. In order for Learner 6 to get to the highlighted course not recommended to him/her, he/she would have a path of length three to get to that course. After reviewing these results, we predict that this path would shorten if we connected learners.

Fig. 7 depicts an alternate view of the adaptive profile network with connected learners. We connect the learners

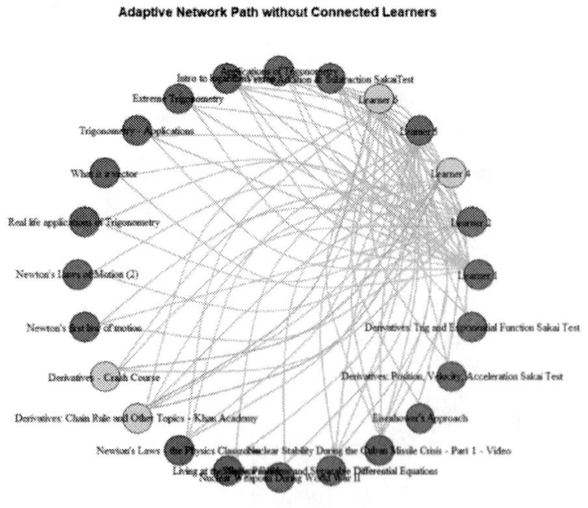

Fig. 6. Adaptive Network Path Showing Disconnected Learners.

through academic disciplines such as mathematics and operations research. What we find is that the minimum path Learner 6 requires to get to the same highlighted course as in Fig. 6, shortens due to the inter-learner connectivity. Therefore, we find it valuable to the educational environment to connect learners with similar qualities. This connection makes activities available to the learner even though they may not have in their profile keywords related to such activities.

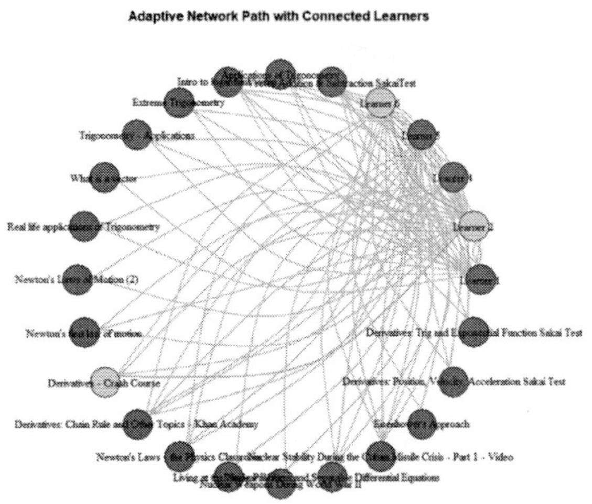

Fig. 7. Adaptive Network Path Showing Connected Learners.

This concept is similar to what Amazon.com users see when shopping on Amazon's App or website. After a user purchases item "W", Amazon connects users who brought item "W" then shows additional items through a section called "Customers who bought item "W" also bought "Y", "X", and "Z"." The adaptive concept offers predictive options given past user behavior. In the CHUNK Learning environment, students may see Learners who completed activity "A" also completed activity "B".

The final incremental change we make to our CHUNK Learning environment network simulation includes analyzing the effects of feedback. We perform this analysis through a simulated activity rating. We randomly assign average ratings to each activity. If the rating is less than three, the activity becomes no longer available in the learner's educational environment.

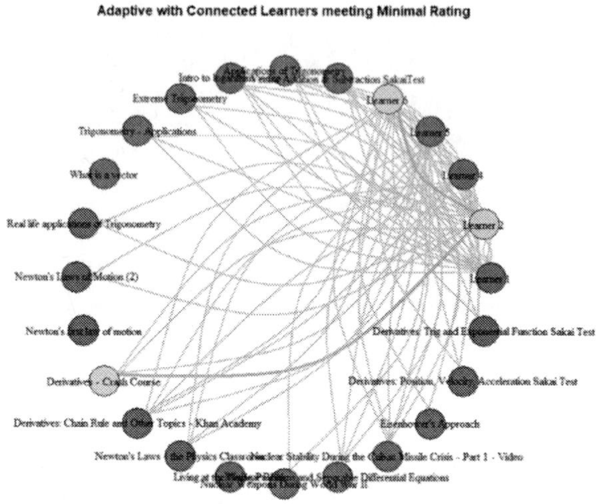

Fig. 8. Path Connecting Learners to Activities Meeting Minimal Ratings.

Fig. 8 is an example of the network with the same path length as found in Fig. 7. As shown in Fig. 8, however, activities with average learner feedback of less than three are no longer present. Since the path from Learner 2 to "Derivatives–Crash Course" meets the required minimum rating value, the connection holds. We find this simulation valuable as feedback provides the CHUNK Learning environment with the ability to continually monitor and update its content to provide the best educational environment for individual learners, concluding that a feedback loop, in the form of average activity rating, enhances a learner's educational experience in the CHUNK Learning environment.

In Fig. 8, three activities fail to meet the rating threshold. As a result, the adaptive simulation disconnects the activity from the network but does not delete the activity from the CHUNK Learning environment. Activities may continue to hold educational value after review and remain within the system. Disconnecting activities from the network inside the CHUNK Learning environment may signal the activity needs maintenance due to a faulty hyperlink, or the delivery of the material fails to resonate with learners. In other words, the activity may be "boring" or the instructor "uninteresting" and the activity should be revamped. Moreover, merely deleting the activity would prevent the analysis of trends for poorly rated content and inhibit overall CHUNK Learning environment improvement and growth.

This concept is similar to Amazon's product review. In the CHUNK Learning environment, learners provide direct feedback for each activity. Amazon rarely offers its shoppers poorly rated products. In turn, CHUNK Learning users would only see exceptional-to-average rated learning activities.

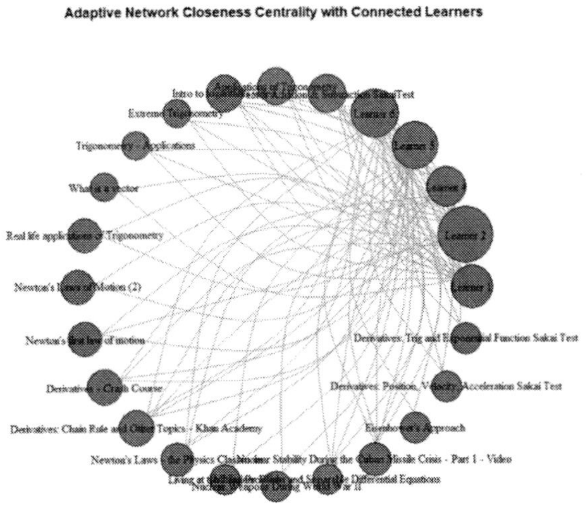

Fig. 9. Normalized Closeness Centrality Network with Unconnected Learner.

B. Network Centralities

Lastly, after running all of our simulations, we find it valuable to analyze centralities on our network. The closeness centrality and eigenvector centrality help measure the effectiveness of node information dissemination. By examining centralities, different node characteristics come into play. These node characteristics are essential when determining how to improve the CHUNK Learning experience.

The network simulations shown in Fig. 9 and Fig. 10 depict the closeness centrality of the adaptive graph without and with learner connections, respectively. While differences exist, the differences yield no significant results which can drastically improve the CHUNK Learning environment.

Fig. 11 depicts the eigenvector centrality of the adaptive network, while Fig. 12 shows the eigenvector centrality of the adaptive network with connected Learners. As expected, Fig. 12 is more densely connected. Our findings indicate that the learner connected adaptive network has advantages over the unconnected network.

Significant to the eigenvector centralities is the shuffle of Learner eigenvalues rankings once learners were connected within the network. The learners' eigenvalues are ranked in Table V.

TABLE V. LEARNER EIGENVALUES.

Unconnected Learner Eigenvalues		Connected Learner Eigenvalues	
Learner 1	1.0000	Learner 2	1.0000
Learner 2	0.7540	Learner 1	0.8370
Learner 4	0.4003	Learner 4	0.6612
Learner 6	0.2206	Learner 5	0.6347
Learner 5	0.1831	Learner 6	0.6249

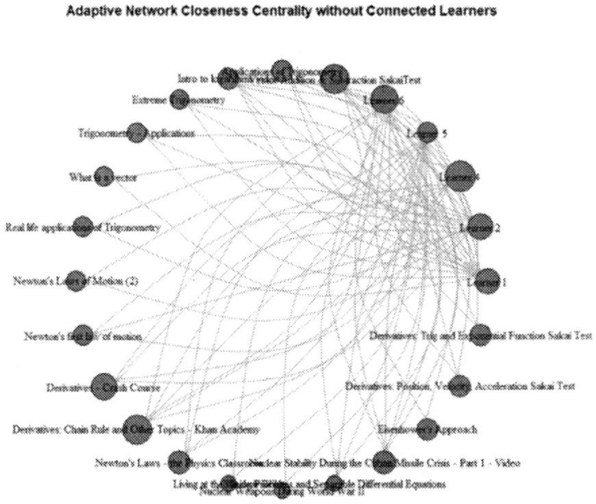

Fig. 10. Normalized Closeness Centrality Network with Connected Learners.

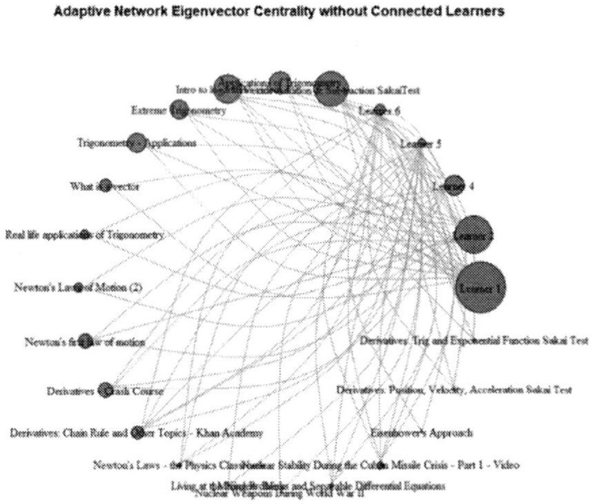

Fig. 11. Scaled Eigenvector Centrality Network with Unconnected Learner.

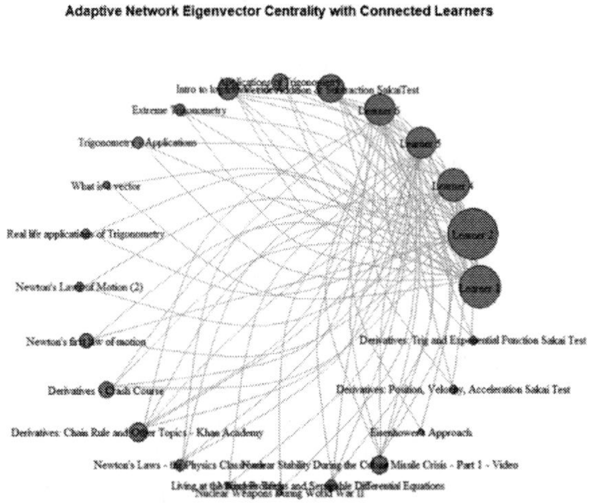

Fig. 12. Scaled Eigenvector Centrality Network with connected Learners.

Eigenvector centrality measures the impact that neighboring nodes have on one another. There are three significant results when comparing unconnected learners to connected learners using eigenvector centralities. First, all but one of the eigenvalues increase, meaning connecting learners results in a significant impact from the weight of the neighboring learner and activity. Second, the re-ranking of eigenvalues showing a learner's individual network connections is imperative during analysis. Learners who connect to other active Learners connect to more information. Moreover, and lastly, by design Learner 2 is a "double major" in Mathematics and Operations Research. Between Learner 2's connected activities and it's neighbors connected activities, Learner 2 is only a maximum of three moves away from any Mathematical or Operational Research activity in the simulated CHUNK Learning environment. This "double major" concept could be applied to a variety of adaptive network characteristics such as learner personal interest, undergraduate degree information, or favorite instructional video.

VI. Conclusions and Future Directions

After reviewing and analyzing the results of the network simulations, we believe more work can be done to enhance the personalized educational experience in the CHUNK Learning environment. Limitations to our experiment were scaling and iterating. We based our analysis on a small sample of randomly simulated learners. To further improve results and provide additional justification for a personalized learning environment, experiments should focus on a much larger scale with real data. Iterating the process over time would also show the effects on learning in the educational environment. Knowing these limitations led to a list of recommendations for future work.

First, feedback is essential to an adaptive, personalized learning environment. A learner rating from one to five could provide a measurable weight to the adaptive list of keywords in a learner's profile. Although a learner may search a particular keyword or use a specific activity, it is possible they may not have an interest in that topic. Therefore, the feedback loop would be a valuable tool to keep the keyword list weighted and updated based on learner ratings.

In addition to a learner activity rating, another area for future work would be to implement statistics in the form of a dashboard within a learner profile. This dashboard will allow the learner to see the derivation of recommendations for certain activities as well as the progress they are making on completing their academic goals.

While we found that connecting learners can be valuable by providing a shortened path to an activity, in the future, it would be useful to analyze the possibility of learner's sharing keywords through their connections. This sharing of information can provide a direct path from a learner to activities through a shared keyword or keywords.

While there is still much work to be done, the results of small scale simulations in an adaptive, personalized educational environment provide valuable insight. An adaptive network within the CHUNK Learning environment would enhance the learner's educational experience by recommending activities most relevant and exciting to the user.

Acknowledgments

The authors would like to thank the U.S. Department of Defense for partially funding this work.

References

[1] R. Gera, M. Isenhour, D. Bartolf, and S. Tick, "CHUNK:Curated Heuristic Using a Network of Knowledge," in The Fifth International Conference on Human and Social Analytics. HUSO, July 2019.

[2] B. Smith and G. Linden, "Two decades of recommender systems at Amazon.com," IEEE Internet Computing, vol. 21, no. 3, pp. 12–18, May 2017.

[3] A. Grewal, S. Rai, R. Phillips, and C. C. Fung, "The e-learning lifecycle and its services: the web services approach," in Second International Conference on e Learning for Knowledge-Based Society, August 2005, pp. 4–1.

[4] M. Šimko, M. Barla, and M. Bieliková, "ALEF: A framework for adaptive web-based learning 2.0," in IFIP International Conference on Key Competencies in the Knowledge Society. Springer, 2010, pp. 367–378.

[5] K. Thyagharajan and R. Nayak, "Adaptive content creation for personalized e-learning using web services," Journal of Applied Sciences Research, vol. 3, no. 9, pp. 828–836, 2007.

[6] Z. Xu, Z. Yin, and A. E. Saddik, "A web services oriented framework for dynamic e-learning systems," in CCECE 2003-Canadian Conference on Electrical and Computer Engineering. Toward a Caring and Humane Technology (Cat. No. 03CH37436), vol. 2. IEEE, 2003, pp. 943–946.

[7] C.-M. Chen, "Intelligent web-based learning system with personalized learning path guidance," Computers & Education, vol. 51, no. 2, pp. 787–814, 2008.

[8] T. Vengattarman and P. Dhavachelvan, "An agent-based personalized e-learning environment: Effort prediction perspective," in 2009 International Conference on Intelligent Agent & Multi-Agent Systems. IEEE, 2009, pp. 1–6.

[9] T.-C. Yang, G.-J. Hwang, and S. J.-H. Yang, "Development of an adaptive learning system with multiple perspectives based on students' learning styles and cognitive styles," Journal of Educational Technology & Society, vol. 16, no. 4, pp. 185–200, 2013.

[10] L. Aroyo, P. Dolog, G.-J. Houben, M. Kravcik, A. Naeve, M. Nilsson, and F. Wild, "Interoperability in personalized adaptive learning," Journal of Educational Technology & Society, vol. 9, no. 2, pp. 4–18, 2006.

[11] P. Brusilovsky, J. Eklund, and E. Schwarz, "Web-based education for all: a tool for development adaptive courseware," Computer networks and ISDN systems, vol. 30, no. 1-7, pp. 291–300, 1998.

[12] M. Rani, R. Nayak, and O. Vyas, "An ontology-based adaptive personalized e-learning system, assisted by software agents on cloud storage," Knowledge-Based Systems, vol. 90, pp. 33–48, 2015.

[13] H. J. Cha, Y. S. Kim, S. H. Park, T. B. Yoon, Y. M. Jung, and J.-H. Lee, "Learning styles diagnosis based on user interface behaviors for the customization of learning interfaces in an intelligent tutoring system," in International Conference on Intelligent Tutoring Systems. Springer, 2006, pp. 513–524.

[14] G.-J. Hwang, H.-Y. Sung, C.-M. Hung, I. Huang, and C.-C. Tsai, "Development of a personalized educational computer game based on students' learning styles," Educational Technology Research and Development, vol. 60, no. 4, pp. 623–638, 2012.

[15] S. V. Kolekar, S. Sanjeevi, and D. Bormane, "Learning style recognition using artificial neural network for adaptive user interface in e-learning," in 2010 IEEE International Conference on Computational Intelligence and Computing Research. IEEE, 2010, pp. 1–5.

[16] J. Liu, C. K. Wong, and K. K. Hui, "An adaptive user interface based on personalized learning," IEEE Intelligent Systems, vol. 18, no. 2, pp. 52–57, March 2003.

[17] J.-D. Cleven, "A MULTILAYER NETWORK APPROACH FOR REAL-TIME ADAPTIVE PERSONALIZED LEARNING," Master's thesis, Monterey, CA; Naval Postgraduate School, 2018.

[18] R Core Team, R: A Language and Environment for Statistical Computing, R Foundation for Statistical Computing, Vienna, Austria, 2013. [Online]. Available: http://www.R-project.org/

[19] M. Bastian, S. Heymann, and M. Jacomy, "Gephi: An open source software for exploring and manipulating networks," in Third international AAAI conference on Weblogs and Social Media, 2009. [Online]. Available: http://www.aaai.org/ocs/index.php/ICWSM/09/paper/view/154